PROFIT AND PUNISHMENT

PROFIT AND
PUNISHMENT

·····················

HOW AMERICA
CRIMINALIZES THE POOR
IN THE NAME OF JUSTICE

·····················

TONY MESSENGER

ST. MARTIN'S PRESS
New York

First published in the United States by St. Martin's Press,
an imprint of St. Martin's Publishing Group

PROFIT AND PUNISHMENT. Copyright 2021 by Tony Messenger. All
rights reserved. Printed in the United States of America.
For information, address St. Martin's Publishing Group,
120 Broadway, New York, NY 10271.

www.stmartins.com

Designed by Donna Sinisgalli Noetzel

Library of Congress Cataloging-in-Publication Data

Names: Messenger, Tony, author.
Title: Profit and punishment : how America criminalizes the poor in
the name of justice / Tony Messenger.
Description: First edition. | New York : St. Martin's Press, 2021. |
Includes bibliographical references and index.
Identifiers: LCCN 2021034260 | ISBN 9781250274649 (hardcover) |
ISBN 9781250274656 (ebook)
Subjects: LCSH: Poverty—Government policy—United States. |
Poor—Government policy—United States. | Criminal justice,
Administration of—United States.
Classification: LCC HV95 .M38 2021 | DDC 362.5/5610973—dc23
LC record available at https://lccn.loc.gov/2021034260

Our books may be purchased in bulk for promotional, educational,
or business use. Please contact your local bookseller or
the Macmillan Corporate and Premium Sales
Department at 1-800-221-7945, extension 5442, or by email at
MacmillanSpecialMarkets@macmillan.com.

First Edition: 2021

10   9   8   7   6   5   4   3   2   1

To my wife and children:

Thank you for sharing me with the world.

CONTENTS

People speak sometimes about the "bestial" cruelty of man, but that is terribly unjust and offensive to beasts, no animal could ever be so cruel as a man, so artfully, so artistically cruel.

—*Crime and Punishment*, Fyodor Dostoyevsky

BY THE NUMBERS

34 million
Number of Americans living in poverty.

$17,420
Highest income a single mother of one child can make to fall under federal poverty guidelines.

80 percent
Estimate of number of people in court system who qualify for public defender.

13 million
Number of misdemeanor cases in the U.S. per year.

$50 billion
Approximate amount of outstanding fines and fees owed various courts in U.S.

$15,900
Amount of money one impoverished Missouri defendant owed court after a year stay in jail that stemmed from a misdemeanor conviction for shoplifting an **$8** tube of mascara.

400 percent
Amount court fines and fees have increased in North Carolina since the Great Recession.

Prologue

· · · · · · · · · · · · · · · · · ·

THE POVERTY PENALTY

Brooke Bergen had $60 in her pocket.

It was November 2018, and the cash was for her court appearance the next day. She hoped to scrounge up another $40 before her morning hearing. She asked me if that was enough.

"Three figures seems more substantial to me," she said. "I'm freaking out. I really am afraid she's going to put me back in jail." Bergen was referring to Dent County Associate Circuit Court Judge Brandi Baird.[1]

Almost every state in America has the statutory ability to charge defendants for a stint in jail.[2] Some jurisdictions make allowances for those who can't afford to pay. Many don't. For roughly a year spent in the Dent County Jail, Bergen's bill was $15,900. It was a sum she could never escape. There was no specific payment plan. She was scheduled to see the judge once a month and pay what she could. If that meant $100 a month, it would take her 159 payments, or more than 13 years, to pay off the debt.

The worst part, though, wasn't even the debt—a large sum, of course, more than she would make in a year—but the requirement to show up in court every month or face the consequences. In other words, every four weeks, Bergen would have to spend half a day in the courtroom, answer to the judge, and agree to pay down her debt little by little. If she didn't show up, a warrant would be issued for her arrest.

We met for the first time at a coffee shop in Rolla, a college town in central Missouri, about thirty minutes north of Salem, where Bergen served time for stealing an $8 tube of mascara from a Walmart. Yes, for a minor shoplifting misdemeanor, Bergen spent a year in a run-down county jail—where water drips down the concrete walls and black mold gathers around damp corners—and, for the privilege of staying there, owed the county five figures. For a person who had never held more than a minimum wage job, it was a mountain of debt, and it weighed on her heavily.

We were in the middle of the country, which is appropriate, because we were talking about a vexing problem affecting both big cities and small towns in every corner of the nation: the intersection of poverty and criminal justice. Bergen, who is white, is poor; has been her entire life. She has long, dark hair, high cheekbones, a toothy smile, and the sort of backstory that has become all the rage on made-for-TV dramas these days. After her mother died, she moved from Florida to the heart of the Ozarks. She never met her father. She married young to get out of the foster-care system, and then divorced. Three years earlier, she lost a baby to sudden infant death syndrome. In a town where everybody knows everybody else's business, people still whispered behind her back. She thought some people blamed her for her baby's death.

This is meth, opioid, and heroin country, a place where people—at the height of the opioid crisis—were consuming more pain pills per capita than most other counties in Missouri.[3] Salem is about an hour east of Plato, which after the 2010 Census was declared the central point of the U.S. population, taking the title from Edgar Springs, just to the north and the east.[4] Imagine every person who lives in the U.S. standing on a massive board that tilts precariously on a fulcrum. This is the place where that board reaches its balance.

Since late 2017, as the metro columnist for the *St. Louis Post-Dispatch*, I've been writing about people like Bergen—residents of small towns like Salem that exist all over the state of Missouri—who have been put in jail because they couldn't afford various fines and fees imposed upon them by the courts.

Wait a minute, seasoned St. Louis lawyers would ask me: *In Mis-*

souri's rural counties, defendants get charged for jail time? Yes, and they often go back to jail if they can't pay. It was an aspect of the criminal justice system that even those whose job it was to know, like lawyers, were unaware of, or at minimum, gave little thought. However, once we began talking, most attorneys found the arrangement absurd. I agreed, and continued writing stories about people caught up in this scheme across the state.

These are not the stories you see in a typical *Law & Order* episode. Such portrayals of the criminal justice system, which may play an outsized role in the public's understanding of the issues, focus mostly on serious felony crimes and how they're prosecuted. "In the criminal justice system, the people are represented by two separate yet equally important groups," says the narrator in the opening credits. "The police, who investigate crime, and the district attorneys, who prosecute the offenders." There is another side of the criminal justice system, perhaps its most significant feature, anchored by the financial burden placed upon poor people caught in its web of fines and fees.

While violent crimes like rapes and murders tend to dominate public attention, about 80 percent of the cases that make their way through the court system—more than 13 million a year—are actually misdemeanors, small crimes like shoplifting, drug possession, speeding, driving under the influence, or simple assault. The vast majority of these cases, much like Bergen's, have some sort of fee or court cost connected to them that a defendant, if convicted, must pay in order to be completely free of their legal obligations.[5] These fines and fees often start at the time of the arrest and can continue even after a person has served their time in jail. In fact, many defendants, like Bergen, don't know how much they owe the court until they plead guilty or, in some cases, *after* they've completed their sentence.

There are fines you may be familiar with, like a $100 penalty for speeding, or a $50 penalty for littering. They're meant as deterrents to minimize traffic accidents or keep our streets clean, for example. Then there are fees you may not be familiar with (unless you've experienced them firsthand), which is what *Profit and Punishment* will study and explore in great detail. They serve a different purpose: money earmarked by lawmakers as a backdoor tax. Some pay for the criminal justice system itself—such as the salaries of clerks and public defenders, or the retirement funds of sheriffs and judges—and others pay for a variety of municipal, county, or state needs. The latter include costs associated with child-abuse investigations, brain-injury funds, law libraries, or courthouse renovations. In most jurisdictions, the largest of these fines is the bill for time in jail, as if one has just spent a year in a hotel. This is what happened to Bergen, and it tethered her to the judicial system for years.

Some of these court costs sound innocuous. Who wouldn't support better sheriff retirement funds or money for child-abuse investigations? But for the people who are the primary target of such fees, it is an unimaginable burden. These costs are nearly always shouldered by the most vulnerable among us: people like Bergen and others who are already teetering on the edge of financial ruin. This debt becomes an accelerant, and the inability to pay means more jail time and additional contact with a criminal justice system that feels more like purgatory than an institution defined by fairness and the rule of law.

Nearly every state in the country has a statute—often called a "board bill" or "pay-to-stay" bill—that charges people for time served.[6] In Missouri and Oklahoma—and in states on both coasts and in the Deep South—these pay-to-stay bills follow defendants arrested initially for small offenses like petty theft or falling behind in child support.[7] Nearly 80 percent of these defendants live below the federal poverty line, meaning they make less than $12,880 a year if they are single, or $21,960 if they are a family of three.[8] They are the working poor: getting by on minimum wage jobs at the local dollar store; seasonal construction workers who get roofing jobs after tornado season; or, like Bergen, they are unemployed, unable to escape the combination of drug offenses and a criminal justice system that follows them everywhere. In some places, like Rapid City, South Dakota, the charges for jail time are small, $6 a day;[9] in other places, like Riverside County, California, they have been as high as $142 a day.[10] For people of little means, these court debts are an albatross they cannot escape or ignore.[11] "This is truly a national crisis," says Lisa Foster,[12] a former California Superior Court judge and co-director of the nonprofit Fines and Fees Justice Center.[13] "This is everywhere. All fifty states."

It's hard not to call this what it is: the criminalization of poverty. The process starts with a powerful punch—the trampling of due-process rights as guaranteed in the U.S. Constitution. What follows is a right hook that takes a defendant to the canvas, a bill of court costs that will bury them in debt. Several forces have collided to create this American reality, which Georgetown law professor and author Peter Edelman calls the "junior sibling to mass incarceration."[14]

The federal "war on drugs," which began in the 1970s with crackdowns on marijuana coming from Mexico and then on the rise of heroin and crack cocaine, fed the nation's "tough-on-crime" policies that followed in the '80s and '90s. When First Lady Nancy Reagan was telling young people to "just say no," her husband, President Ronald Reagan, was filling jails with those who didn't heed the advice.

"In two short decades, between 1980 and 2000," wrote author and law professor Michelle Alexander in her ground-breaking book, *The New Jim Crow*, "the number of people incarcerated in our nation's prisons and jails soared from roughly 300,000 to more than 2 million. By the end of 2007, more than 7 million Americans—or one in every 31 adults—were behind bars, on probation, or on parole."[15] Alexander ties the rise in mass incarceration in the country—particularly among African Americans—to the aforementioned drug war and the rise of tough-on-crime policies. Those policies also contributed to a massive spike in court fines and fees.

As America began prosecuting this war, the cost to state court systems rose dramatically, mirroring the increase in prison population. Between 1980 and 2013, state corrections costs jumped from about $6 billion to more than $80 billion.[16] Meanwhile, at least in part because of gang activity related to the drug trade, homicide and other violent crime rates were spiking across American cities. The U.S. homicide rate grew annually by 4 percent between 1987 and 1991.[17]

As a result, President Bill Clinton pushed his signature crime bill through Congress in 1994 with the help of then Senator Joe Biden.[18] Clinton proposed a bill that would increase funding for police, create tougher sentencing—highlighted by the federal "three strikes" policy that increased prison stays for repeat offenders—and fund new prisons.[19] The massive bill, known as the Violent Crime Control and Law Enforcement Act, passed in 1994 with bipartisan support.[20]

In 1996, Clinton would also sign a controversial welfare reform bill pushed by Republicans that would, in retrospect, sentence an entire generation to poverty.[21] The worst parts of the bill came out of Speaker of the House Newt Gingrich's "Contract with America," which pushed old GOP bromides about "welfare queens" in American cities abusing federal aid programs, using food stamps for drugs, or preferring to live off the government's charity than look for work. The result was that federal aid was denied to pregnant teenage mothers and strict work requirements were imposed.[22] The bill, known as the Personal Responsibility and Work Opportunity Reconciliation Act, would make it impossible for those convicted of drug crimes to obtain food stamps or other forms of government aid.[23] In return, it left single mothers often making difficult choices: even if they wanted to, they couldn't live with the father of their children, since it would disqualify them from obtaining the aid they needed to survive.[24]

Many years ago I wrote a series of columns in the *Columbia Daily Tribune* about a couple living in public housing in Columbia, Missouri. Both had either a high school diploma or its equivalent and were working. They were good at their jobs and got promoted. But the promotions created a conundrum. In most public aid programs, there is no sliding scale, just a hard cutoff. With the promotions, their total family income exceeded the threshold required to stay in subsidized housing. In addition, they would lose their subsidized childcare. Ironically, the family would have been better off *without* the promotions, as the slight pay increase would upend their lives entirely. So they compromised: one of them didn't take a promotion, to keep their pay intentionally lower. Poor people make these impossible decisions—diapers or gas, child support or court costs—all the time, but their difficult choices are often exacerbated by the ones made by policy makers.

As corrections costs went up in the late twentieth century, lawmakers sought to collect from the very people they were putting away, and those additional costs pushed people deeper into poverty, which further compromised their ability to pay. Over the past four decades, this vicious cycle has become fully baked into the criminal justice system. During the 2020 presidential election, debates on the merits and demerits of the crime bill and its effect on mass incarceration resurfaced once again, with at least some prominent Democrats who previously supported such measures willing to question their prior positions. "I do think we need to revisit some of what we did in the '90s," Speaker of the House Nancy Pelosi told me during the run-up to the election.[25]

In the mid-to-late 2000s, additional forces combined to create a toxic stew of public policy decisions that would accelerate the expansive use of fines and fees in American courts. After the subprime mortgage crisis in 2008, the Great Recession that followed devastated state budgets across the country. For instance, Oklahoma's overall tax revenue dropped about 21 percent during the first year of the crisis and didn't fully recover until the second quarter of 2019.[26] That massive drop in the state coffers was, in turn, passed on to cities and counties to reckon with. Missouri faced a similar, if less dramatic, downturn: a 14 percent drop in 2010, and the state would not return to precrisis revenue until 2016. Nationally, according to the Pew Research Center, state-by-state revenue declined more than 12 percent by late 2009 and didn't recover until 2013.[27]

As that revenue declined, other expenses, such as Medicaid and corrections costs, went up.[28] Lawmakers had to find new revenue to balance budgets. Unlike the federal government, most state governments can't deficit-spend (meaning, they can't borrow; they have to raise what they wish to spend). Some states raised taxes, which is the traditional solution. But many state legislatures, particularly those controlled by Republicans, followed party orthodoxy: no new taxes.

This was in part because of the rise of political operative Grover Norquist's "Taxpayer Protection Pledge," which was becoming GOP dogma.[29] Norquist, a former speechwriter for the U.S. Chamber of Commerce, is the founder of Americans for Tax Reform, and had played a role in crafting Gingrich's Contract with America.[30] In the 2012 GOP presidential primary, all but one of the Republican candidates signed the "no new taxes" pledge, which became the standard in Republican-leaning states like South Carolina, Oklahoma, and Missouri.[31] But since they still needed to balance state budgets, what did they do? They turned to court fines and fees. Put another way, lawmakers found a backdoor tax, and poor people paid the price. This is the cautionary tale to keep in mind when elected officials offer economic nirvana by cutting taxes: Somebody, somewhere, is always paying the price, whether it's middle-class families stuck with higher college tuition bills, truckers navigating crumbling highways, or poor people stuck paying the bill of a criminal justice system that used to be funded by taxes.

Court fines and fees have been a part of the American court system since the beginning. Civil rights icon Rosa Parks, for instance, was fined $10, plus an additional $4 in court costs, when she was cited for a municipal ordinance violation in Montgomery, Alabama, in 1955 for sitting on a bus reserved for whites. After the Great Recession, lawmakers increasingly turned to fines and fees to fund court services and other elements of government. "Over time, lawmakers started to use the courts as a piggy bank," Foster said. "The results are truly staggering."

"For a person who may be justice-involved and on the lower socioeconomic scale, the punitive consequences for the inability to pay these fees and fines lends itself to additional involvement in the criminal justice system," Kris Steele, executive director of Oklahomans for Criminal Justice Reform, told *Tulsa World* in 2019.[32] "And we reach a point where we begin to criminalize poverty. And that should be unconscionable for any Oklahoman." In the past decade, forty-eight states have increased their court fines and fees, and the rate of the hikes are shocking.[33] According to Foster, the state of California, for example, has $10 billion in unpaid fines and fees.

In 2009, Kendy Killman, a white, fifty-year-old single mother of a disabled child, picked up a misdemeanor drug charge after a questionable traffic stop in Norman, a university town south of Oklahoma City. She has been hounded by it for more than a decade. What started as $900, all set by state statute, more than tripled over the years: she was handcuffed and detained for her inability to pay and the costs kept rising. Throughout it all, she never committed another crime. But she continues to live in fear of arrest and struggles to make ends meet.

Sasha Darby of South Carolina lost her baby after a stint in a Lexington County jail.[34] She was convicted of a misdemeanor assault charge that stemmed from a spat with her roommate. But she was locked up more than a year later, because she couldn't afford the court costs foisted upon her. At twenty-six, she lost her job, her home, and, eventually, her baby, all because she was a poor, African American single mother who couldn't afford the $1,000 court bill. In many urban areas, and some parts of the rural south, it's people of color who are disproportionately affected by these court collection schemes.[35] In fact, a 2019 study by the Criminal Justice Policy Program at Harvard Law School found that the prevalence of fines and fees in overpoliced Black communities contributes directly to the wide racial disparities in incarceration in the United States.

Remember Philando Castile? Video of him being shot to death during a traffic stop in St. Paul, Minnesota, went viral in the summer of 2016. He warned the officer that he had a firearm in the car, which he was licensed to carry, but the officer—who a grand jury declined to charge—fired several shots almost immediately, killing him while his girlfriend and her daughter were in the car. But Castile's plight began much earlier. From age nineteen to the time of his death at thirty-two, Castile had been pulled over by police forty-six times, which resulted in more than $6,000 in fines and fees. He never got ahead of this debt while he was alive and, as we'll see, hardly anyone ever really does.

All over the country, in cities and rural enclaves, in blue states and red states, people charged with minor offenses find themselves paying what criminal justice reform advocate Joanna Weiss calls the "poverty penalty." The connection between the courts and people living in poverty—an entanglement that can continue for decades—is an intentional one.[36] Too often, the victims of this scheme are not viewed through an empathetic lens—as people simply lacking financial resources. Instead, the system brands them as criminals and uses them as a means to an end, a more politically palatable way to pad sheriff's salaries, for instance, than asking the taxpayers to vote for a tax hike. The problem of backdoor taxation involves all three branches of government. Lawmakers who pass these laws end up financially squeezing the poor while publicly telling their constituents that they aren't raising taxes.

The system, as it currently operates, ruins vulnerable people at nearly every stage. Consider the fact that the United States is one of only two countries, along with the Philippines, with its cash bail system tied to a for-profit industry. After someone is arrested, a judge determines bail (the amount required for temporary release as a defendant awaits trial), which, if you're poor, means very little. You can't afford to pay a bail bondsman—or know someone who can afford to do so on your behalf—for temporary release. In many ways, in a criminal justice system that purports innocence before proven guilty, poor defendants are treated as guilty from the moment they are handcuffed.

Let's say you're a single mother arrested on a misdemeanor theft charge, and the judge sets bail at $500, which you can't afford. You apply for a public defender but it takes a few days before that office assigns you an attorney (public defenders are expected to manage an absurd caseload, which we'll explore in detail later). Once assigned, the attorney takes another week or more to arrange a time to meet you in jail. You might be in jail for thirty days, away from your job and your children, when the prosecutor offers you a plea bargain, an opportunity to get out of jail on a reduced charge as long as you agree to a conviction: Plead guilty to time served and you can go home. Who wouldn't take that deal?

What the prosecutor and judge often don't explain to defendants is that with a conviction comes a bill for court costs, as well as a pay-to-stay bill for time in jail. And in some states, there is probation, supervised by private, for-profit companies. They require drug testing, check-ins, and monthly fees.[37] These companies' profit motive incentivizes them to hunt for defendants who violate the terms of their probation, thus keeping county jails full of repeat offenders. The plea bargain, which initially felt like the right move, becomes more of a devil's bargain, as additional jail time linked to failure to pay down the debts comes calling.

In 2014, after protests erupted in Ferguson, Missouri, in the wake of Michael Brown's death, the issue of oppressive fines and fees in traffic-stop cases sparked a national debate. Brown was a Black teenager killed by a white police officer on August 9. Many of the young, Black people who marched in protest of his death, raising awareness of the larger issues of police brutality and systemic racism, were themselves victims. They were the targets of the overpolicing that exists in communities that rely on their police departments as revenue streams, like quotas for traffic-ticket violations, which then lead to additional fines and fees for those caught up in the fundraising scheme. State Senator Eric Schmitt would summarize the problem with a catchy phrase: "taxation by citation."[38]

Schmitt, a Republican, later became the state attorney general, and in one of his first acts on the job, in 2019, wrote an amicus brief supporting a Missouri Supreme Court case that sought to undo this scheme. "No statute authorizes this practice," Schmitt wrote. "It lends itself to abuses that threaten the constitutional rights of Missouri citizens ... It does little good, and potentially much harm, to threaten indigent persons with more jail time and debt when they are unable to pay."[39] On February 6, 2019, a young public defender named Matthew Mueller brought that case before the Missouri Supreme Court and explained why his client had been behind bars. "He sat in jail because he's poor," Mueller told the judges.[40] In one sentence, Mueller highlighted an American epidemic.

This book explores that epidemic, and the movement to end it, primarily through the stories of three single mothers living in poverty—

Bergen, Killman, and Darby—who were abused by a judicial system more focused on collecting debts than public safety. Their stories, emblematic of a broader phenomenon, offer a window into the tragic cycle of profit and abuse that begins with an arrest for a minor offense, and continues long after a guilty plea, sentencing, and time served.

For too many people, this is their relationship to America's system of justice. The good news is that a growing coalition of attorneys, nonprofits, and advocates for the poor, many of them victims of the system themselves, are rising up and trying to end this cycle of abuse by filing civil rights lawsuits and pushing legislation to change the status quo. In some capacity, nearly every state is facing pressure from civil rights advocates or lawmakers from both sides of the political spectrum to end these practices, whether it's charging for jail time, collecting excessive fees, or seeking punishment for the inability to pay court costs, including suspended driver's licenses. This book also tells the stories of these advocates—their successes and their failures—and points to a path forward toward reform that will fix America's two-tiered (and often invisible to most of us) system of justice.

A sense of hopelessness is palpable when you walk into the Dent County Courthouse on payment review days. Those are the days when Judge Baird requires people who have already served their time to return to court to either pay the court costs they owe or explain why they can't.

Many Americans have never seen this side of the criminal justice system. Let's say you are an average middle-class person who gets a speeding ticket. Maybe you go to court to plead it down to something smaller, to limit the damage to your driving record, and you cut a check that day for the settled amount. You're done and go on with your day.

Bergen had already pleaded guilty and been sentenced. She had already done her time. She had paid her debt to society, but not her monetary debt to Dent County, and for that, she was still tethered to Baird's courtroom and would be for years. In fact, nearly everyone in the courtroom that day—thirty people at a time, with a line out the door—were there for similar reasons.

Judge Baird, like many rural Missouri judges, employs an extrajudicial process not outlined anywhere in state statute—a payment review hearing—to collect costs foisted upon defendants by county commissioners and the state legislature.

Once a defendant has served his or her sentence and receives the bill for their time in jail, Baird schedules monthly hearings to collect the debt. If the defendant pays something, say $50, they're good for another month. If not, or if they miss their hearing, they're back in jail.

Twice in the previous month I had written about cases where Baird had sent people to the Dent County Jail for their failure to pay various court costs or the board bill for jail time.[41] There was Bergen, Leann Banderman, and Amy Murr, each with their own misdemeanor offenses that turned into jail time, a bill for that time, and a recurring date in court to pay it off.

On the day of Bergen's hearing, the bailiff tried to stop me from observing the proceedings.[42]

"Wait here," he said. He wanted to alert the judge that I was there.

Baird, who declined several interview requests for this book, didn't want me in her courtroom to view the proceedings up close. I was bringing her the sort of public attention judges don't like, and it was causing the local weekly newspaper to ask questions during an election year. This was her courtroom, and she didn't need some reporter from the big city poking around and causing her trouble.

"You can't come into court today," the bailiff, with his thick country drawl, told me. "You didn't follow the supreme court rules."

Presumably, he was referring to a rule in Missouri courts that if reporters want to record audio or take photos, they must ask a court coordinator for permission.[43] But I had no camera. I left my phone in the car. All I had was a pen and notebook. And there is no rule that you can keep a reporter—or anybody else, for that matter—out of public court proceedings.

My adrenaline kicked up a notch. These are the moments watchdog journalists live for: standing up to public officials who question the role of transparency in these proceedings, which should be made available to the public.

I told the bailiff that he and the judge were wrong. I was going to sit in the courtroom that day and if he tried to stop me, I'd need time to call the newspaper's attorney to file a writ with the court.

The bailiff went back to the courtroom for a few minutes. Then he waved me in.

"Sit over there."

I was there that day to report on what happened to Bergen. Would she show up? Would she go to jail if she didn't come up with enough money? I also wanted to see how the other cases were handled, how the judge interacted with the prosecutor and the public defender, and what role the local for-profit private probation company played throughout the day.

One by one, the long line of downtrodden defendants made their way before the judge. Some offered up a fistful of crinkled-up cash to the probation officer right before their name was called. One man tapped me on the shoulder and whispered in my ear. His mom lived in St. Louis and had been sending him copies of my columns. There were dozens of people like him, he said, like Bergen, in the same boat, forced to come to court every month with money. Some people had been sentenced years earlier and were still coming regularly to pay it off. I watched them go before the judge and explain how much they could pay.

On this day, nobody went to jail.

"She was in a good mood," Bergen told me later, referring to the judge. "She knew you were there."

Bergen had asked every friend she had in town to help her come up with some money, and she raised $100. She paid it and was sent on her way. Only $15,800 to go.

PART I

GOING TO COURT

1

....

THE ARREST

Norman, Oklahoma
April 2009

Kendy Killman was about four miles from her apartment in Norman,
Oklahoma, when she saw the police officer in the rearview mirror. Her
boyfriend, Steven, sat in the front seat. Her father was in the back.
Everybody was tired. For the past two days, they had driven nearly 480
miles, to Springdale, Arkansas, and back, after an unexpected trip to see
her grandmother in the hospital. The whole trip was last minute; she
was driving in pajamas.

Her father got the call on April 17, 2009. His mother was in the
hospital and the diagnosis wasn't good. Killman's car was fine for trips
to the grocery store or to take her stepchildren Bubba and Brittany
to school, but it wasn't going to handle a trip out of state. Desperate,
she called Kenny, her ex-husband and the father of their children. He
had a blue 1996 Chevy Lumina. It was a bit beat up, but he said she
could have it for $400. Killman gave him the money, stuck the title in
the glove compartment, and went to pick up her boyfriend and father.
The drive to Arkansas wasn't complicated. North on Interstate 35 to
Interstate 44. East to Tulsa, then a straight shot on Highway 412 all
the way to Springdale.

After a short visit at the hospital, Killman and her clan spent the night
at Grandma's house. They went back to the hospital on the eighteenth.

Grandma was taking a turn for the better. Killman's father and boy-friend had to work on Monday. So they headed back to Norman, with one extra traveler on the ride home: Grandma's dog. Dad didn't want to leave the dog home alone while Grandma was recuperating.

On the drive home, Killman turned off Interstate 35 earlier than she normally would. Because of an accident, a news alert on the radio warned of a traffic backup on the highway near Oklahoma City. She was heading south on Sooner Road when she saw the cop. Killman wasn't speeding, and she knew it.

"I wasn't worried," she told me later.

At first, the police car drove up beside her. Then, as they were about three miles from home, the officer dropped back, and turned on his flashing red and blue lights. Killman pulled over. The officer ambled up to her car and asked her to step outside.

As she got out, the officer told Killman that she was drifting a bit left of center, but that's not why he pulled her over. Rather, while they were driving, he noticed what he thought was a crack in the windshield. Indeed, there had been one, but it was repaired, enough to not be a hazard. He could see that now. Pivoting, the officer asked Killman if he could search the vehicle. This is not an uncommon occurrence, but at least in theory, a police officer is supposed to have probable cause for such a search. They smelled marijuana, for instance, or witnessed erratic driving. This police officer didn't mention any of those things, and Killman didn't push it.

Standing there in her pajamas, tired from hours of driving and wanting to see Bubba and Brittany, who were staying with her mother, she consented. Never mind that she had only owned the car for less than two days, or that she bought it from her ex-husband, whom she had left in part because of his drug use.

As the officer and his partner looked through the vehicle, the three of them—Killman, her father, and Steven—sat on the curbside. In the trunk, under the carpet, one of the officers found something and placed it on the roof of the car. It was a pipe for smoking weed.

"Whose is this?" the officer asked. There were no drugs in the car.

Just the pipe, which showed signs of previous use. There was residue in the bowl. Killman explained that she had just bought the car on Friday specifically for their trip to Arkansas. Keep in mind, she had no criminal record. She'd never been arrested. Though booze and drugs were constants in her life, she stayed away from them, having seen up close the impact it would have on loved ones. The officers were not swayed. Killman was cuffed and put in the back seat of the police cruiser. A tow truck was called for the Chevy. Her dad, Steve, and Grandma's dog were left on the side of the road. It was around lunchtime.

"I was headed to jail for the first time ever," she said.

In Cleveland County, the jail was in the basement of the courthouse. For seven hours—noon until 7:00 p.m.—Killman sat cuffed to a bench as the officer filled out paperwork and processed the evidence. Finally, they issued her a summons for a court appearance and let her go home. Without money or a car, she walked the distance herself, which was about a mile, southeast from the courthouse to her apartment on the back side of the Cottonwood Ridge complex. She was expected to be in court on Monday and appear before a judge.

Born to Kendall and Deborah Garrett on May 7, 1969, in Bartlesville, Oklahoma, Kendallia, who goes by Kendy, was named after her father. Her parents had her young. Kendall, a construction worker, was nineteen. Deborah was eighteen and worked as a waitress. Bartlesville was an oil boomtown, the home of the Phillips Petroleum Company, which was good if you worked for the company, the largest employer in town, and not so much if you didn't.[1] Few other employers in town could pay oil-industry wages.

Killman's middle name, Wynette, was inspired by the country singer Tammy Wynette, whom her mother adored. Known as the First Lady of Country Music, Wynette was one of the first women to achieve commercial acclaim in country music, landing twenty songs at number one on the country charts from the late 1960s through the 1990s. Her songs, especially the sad ones, match parts of Killman's story: "Stand by Your Man," "'Til I Can Make It on My Own," "D-I-V-O-R-C-E," "My Elusive Dreams."[2]

Killman had two siblings, a brother and a sister. Killman was five when her two-year-old sister died. It was a Sunday afternoon, and the family was gathered for her uncle's birthday. The men were working on her papa's truck. Papa was her mom's father. The pickup truck was lifted on one side with a jack, so Papa could work on it, and several of the kids were in the bed playing together.

There was too much weight on one side of the truck as the kids were playing, and the truck started rolling backward off the jack, toward the street. Killman, her brother, and her cousin all jumped out. Carrie Alaine Garrett, who was two weeks from her third birthday, fell backward out of the truck. It rolled over and crushed her. Later, at the hospital, she was confirmed dead.

"Our lives were changed forever," Killman says. "I was only five. I didn't know what it meant, just that she was never coming home, and I would never see her again."

Her parents filed for divorce (though they would later reunite) and, as Killman recalls it, boozed the pain away. They kept moving and uprooting the family: Killman went to two different schools for kindergarten, another for first grade, two for second—a trend that continued throughout her elementary school education. They moved in and around Bartlesville, then to Jet, off to Snyder, back to Bartlesville, and then in with her grandparents on her mom's side. When she was in junior high, they moved to Dewey, just north of Bartlesville on Highway 75, in the northeast part of Oklahoma. The town of about 3,400 people sits just west of the Native American Osage Reservation.[3] Killman had her own bedroom in the Dewey house, which was a first. It's one of those little details that might seem insignificant, unless you happened to grow up poor and understood space as a scarce commodity. Getting her own room was a concrete sign that "we were doing okay."

Being on the move was normal for the Garretts, as it is for many working American families. They follow jobs, or chase them, and end up in low-end apartments because they can't afford much more, or because a history of broken leases makes them a bad credit risk.[4] But for people living in poverty, mobility means something different than for folks with disposable incomes and stable careers. Too often, for poor people, mobility is involuntary, as a result of eviction, rather than a choice.

Killman didn't grow up thinking of her family as poor. Her parents were always working. They had a roof over their heads. "I have lived from paycheck to paycheck my whole life," she told me. "I wouldn't know how to act if it was any different. What is poverty? It's a thin line. I do have somewhere to live and I am not on the streets. But I still need food stamps to make sure everyone in my home gets enough to eat every month."

In his 2004 book, *The Working Poor*, Pulitzer Prize–winning author David K. Shipler describes American poverty this way:

> For practically every family, then, the ingredients of poverty are part financial and part psychological, part personal and part societal, part past and part present. Every problem magnifies the impact of the others, and all are so tightly interlocked that one reversal can produce a chain reaction with results far distant from the original cause. A run-down apartment can exacerbate a child's asthma, which leads to a call for an ambulance, which generates a medical bill that cannot be paid, which ruins a credit record, which hikes the interest rate on an auto loan, which forces the purchase of an unreliable used car, which jeopardizes a mother's punctuality at work, which limits her promotions and earning capacity, which confines her to poor housing.[5]

It is a cycle that can be difficult to escape, particularly when the criminal justice system is conspiring to keep you poor.

All day Sunday, Killman fretted over what to expect the next day in court. It was all speculation; she'd never been before. The Cleveland

County Courthouse is a three-story, classical revival structure built with funds from the Public Works Administration in the late 1930s.[6] It sits at the corner of South Jones Avenue and East Eufala Street, across from Legacy Trail Park. Designed by architect Walter T. Vahlgert, it is the third such courthouse built in Norman. The first one burned down in 1904.

When she arrived Monday morning, the courtroom was packed. This is a common sight in municipal and county courthouses across America on what many jurisdictions refer to as "law day." It's the day the judge goes through a massive list of folks who have been arrested on ordinance violations or misdemeanors: traffic tickets, driving under the influence, noise violations, shoplifting and petty theft, bar fights, and minor indiscretions. These are the cases that clog the American courts. A few defense attorneys mull around a table near the prosecuting attorney, or sometimes they hang out in the empty jury box, waiting to hear their client's name.

It's a cattle call. There are dockets like this for traffic court, evictions, and criminal arraignments everywhere in America. Here's how it usually goes: The judge calls your name, confirms that you are in attendance. You'll be asked if you have an attorney. Then you wait to hear your next court date, which is set for a trial or a plea. When you sit in such courtrooms, it often takes half a day or more for the few minutes you'll get with the judge. There might be a few inmates brought in, shackled and in orange jumpsuits, who are there to appear on a felony arraignment or to make a plea, but in most courtrooms in America, the overwhelming number of these cases are misdemeanors.[7]

In her book *Punishment Without Crime*, which examines the failures of the criminal justice system to deal with such misdemeanor dockets, law professor Alexandra Natapoff writes, "Because the petty-offense process is so large, it tends to move cases fast," and thus "has earned it some choice nicknames like 'cattle herding,' 'assembly-line justice,' 'meet 'em and plead 'em' lawyer, and 'McJustice.' The Supreme Court has worried that the sheer volume of misdemeanors 'creates an obsession for speedy dispositions, regardless of the fairness of the result.' In practice, this speedy volume means that people's rights and dignity often get trampled."[8]

As Killman told me, describing her first such court experience, "Nothing is sacred. Everybody knows everyone's business." Over the years, as she ended up in the same courtroom time and time again, she would come to recognize some of the same faces. They were faces of American poverty, tethered to a system seeking payment for alleged sins.

Finally, it was her turn. "Kendallia Killman?"

She stood and told the judge she didn't have an attorney and couldn't afford one. "Fine," he said. "Fill out an application for a public defender and bring it back with $40." The Sixth Amendment to the U.S. Constitution guarantees federal criminal defendants the right to an attorney, even if they can't afford one.[9] It says: "In all criminal prosecutions, the accused shall enjoy the right to a speedy and public trial, by an impartial jury of the state and district wherein the crime shall have been committed, which district shall have been previously ascertained by law, and to be informed of the nature and cause of the accusation; to be confronted with the witnesses against him; to have compulsory process for obtaining witnesses in his favor, and to have the assistance of counsel for his defence."

It wasn't until 1963, though, in *Gideon v. Wainwright*, that the U.S. Supreme Court determined that the right to counsel applied to state courts, not just federal ones.[10] In 1961, Clarence Earl Gideon was accused of stealing money from a vending machine in a pool hall in Panama City, Florida. He told the judge that he couldn't afford an attorney so it was decided that he would have to represent himself. After he was convicted, Gideon filed a habeas corpus petition with the Florida Supreme Court, seeking his freedom because his constitutional right to a defense had been denied. The U.S. Supreme Court agreed, and in its ruling made clear that the Sixth Amendment also applied to states in felony cases. Gideon was eventually appointed an attorney and retried. He won. In 1972, the nation's high court extended that protection to any case in which imprisonment is a possibility.

Since then, every state has developed a public-defender system of some kind, though how they operate, and who funds them, varies wildly.[11] Twenty-six states, for instance, operate state-funded public-defender systems. Their funding, like those of prosecutors and judges and law enforcement, comes from a statewide tax base. Most other states use a combination of state-funded and contract systems, the latter being where private attorneys are paid a flat fee to represent indigent clients. These attorneys are not exclusively tied to such contracts. They also maintain a private practice with other, higher-paying clients.

Oklahoma is one of the states that uses the latter system. The two most populous counties in the state—Oklahoma County and Tulsa County—have dedicated public defenders, funded by county taxes.[12] For the other seventy-five counties, including Cleveland County, there is the Oklahoma Indigent Defense System, which uses private attorneys paid flat fees on contract. Both systems are woefully underfunded, leaving these lawyers tasked with defending poor people with unmanageable workloads and a financial incentive to move through them quickly, often at the expense of individual cases.[13]

"Chronic underfunding has led to drastic resource disparities between prosecutors and defenders, undermining the very basis of our criminal legal system," determined the Brennan Center for Justice, in a report issued in 2019 titled "A Fair Fight: Achieving Indigent Defense Resource Parity."[14] It found that between 2008 and 2012, as court costs were rising, public defender budgets dropped in twenty-six states. And seventeen states provide only county funding for public defenders, leading to wide disparities in representation. Why? Because prosecutor offices are exponentially better funded. If you think of prosecutors and public defenders as opposite sides of a mathematical equation, where both sides are supposed to be equal, the problem is out of balance, tilted in favor of the side of the equation that seeks to put people in jail, and against the side that seeks to protect defendants' constitutional rights.

In some states, like Louisiana, public defender budgets are actually funded by court costs, creating a double tax on the poor, since they are the only people who need, and qualify for, public defenders.[15] That leads to even deeper levels of underfunding, which leaves indigent defendants who can't afford bail stuck in jail for long periods as they wait for understaffed public defenders to find time for them. At one point in New Orleans, a typical public defender handled up to 19,000 cases per year, meaning he or she would have about 7 minutes per client. In Missouri, the situation is similar. In 2017, the state's 370 public defenders handled about 82,000 cases, spending about 9 hours per case, about 5 times less than the American Bar Association recommends.[16]

"If I had a nickel for every Constitution-loving lawmaker who claimed support for a fair system of justice and liberty but then voted for wildly disparate resources for constitutionally required lawyers who fight the government to ensure justice and preserve liberty, well, we'd be pretty well-funded," says Michael Barrett, who was the head of Missouri's public-defender system between 2015 and 2019. In 2016, Barrett was so frustrated by the anemic funding and massive workloads the public defenders in Missouri had to carry that he assigned Governor Jay Nixon a case.[17] This was a shocking move by a man hired by a commission of Nixon appointees, but Barrett was desperate. Though he had made a bit of progress, convincing the Missouri Legislature to up the public defender budget by $4.5 million,[18] it was only a fraction of the more than $20 million Barrett believed the office really needed.

But Missouri, with one of the lowest tax rates in the country, was in a fiscal crunch. Nixon withheld $3.5 million of that increase to balance the budget. It's always easier politically to take money away from criminal defendants than, say, schoolchildren.[19] There is a law on Missouri's books that gives the head of the public-defender system power in certain extraordinary circumstances to appoint a case needing a public defender "to any member of the state bar of Missouri." Turns out, the governor was also an attorney, and therefore qualified.

Nixon protested, and the court took his side, relieving him of the responsibility, but Barrett won the national headlines he sought.[20] The governor, who was already serving a second term of office and couldn't run for reelection, may have missed a big opportunity. Imagine the attention paid to the case if the governor showed up on behalf of a client living in poverty who needed a competent defense. But Nixon was a tough-on-crime former prosecutor. He passed on his big chance.

Did you know that in most states, defendants who require a state-appointed defense can ask for the fees associated with their representation to be waived? Most don't know this, and thus don't ask. Certainly Killman didn't. It's the ultimate contradiction. To avoid the crushing debt of fines and fees, a defendant needs representation, but to get representation, they have to pay a fee, the first of many court costs that could end up costing a defendant thousands of dollars, for what began as a minor crime like a traffic ticket. What Killman knew as she stood in court for the first time was that her money all went to buying that $400 car, which put her in this position to begin with. She just didn't have the $40 she needed for an attorney, and that's what she told the judge.

"He looked at me like I was lying and told me to have a seat in the jury box," Killman said. "Here I was, I thought, going to jail." She was there about four hours. Finally, the judge summoned her again, told her the $40 fee was waived and that an attorney would be in touch. She had to return to court on June 9.

Columbia, South Carolina
August 2016

Twenty-six-year-old Sasha Darby couldn't afford an attorney, either. She never imagined she would need one. At the time, Darby was living in the Landmark Apartments in Columbia, South Carolina, with a couple of roommates. She was making $10 an hour working as a forklift driver at Michelin tires. It wasn't a lot of money, but it was a good job, better than the ones she had the year before.

This is the thing about poverty in America: It's relative. Add to the mix being an African American single mother, and the physics begin to scramble. Darby's family had moved to Columbia from New Bedford, Massachusetts, outside Boston, where Darby grew up. In New Bedford, she had qualified for various state aid programs, such as Temporary Assistance for Needy Families, food stamps, and Medicaid. Now she had a decent job, making more than minimum wage, but overall, in the past year, she was still bringing in less income (slightly below $17,000) than the federal poverty level for a single mom. When Darby's mom could watch her three-year-old son, things were manageable (she couldn't afford childcare). But then her mom got sick. So Darby had to make the difficult decision of sending her son back to Massachusetts to live with his paternal grandparents. Meanwhile, she would send money to support him and save for a visit.

In South Carolina, the average cost of childcare for a four-year-old is more than $500 a month, according to the Economic Policy Institute. In every state in the country, for people living below the federal poverty level, the cost of childcare surpasses the percentage of income that the federal government would classify as "affordable."[21]

For Darby, things were manageable—not great, but not awful—all things considered, though she missed her son. Then things got complicated at home: she and her roommate got into it, arguing over money, made all the worse because they both worked at Michelin. So Darby decided to look for a new place. But before she could officially move out, she and her roommate got into an argument that turned physical. For Darby, this was no small thing: as a child, she had been abused and suffered an assault, and she was later diagnosed as having post-traumatic stress disorder (PTSD).

"It started out as a discussion," Darby said. But it escalated. "I thought she was going to hit me. So I hit her." A fateful decision, though it didn't feel like it at the time. Her roommate called the police, and Darby waited on the porch until an officer arrived. When the police arrived, Darby explained what happened. The officer issued her a summons for misdemeanor assault and stood by as she packed up her things. She stayed on her sister's couch for a bit until she could find a place.

The following Monday, Darby ended up before Magistrate Rebecca Adams. The first thing she did when she walked into court was waive her right to an attorney.[22] On the information sheet she was handed, there was a box to check to request a public defender. The fee was $40.

"I didn't have $40," Darby said. Who could fault her for checking the box that didn't involve a fee? Far too often, defendants like Darby check the wrong box as they walk into a courtroom for the first time, stressed out, with no money, hoping mostly to find a way to stay out of jail. What Darby didn't know, and what nobody told her, is the judge had the ability to waive that fee.

Darby was unsure of herself as she stood before Adams. Not only had she never been to jail, she had never been to court. She didn't understand what was happening—and she had no one there to speak on her behalf, as an attorney would.

"You have the right to remain silent. You have the right to an attorney and the right to request a jury trial," Adams said. "You are charged with assault. Do you understand what you're charged with? Do you understand your rights?"

"Yes, ma'am."

"How do you want to plead?"

"Not guilty."

"Do you want a bench trial or do you want a jury trial?

"A bench trial."

"Are you ready to proceed now?"

"Yes, ma'am."

"Is the state ready?"

Yes, the prosecutor said. And that was it. The entire trial would take eleven minutes and Darby would convict herself with her own words.

She told the judge the same thing she told the police officer. Yes, she hit her roommate, but she was afraid and acted accordingly. A defense attorney likely would have turned that into a self-defense argument, which, at the very least, could have gotten the charges reduced. But Darby didn't have an attorney, and when she started to make the argument, Adams cut her off.

"You did hit her?" Adams asked. "We're having this trial, why?"

"I'm not sure," Darby said, confused. "I'm not really familiar with legal terms."

The end was swift.

"I'm going to find you guilty by your own admission," Adams said. "Why would you do that? Why would you hit her like that? That's just stupid.

"You got a job?" Adams asked.

"Yes ma'am, I do."

"So you can pay my fine? Or would you rather do jail time?"

Those last two sentences say a hell of a lot about the state of today's criminal justice system. It might seem insignificant, but the magistrate's choice of "my" is meaningful. The fines aren't personal but established by state statute. They are meant, in theory, to punish people for breaking the law, to deter such behavior, or both, but that is not how many judges see it, and it's not by accident.

In the early 1990s, the National Center for State Courts, an organization of state court officials such as judges and clerks, published a "Handbook of Collection Issues and Solutions," for its membership. This training manual of sorts came out of a series of workshops across the country put on by the organization titled "Collecting Fines and Fees in Traffic Cases." Such training, Foster says, has little to do with judges understanding the finer points of the law, or their role in protecting civil rights. This is about making sure judges are good at collecting backdoor taxes paid by poor people at the request of the executive and legislative branches of government. Too many judges, rather than being offended by the loss of judicial independence, take it personally when the money they are collecting for others isn't paid.

In 1999, for instance, Nevada established a statewide task force "to improve the collection of court-imposed fines, fees, forfeitures and administrative assessments."[23] For too many judges in too many cities and counties across the country, their job is defined by this.

Then there is the question about jail.

Some states—Mississippi and South Carolina among them—specifically penalize defendants who can't manage the ensuing debt with jail time.[24] Adams was offering Darby an "opportunity" to go to jail instead of paying a fine, which is a devil's bargain only a poor defendant would have to consider.

"I'd rather pay the fine," Darby said.

"All right, your sentence is thirty days in jail, suspended, and the payment of a fine of $1,000."

Darby wrote a check for her first $200 payment that day. She wasn't sure the check would clear—hence her previous decision to decline to pay $40 for a public defender—but she didn't feel like she had a choice. Darby left the courthouse agreeing to pay $175 a month until her court debt was paid off. She knew it was more than she could afford.

The entire experience was dumbfounding. "I just didn't know I had the option of having an attorney," she said. "I had no idea that we were going to trial right there. I never would have thought this was going to cost $1,000. I agreed because she's the judge and I didn't want to get in trouble. I was going to do the best I could to make the payments."

Salem, Missouri
April 2016

If you were trying to find the picture of a town to define poverty in rural America, Salem would be about as good a place as any. Nearly 30 percent of the people who live there survive on income that is below the federal poverty line, more than twice the national average.[25] That means living on less than $12,760 a year, or $17,420, if you are a single mom with one child.[26] In the woods east of town, nestled up against the rolling hills of the Mark Twain National Forest, are remnants of homeless camps that come and go, a sign of the poverty that is pervasive in Salem.[27]

There was a time when good factory jobs existed in Salem, at the bottling plant or the shoe factory, but those days are mostly gone. Walmart is the biggest employer, followed by the local hospital and various government jobs.[28] Some people drive thirty minutes north to Rolla, a college town, to find work.

Nestled up against the pines, along dirt roads, there are abandoned shacks and trailers that used to serve as meth labs, before laws limiting the sale of Sudafed shut them down. Now the meth comes mostly from

Mexico,[29] and it's been replaced as the drug of choice by opioids—
Oxycontin and Vicodin—which often serve as a gateway to heroin.[30]

There is evidence that the very presence of a Walmart Supercenter
actually makes poverty worse in towns like Salem, where they drive out
mom-and-pop stores, pay their employees wages that still qualify them
for food stamps, and undercut prices in the stores that stay open. In
2006, researchers Stephan J. Goetz of Pennsylvania State University and
Hema Swaminathan of the International Center for the Research on
Women found that even after controlling for other factors, the presence
of a Walmart often increased poverty in a community, or at least made it
harder to recover from poverty during strong economic times.[31]

This is where Brooke Bergen ended up on a day that would turn out
very badly for her. Wide awake at three in the morning and unable to
sleep, she decided she needed to get out of the house. There are a couple of dollar stores on one side of Salem, the Town & Country grocery
store on the other, but if you're awake at three in the morning, Walmart
is the only place to go.

Nine months earlier, Bergen's life had been turned upside down
when her four-month-old infant girl, Amaya Jaine, died in her sleep.
She was twenty-seven when she lost her child, but sadly grieving a
loved one was nothing new to her at that tender age. She had lost her
mother and a brother already. But this death, coming as she was turning
a corner after a prison stint for abusing opioids, when she was happy
and thought she was beating her addiction, this one was too much too
handle.

"I was crazy."

Aisle to aisle she went in the near-empty store. Bergen had packed
her grocery cart with food, household items, and some makeup. She
stopped in the aisle with bulk deals and picked up a box of mascara for
$8.74. As she headed toward the checkout, the mascara fell out of its
box, which was annoying, so she absentmindedly put the tube in her
pocket and threw the box away.[32] But then she forgot about it. While

she was paying for her items, she never pulled the mascara out of her pocket. As she was leaving, an employee stopped her and asked about the makeup in her pocket. Bergen panicked.

"I freaked out," she said. "I tried to run. I knew it was stupid."

Unlike Killman and Darby, this wasn't Bergen's first brush with the law. Though she lived in Missouri, her struggles started in Florida, where she grew up. "We were poor," Bergen told me. Her mother lived mostly off various state aid programs, including food stamps. They lived in the Henry Kirkland Garden Apartments, a public housing project on Everitt Avenue in Panama City.[33] It was an area of town referred to by the locals as Millville, which was built up in the late 1800s around lumberyards that have long since closed down.

She was twelve when her little brother died. He was eight, playing outside, when he was crushed and killed by a rampaging truck that jumped a curb. Bergen was just entering middle school. She didn't know her father. He died when she was little. The typical angst of any preteen was accelerated by so much trauma early in her life. "I was really angry, all the time," Bergen remembers.

So angry that when she was thirteen, she got into a fight with another girl in middle school, injuring her severely. It was her first brush with trouble, and she ended up at a girls' juvenile facility on the grounds of the notorious Greenville Hills Academy. It was a dark place.

Located in an old railroad town on Highway 90, east of Tallahassee, just a couple of hours from the panhandle city where Bergen grew up, Greenville Hills Academy at the time looked almost pastoral, though it was surrounded by barbed wire fencing. The series of brick and concrete-block buildings with blue metal roofs are spread across hundreds of acres. But it's difficult to describe it innocuously as an "academy" while Bergen was there in 2003 and 2004. Just a couple of years after she left, Greenville was investigated by multiple state agencies for abuse and endangerment of its teenage student population. There were more than two hundred calls to a state abuse hotline over a two-year period including complaints of physical restraints that could break bones.[34] Bergen witnessed it. She was on the other side of a door when she heard a couple of officers at the boot camp restraining another girl. "All I could hear was her crying, and screaming in pain," Bergen says. "Then I heard the bones breaking, I think in her arm.

"It was the worst sound I ever heard."

For too many young people across the South, this is what juvenile justice looks like. Author Colson Whitehead addressed such horrific conditions in his Pulitzer Prize–winning novel *The Nickel Boys*, which was based on real tales of abuse from the Dozier School for Boys, located in Marianna, Florida, just northwest of where Bergen was sent.[35] After a damning Department of Justice report in 2011 that documented years of abuse, violence, and death, the Dozier School was shut down.[36]

When Bergen walked out of that academy, everything changed. She had seen things, heard things, at the juvenile boot camp that would change her forever. It was April 27, the two-year anniversary of her eight-year-old brother's death. While she was inside, her mother had died of a heart attack. The little family she had was gone. A relative she barely knew lived in Rockaway Beach, Missouri, a tiny town on the shores of Lake Taneycomo just northeast of Branson. She moved and never looked back. She would be there until she finished high school.

As soon as she was old enough, she found a job. The family member who took her in drank heavily and could be abusive, Bergen said. Work was her place of respite. She worked first at the Sonic Drive-In in Forsyth, a town just east of Rockaway Beach. In high school, she worked at an Old Navy in the Tanger Outlets mall in Branson, the family-oriented entertainment mecca and tourist spot in southwest Missouri. "I worked, and worked, and worked," she said. "All the time." The day after she turned seventeen, Bergen moved in with her boyfriend. They got married a year later and moved to Salem.

When she got hooked, it started slow. First a joint. Then, softening the pain of a toothache, a Vicodin pill. Before long, an opioid addiction took hold of her. She was hardly unique. Between 2012 and 2017, the nation's three largest opioid producers distributed more than 1.6 billion pain pills in Missouri, at the height of what had become a national crisis of addiction.[37] As this crisis percolated, every state in the nation except one—Missouri—developed a prescription drug monitoring program, where physicians and law enforcement could track the abuse of opioids. These databases are used to cut down on "pill-mill" shopping, where a drug abuser might go to several doctors or pharmacies to fulfill narcotic prescriptions. Missouri's lack of such a database—blocked by a few Republicans in the state senate—exacerbated the opioid crisis in the state. At one point the biggest opioid producers were sending more than sixty pills per person in Dent County a year to the area, one of the highest rates in Missouri.[38]

Opioid addicts often graduate to heroin when getting pain pills becomes too difficult or too expensive.[39] So it was for Bergen.

In 2009 Bergen was charged with drug possession and served 120 days in state prison. A year later, she still wasn't clean, and she violated her probation multiple times. She headed back to prison for another 120 days. Missouri's prisons are full of people like Bergen: sent there first on nonviolent drug offenses, and then again on probation or parole violations. As of 2018, about 54 percent of the men and women in Missouri prisons were there on the latter, tied with Arizona for one of the highest percentages in the country (Idaho tops the list).[40]

In December, Bergen pleaded guilty to the misdemeanor theft charge that stemmed from shoplifting the $8.74 tube of mascara.[41] She was sentenced to a year in jail and two years of probation. The year in jail would be suspended if she stayed out of trouble. This is the double-edged sword of justice in rural Missouri. It is very common for rural judges to issue what sounds like a tough sentence—one year for shoplifting, for instance—and then suspend the sentence. The idea is that if the defendant doesn't get into trouble, they won't ever serve any time in jail. Such sentences sound both tough and humane at the same time.

The reality, for most folks, is something different.

Unlike a state felony charge—in Missouri and elsewhere—misdemeanor probation is supervised by private companies with a profit motive.[42] These companies sprang up after state legislatures made cuts to state probation departments and left the problem to counties, who then turned to the private sector. Just like that, the cost moved from the taxpayer to the defendants themselves. The probation company in Salem, MPPS, was run at the time by Lisa Blackwell, who was a longtime friend of Judge Brandi Baird, who had been the prosecutor on Bergen's first drug charge.[43]

In the Dent County Courthouse at the time, Blackwell had her own chair next to the prosecutor. This is remarkable. An unelected person who does not work for the state was elevated to a position of power, as though she were an official part of the judicial system. In reality, she managed a private company that could benefit financially when the people in the courtroom return to jail and stay in the probation system. When Baird would call up a defendant for a payment review hearing, the judge would turn to Blackwell, who with a simple word or a thumbs-up or -down could decide whether somebody was going back to jail.

Bergen didn't know it, but, at the time of her sentencing, her cycle of jail and debt was just beginning. The same was true for Killman and Darby. Indeed, the real trouble was just starting.

2

· · · · · · · · · · · · · · · · · ·

TAXATION BY CITATION

Norman, Oklahoma
June 2009

Killman returned on June 9 to the Cleveland County Courthouse for her second hearing. As she waited, "A guy I've never met pokes his head into the courtroom and yells a version of what I believe is my name." It was Henry Herbst, a personal-injury attorney who took indigent cases on contract basis from Cleveland County. This was the first time she was hearing from her "court-appointed" lawyer. She told Herbst her story: She bought the car for a trip to Arkansas and got pulled over on the way home. Police found the marijuana pipe with residue. She has no idea who it belongs to or how it got there. Herbst tells her to plead "no contest."

Similar to an "Alford plea" in some states, when a person pleads no contest, they are admitting the prosecutor can probably win the case, but they are not admitting they are guilty of the crime. It is a compromise of sorts, with the basic effect of a guilty plea.[1] In many states, defendants use such pleas to avoid the potential of a harsher sentence were they to be convicted at trial. Killman didn't want to put up a fight. She wanted it to be over. Herbst did all the talking. Killman describes the day as an out-of-body experience. Through her attorney, she pleaded no contest to two misdemeanors, possession of drug paraphernalia and possession of marijuana. In Oklahoma, pipe residue is enough evidence to establish possession.

Sentencing was set for August 21. On that day, the judge sentenced her to a year in jail on each count, but the sentence was deferred. A deferred sentence is common in misdemeanor cases. In effect, it means that the defendant won't actually go to jail, as long as they don't violate the terms of their probation.[2] Judges like deferred sentences for a variety of reasons. In many jurisdictions, the jails are crowded, and there is simply no room for everybody. But judges don't want to look weak on crime, so they impose sentences like the one Killman got, but defer them, holding the possibility of jail over a defendant's head for as long as they are on probation. If Killman did everything the judge asked her to do, she wouldn't actually go to jail. The judge also ordered Killman to perform forty hours of community service and pay court costs.

Court costs. To this day, those two words haunt her.

A few of those costs are outlined in the document she signed after sentencing. There was a $100 court assessment, $100 for a victims' compensation fund, $40 a month in probation costs, $100 in a mental health fee.[3] Killman had to pay $100 for a trauma care assistance fund; $25 for the Oklahoma court information system; $15 to the district attorney council; $10 for courthouse security; $6 for a law library fee; $5 for a sheriff's service fee; $27.50 to the county clerk; $17 for a collections fee. The costs were charged on each count, meaning she had to pay each one of them twice. This is a clever little trick cities and counties pull as part of their criminal justice fundraising machine. It's not like Killman cost the courts any additional money because she faced two charges. Both charges were handled by the same judges and clerks and prosecutors in the same court at one time. But by charging twice the county doubles its financial haul while burying a poor person in debt.

Killman was shocked by the amount, which, she says, hadn't been described to her before her plea by either her attorney or the judge. The judge put her on a payment plan. When Killman signed the papers agreeing to pay $100 a month, she saw the total owed: $1,150.

There are more than 120 separate fines or fees called for in municipal, county, or state law in Oklahoma depending on the circumstance, and the burden of paying these fees falls mostly on the poor people who crowd the state's misdemeanor dockets.[4] There are law library fees, clerk fees, jury fees, and district attorney fees.[5] It's overwhelming, certainly. But this is the "backdoor tax"—this is what happens when you need to raise capital for local spending but refuse to increase taxes on the local residents. Good politics, perhaps, and devastating for those stuck with the bill. Loretta Radford, the legal director at the Center for Criminal Justice at the Oklahoma City University School of Law, calls all these fines and fees in Oklahoma a form of double taxation. "It is not helping public safety in any way by burdening individuals with all this debt," Radford says. It is nearly impossible to track how much is owed to municipal and county courts, which don't keep consistent, easy-to-track records of these fines, but nationally, there is likely somewhere around $50 billion in outstanding debt associated with this phenomenon.[6]

At the time of her sentencing, Killman and two of her children, her father, and her boyfriend were all sharing a two-bedroom apartment, funded mostly by the federal Housing and Urban Development's subsidized Section 8 housing program. She received a $543 federal disability check every month for Bubba, who is intellectually disabled. It is her primary source of income. She can't work because she's his primary caretaker. The family receives $306 a month in food stamps. After gas, car insurance, and utilities, she has to make sure everyone stays fed with the food stamps. Now this. "The court thing never goes away," she says. "They just keep adding to it. It's never ending." Yes, she agreed to $100 a month, but how long would she be able to manage it?

Ferguson, Missouri
August 2014

I became familiar with this issue amid unrest in the streets of Ferguson and St. Louis in the summer of 2014, nearly five years after Killman's personal brush with the indignity.

If you are Black, poor, and live in St. Louis County, then having traffic tickets and outstanding warrants are simply facts of life.[7] The county is a patchwork of eighty-eight municipalities, each with their own police departments and traffic courts.[8] It isn't uncommon for a person to get multiple tickets on a single drive down Interstate 70, especially near the airport, as they move through several municipalities in less than a two-mile stretch.[9]

Here's how bad it was in 2014, before the protests:

- Pine Lawn, a tiny town of 3,500, which is more than 96 percent Black and has a per capita income of $13,000 a year, collected $1.7 million in traffic fees in 2013. At the time it had more than 23,000 outstanding warrants, many for failure to pay.[10]
- In 2015, Ferguson was bringing in about $2 million a year in fines and fees, mostly from traffic offenses, about 23 percent of its city revenue.[11] A city of about 21,000 people[12] issued more than 90,000 citations between 2010 and 2014.[13]
- An analysis of public records in 2014 by the *St. Louis Post-Dispatch* found that the municipalities in north St. Louis County issued more warrants and traffic fines per capita than the rest of Missouri. "Of the 25 courts that saw the greatest increase in collection between 2008 and 2013, 12 were in St. Louis County," the newspaper found.[14]

Where does all this money go? It mostly goes right back into police departments and courts, funding all their operational needs. It does not go to building schools or funding roads, erecting bridges or breaking ground on new public parks.[15]

Much of the angst that fueled the 2014 protests was driven by the experiences of Black people who had been overpoliced for decades. The reasons for this are wide-ranging, but also, in some ways, humiliatingly banal: a patchwork of municipalities used their courts as a revenue source because they didn't have much of a tax base, and the burden was unduly placed on their Black residents.[16] The protests resonated nationally, in part because this experience is so common in cities everywhere. Police officers are given quotas on traffic enforcement, so they issue an exorbitant number of tickets, which in turn balance municipal budgets.[17] Nearly every one of the African American residents of the St. Louis region who took to the streets, both young and old, had experienced the process of being in and out of municipal jails for falling behind on outstanding debts emerging from traffic tickets.

In the days after Michael Brown's death, attorneys Michael-John Voss, Thomas Harvey, and John McAnnar—the founders of a nonprofit law firm in St. Louis called the ArchCity Defenders—published a white paper that outlined the municipal court scheme they had been seeing over the years. "Clients reported being jailed because they were unable to pay fines," they wrote. "Some who have been incarcerated for delinquent fine payments have lost jobs and housing as a result. Indigent mothers 'failed to appear' in court and had warrants issued for their arrest after arriving early or on-time to court and being turned away because that particular municipality prohibits children in court. Family members were forced to wait outside courtrooms while loved-ones represent themselves in front of a judge and a prosecutor."[18]

I met one of Voss's clients, Keilee Fant, at a funeral for her friend; both women were victims of the scheme, and both had Voss as their attorney. For Fant, who is Black, her legal troubles stemmed from years of traffic tickets and warrants and stays in municipal and county jails in north St. Louis County. It started when she was a teenager. Sometimes, she would spend weeks at a time locked up—in St. Ann, in Jennings, in many of the municipalities in North County—and, as a result, lose jobs and miss car payments, all because she was too poor to afford the traffic fines—and there was nothing unique about her case.

Now Fant was the lead plaintiff in two lawsuits filed by ArchCity Defenders, the Civil Rights Corps, and the St. Louis University School of Law Legal Clinics—one against the city of Jennings, another against Ferguson. Both lawsuits alleged multiple civil rights violations of Fant and thousands of other defendants over decades in which the system worked to exploit their poverty for government profit.[19]

"The Plaintiffs in this case are each impoverished people who were jailed by the City of Ferguson because they were unable to pay a debt owed to the City from traffic tickets or other minor offenses," reads the lawsuit.[20] "In each case, the City imprisoned a human being solely because the person could not afford to make a monetary payment. Although the Plaintiffs pleaded that they were unable to pay due to their poverty, each was held in jail indefinitely and none was afforded a lawyer or the inquiry into their ability to pay that the United States Constitution requires. Instead, they were threatened, abused, and left to languish in confinement at the mercy of local officials until their frightened family members could produce enough cash to buy their freedom or until City jail officials decided, days or weeks later, to let them out for free."

Like many people who live in poverty, Fant had to make a series of difficult choices to survive. For instance, because she couldn't pay her fines, her driver's license had been suspended. There is little effective public transportation in north St. Louis County. Plans for the region's long anticipated north–south transit line has yet to materialize. In other words, to get to work as a nurse's aide, Fant needed to drive.

So she did. One day, in October 2013, while dropping her children off to school, she got pulled over in Jennings. Because of outstanding warrants on traffic tickets, she was taken to jail and told she could get out if she could pay $300.

"I didn't have it," Fant told me. Unable to pay, she sat in jail for three days until the city needed the space for somebody else, and let her go. But she wasn't exactly free. Here's how the federal civil rights lawsuit against the cities of Ferguson and Jennings described what happened next:

> Ms. Fant's supposed "release" from Jennings's custody was just the beginning of a Kafkaesque journey through the debtors' prison network of Saint Louis County—a lawless and labyrinthine scheme of dungeon-like municipal facilities and perpetual

debt. Every year, thousands of Saint Louis County residents, including the Plaintiffs in this case, undergo a similar journey, buying or waiting their way out of jail after jail.

From Jennings to Bellefontaine Neighbors to Velda City to St. Louis County to Normandy to the city of Beverly Hills—which is nothing like the glamorous city of California—Fant was moved to different jails over the course of eight more days. But it still wasn't over.

St. Louis County eventually sent her to Maryland Heights, and then, finally, Ferguson, where jail officials told her they would set her free for the princely sum of $1,400, which she obviously couldn't pay. She sat in the Ferguson jail for three more days before they let her go.

Jennings settled the lawsuit against it for $4.7 million in July 2016, the largest such payout in the country at the time.[21] Further, the city canceled outstanding debt and warrants, and agreed to multiple reforms, including holding "ability-to-pay" hearings. Such hearings are required by law before bail is set, or in a case where incarceration is possible. But municipal judges were regularly skipping this step.[22] All in all, Fant pocketed about $1,200, and had her outstanding warrants erased. The city of Ferguson has denied that it violated Fant's civil rights, or any other citizens' who might be affected by the class action. The lawsuit is ongoing.

"I'm not where I want to be," Fant says. "But I'm not where I used to be."

The white paper drafted by ArchCity Defenders was focused on the tiny municipalities that dot St. Louis County, and its victims were mostly poor and Black, but don't be tricked by this regional specificity. As I wrote in an editorial in 2014: Ferguson is everywhere.

A 2019 analysis by *Governing* magazine found that nearly 600 cities and counties in the U.S. collect more than 10 percent of their budgets from these types of fines and fees through their court system. The states where the situation is most prevalent are in the South: Georgia, Louisiana, Oklahoma, Arkansas, and Texas.[23] In Georgia, where, unlike most states, traffic violations are criminal misdemeanors, not civil offenses, fines can be between $500 and $1,000. It also has some of the highest surcharges in the country, meaning an additional several hundred dollars added to the statutory fine.[24]

One small Georgia town outside of Atlanta, LaGrange, until 2020 would turn off your water and electricity if you couldn't afford to pay your traffic fines.[25] Just over half of the city's residents are Black.[26] In 2017, the Southern Center for Human Rights sued the city over that policy, arguing it was discriminatory and a violation of the federal Fair Housing Act.[27] Passed in 1968, the Fair Housing Act prohibits racial discrimination in public housing. "Residents in LaGrange who have court fines and health issues live in constant fear," said Atteeyah Hollie, one of the attorneys who filed the lawsuit.

One of the plaintiffs is April Walton, a forty-year-old single mother of three who also takes care of her disabled mother.[28] In 2015, she pleaded no contest to possession of less than an ounce of marijuana (a misdemeanor). The charge stemmed from a traffic stop. Her court debt was $1,200. By the time she completed her twelve months of probation, she still owed $853.60. That debt was then attached to her utility account, which was operated by the city. In 2016, when she fell behind on her payments, her water and electricity were cut off. Ninety percent of the residents of LaGrange who are threatened with a utility cutoff because of outstanding debt are people of color and mostly Black. In court filings, the city denied any violations of the Fair Housing Act and said the provisions of the federal law didn't apply to the utility cutoffs because they occurred after service had already been provided.

The lawsuit was dismissed by a federal judge in late 2017 but was reinstated by an appeals court in October 2019.

"Plaintiffs who have utility services but have acquired municipal debt are at risk of having those services terminated without notice," the court wrote.[29] "As a result, even if the plaintiffs are able to purchase or rent a dwelling, they are unable to live in it due to being unable to obtain or maintain basic utility services."

In October 2020, the city reached a $450,000 settlement with the plaintiffs, agreeing to reverse the utility shutoff policies.[30]

In the *Governing* study, Louisiana was cited as one of the nation's worst offenders of the backdoor tax. Across the U.S., the eight municipalities that collect the largest percentage of their overall budget from traffic fines and fees were all in Louisiana: Georgetown, Fenton, Baskin, Henderson, Robeline, Reeves, Pioneer, and Tullos. All depended on traffic revenue for at least 75 percent of their budgets.[31] A Louisiana state audit completed in 2018 found that in one of these cities, Fenton, the traffic revenue was padding additional compensation for various officials, including the mayor, who blamed the situation on a clerical error, but reimbursed the city for the extra pay.[32] That sort of connection between what is supposed to be a public safety function and the actual compensation of public officials highlights how the profit motive leads to an abuse of the justice system, says Samuel Brooke, deputy director of the Southern Poverty Law Center. "The idea of a user-funded model is backward. Society is paying for this," he said. "The problem is the money is coming out of the pockets of its poorest citizens."[33] In Oklahoma and Texas, each has thirty-three communities that obtain more than 30 percent of their annual budgets from court fines and fees.[34]

As Ferguson was unfolding, with nightly images on cable television of the standoffs between protesters and police dressed head-to-toe in riot gear and backed by armored vehicles manned by snipers, I became angry. At the time, I was the editorial page editor, writing daily about the underlying causes of the nightly unrest, the police brutality, the awful racial profiling statistics in Missouri, and the broken municipal court system.

Stuck in traffic on Interstate 64 one morning during my commute, I turned on the voice recorder on my phone and started ranting. "This is not St. Louis!" I screamed. "We are not tear gas and sniper rifles, pointed at young, African American men, protesting the death of their friend and community member, eighteen-year-old Michael Brown . . .

"This is not St. Louis, where the governor can't be found and night after night, our paralysis is played out over national airwaves for the world to see . . .

"This is not St. Louis. This is not the United States of America. We are not a police state."

I linked the words to photos taken from that night's protest to create a video editorial that I released on the newspaper's website.[35] It was emotional and it was real, but I was, of course, wrong.

This *was* St. Louis.

Particularly for young Black drivers who felt like they had to gear up to survive a gauntlet every day, hoping not to get pulled over for a broken taillight or expired tags or simply Driving While Black, doing what everyone else does: headed to school or work or their grandmother's house.

At the time of Brown's death, Missouri's racial-profiling statistics had gotten worse in eleven of the fourteen years they had been kept. In 2013, for instance, Black Missourians were 66 percent more likely to be pulled over by police than white drivers. In November 2014, the Reverend Starsky Wilson helped bring some focus to what Americans were seeing on their television screens. He organized a panel event to give leaders of prominent Black nonprofits across the country a sense of what was happening on the ground in Ferguson.

"What does justice look like?" Wilson asked the audience he had gathered in St. Louis at a Grand Center jazz club.[36] Wilson was the CEO of the Deaconess Foundation and would soon be named the co-chair of the Ferguson Commission, which Governor Jay Nixon created to address the underlying causes of the unrest and develop a path forward.[37] Patricia Bynes and Tory Russell were panel speakers that night. They shared their stories of living in north St. Louis County, of what drove them to protest, of what—all in all—things were like on the streets.

Justice, I wrote in a column that was jointly published by the *Post-Dispatch* and the *Guardian*, is "about Ms. Bynes driving to work in Chesterfield without having to navigate a patchwork of municipalities, most of which shouldn't exist, that rely on traffic stops to pay their bills. It's about her neighbors having that little extra money in their pockets to feed their children, or put gas in their cars, rather than pay fine upon fine in city court upon city court that prey upon blacks in ways most whites in the community don't understand."

Wilson's Ferguson Commission would eventually issue a report that included several recommendations to fix the broken municipal courts by focusing on public safety, not debt collection.[38] "More than half the courts in St. Louis County engage in the 'illegal and harmful practices' of charging high court fines and fees on nonviolent offenses like traffic violations and then arresting people when they don't pay . . . The Commission and Working Group heard numerous examples of people who were unable to pay their fines for a minor ordinance violation, missed their court dates because they did not have the money, had warrants issued against them, and/or ended up in jail for failure to appear."

This last part demands a revision to court hearings so that a defendant's ability to pay is always taken into consideration, for courts to treat fines and fees like civil debts, not criminal issues, to cancel failure-to-appear warrants, and to cap the amount of money cities could collect from traffic revenue.[39] On the latter, the commission would need help from the Missouri Legislature, which was dominated by white, rural Republicans.

Enter Eric Schmitt.

Jefferson City, Missouri
January 2015

The Senate lounge is more courtroom than place of respite. Located on the third floor of the Missouri Capitol, it's a grand room with wood paneling, historic chandeliers, witness chairs, and tables where various panels hear testimony for or against bills. In January 2015, Schmitt, a Republican from Glendale, a West County suburb of St. Louis, stepped down from the dais and sat in the witness chair to face his colleagues.

He was presenting Senate Bill 5, a rewrite of the 1995 Macks Creek Law that would lower the cap on the amount of revenue cities could collect from traffic fines.[40]

I got to know Schmitt during his first term. One of the first times I wrote about him, I was alone in the senate chamber, typing away on my laptop. It was quiet and was sometimes my favorite place to work. At the time, reporters had a small table to the side, right on the floor of the senate, where they could observe and do their work. Schmitt came in with some elementary students. He was giving them a tour, and I could overhear him telling the kids about some legislation he was working on.[41]

That year, Schmitt was sponsoring a bill that required insurance companies to pay for certain treatments and services for children with autism.[42] For Schmitt, this was personal: his son, Stephen, has autism. Schmitt choked up as he told the students one of those "why I became a politician" stories. I stopped what I was working on and listened, and later wrote a column about it.[43] Schmitt struggled to get the bill passed. The insurance lobby, among the most powerful special interests in the state capitol, had blocked the bill in a previous session.[44]

By 2015, Schmitt had risen in seniority and began eying statewide office. Ambitious by nature, he is the sort of person who seemed destined for a life in politics: tall and athletic, he played baseball and football at Truman State University in Kirksville, Missouri.[45] He came back home for law school, where he graduated from St. Louis University School of Law.[46] Schmitt also had something else, so uncommon nowadays: he got along with people on both sides of the aisle. Now Schmitt would take on the "backdoor tax" issue directly. He would introduce Senate Bill 5, and it was the kind of move that could make him a national figure.

In his first hearing for the bill, Schmitt read an email that had been sent the preceding April from the mayor of Edmundson, a tiny municipality near Bridgeton, where Schmitt grew up. The email told the police force to double down. Schmitt was exposing it.

"I wish to take this opportunity to remind you that the tickets that you write do add to the revenue on which the P.D. budget is established and will directly affect pay adjustments at budget time," wrote Mayor John Gwaltney.[47] "As budget time approaches, please make a self-evaluation of your work habits and motivations, then make the changes that you see that will be fair to yourself and the city."

In April 2014, urged by their mayor, police officers in the town of about eight hundred people doubled their traffic ticket issuances. A year later, after Schmitt read that email, he convinced his fellow lawmakers that it was time to stop taxation by citation.[48] Nonetheless, it wasn't easy to get Senate Bill 5 over the finish line.

About midway through the session, I sat with Schmitt in his office and talked about the hurdles. Ironically, opposition was coming from mayors in the places that needed the bill most: those who ran primarily Black cities in north St. Louis County and those who headed small rural cities in tiny outposts throughout Missouri that relied on speed traps for revenue.[49] The underlying law that Schmitt was trying to amend was named after a town in the south-central part of the state once known for its speed traps.[50] Macks Creek is no longer even a city, just a place on a map, southwest of Lake of the Ozarks along Highway 54. But for a long time in the '80s and the '90s it was the most notorious speed trap in the state. In fact, it was so well-known that it appeared in a 1991 national publication called *The Safe Motorist's Guide to Speedtraps.*[51] The problem started in 1987, when Macks Creek decided to add a police department, not because it had a safety problem, but as a source of revenue.[52] It dropped the speed limit on the highway from sixty-five miles per hour to forty-five in the city limits. Then the money started flowing in.

By the time the Missouri Legislature got involved in 1995, about 80 percent of Macks Creek's revenue was coming from traffic tickets.[53] Not even the lawmakers were spared: some of them who had to drive through town on their way to the state capitol were issued tickets. In 1995 the legislature passed a law that would limit cities from collecting more than 45 percent of their budget from traffic fines and fees. Rep. Delbert Scott, a Republican from Lowry City, who had also been pulled over in Macks Creek, sponsored the bill.

"There's something unjust about highway robbery, literally, when it's not for safety issues but to strictly raise revenues," he told the *Kansas City Star* after the bill's passage.[54]

After the law took effect, city leaders found a workaround: all speeding fines were changed to parking violations. But once a state audit uncovered the scheme, city leaders resigned, the town went broke, and now it's back to being what it was before, a blip on the road on the way to the lake.[55] Of course, that all happened twenty years before any current lawmakers were in the capitol, so old fights had to be revisited.

"It would really hurt our town," Edgar Springs city administrator Paula James told a local newspaper during the Senate Bill 5 debate.[56]

Anybody who drives through mid-Missouri regularly, as my family does, knows that Edgar Springs is the new Macks Creek. My wife's family lives in Ozark County, which borders Arkansas in the heart of the Ozarks. It's cattle country, with beautiful rolling hills and fresh-water streams that feed historic old mills that dot the landscape. On our way to spend time on the farm, we drive through Edgar Springs. The town of about two hundred has a stoplight on the highway, with a convenience store on either side.[57] Like Macks Creek, city leaders dropped the speed limit from sixty-five to forty-five, with little warning.[58] When I'm driving, my wife always reminds me to slow down before we get near the town.

A couple of years ago, we were driving near another speed trap, headed east on state Highway 70, into New Bern, North Carolina. We were on the way to see my son, a Marine officer who was based at Cherry Point, the base near the Atlantic Ocean in the northeastern part of the state. To get there, we drove through New Bern (notable for being the place where PepsiCo was founded).[59] My two youngest children, sitting in the back seat, saw the flashing lights first. I pulled over. My wife recorded me getting the ticket on her phone, just so the family could make fun of me later. It was a hefty fine: if memory serves, it was $350. The most memorable thing about it, however, was what was in my mailbox when we got home a week later: seven solicitations from attorneys in and around New Bern. One was from a former mayor of the town.

"In most cases we can take care of everything in a single phone call," he wrote.[60] It's likely that he was responsible for creating the scheme in the first place. I put my check in the envelope and paid the fine. It hurt, but I didn't want to give the New Bern scheme the satisfaction of playing by their rules and paying some attorney an extra bundle of cash to drop my speeding ticket to a parking fine. It also helped that I had the cash—I could pay my way out of it.

In North Carolina, court fines and fees have risen by 400 percent in the past two decades.[61] That models the trend across the country.[62] What happens to those people who can't afford to pay their fines? They lose their driver's licenses.

According to a 2017 study, more than 1 million people in North Carolina have had their licenses suspended over nonpayment of fines and fees. In Texas, it's 1.8 million.[63] Four million in California.[64] Between 2016 and 2018, the state of New York suspended more than 1.7 million driver's licenses because of the failure to pay traffic debt.[65] In Florida, nearly two million drivers have had their licenses suspended. In Orange County, Florida, nearly 15 percent of its driving population has a failure-to-pay suspension, the highest such rate in the country.[66]

In the U.S., "35 states and the District of Columbia suspend driver's licenses for nonpayment of fines and fees from previous court cases, traffic or otherwise," Lisa Foster, of the Fines and Fees Justice Center, said. Her organization estimates that this scheme affects 11 million people nationwide. "Probably the most famous example is Ferguson," she said. "But it's happening all around the country."

Ashley Gantt is an activist with Action Together Rochester, a group that formed to help battle the criminalization of poverty in Rochester, New York, which has historically high rates of driver's license suspension for failure to pay, especially among people of color.[67] "People are going to prison over this," she said. For Gantt, who is Black, this is also personal. When she was sixteen, she received two tickets, one for speeding and another for not coming to a complete stop.

"I couldn't afford to pay the tickets," she said. Eventually, her inability to pay the fines led to the suspension of her driver's license. A few years later, she was pulled over on the suspended license and served fifteen days in jail. After a while, it's not where to look, but where *not* to look.

For three years, for instance, Minnesota state representative Nick Zerwas, a Republican from rural Elk River, tried to end this whole phenomenon in his state.[68] The problem, as Zerwas sees it, is that the punishment is worse than the crime.

"It's a huge, huge impact on less affluent communities," Zerwas said. "If you're from where I live, if you can't drive, you can't get to work. You can't get to the store to buy milk for your kid. How ridiculous is it that we're going to take away a person's ability to work because they haven't made enough money to pay a fine or fee?"

In other words, you're stacking fees on people who can't pay them anyway—so how else to view this? You're not simply ruining lives; you can't even collect on the fees themselves. Zerwas failed to get his Minnesota bill across the finish line before he left the legislature in 2019. In Missouri, however, Schmitt succeeded.

"The purpose of municipal courts is to protect our communities, not profit from them," Governor Nixon said as he signed Schmitt's bill into law on July 9, 2015.[69]

In the spring of 2015, a nonprofit in St. Louis called Better Together hired the Police Executive Research Forum (PERF) to study the balkanized nature of police agencies in St. Louis County.[70] They hoped to lay the groundwork to eventually consolidate most of those municipalities into a more unified government, similar to what had happened in Indianapolis, Nashville, and dozens of other cities over previous decades.[71] Part of the group's plan was to get rid of most of the municipal police departments and municipal courts that were nickel-and-diming residents to death in order to fill city coffers with cash.

To help make its case, Better Together pointed out that many of the cities lacked a reasonable tax base, and the poorest of those cities turned to its police department to supply revenue.[72] This, PERF found, goes against good policing principles.

"In many municipalities, policing priorities are driven not by the public safety needs of the community, but rather by the goal of generating large portions of the operating revenue for the local government," PERF's report said. "This is a grossly inappropriate mission for the police, often carried out at the direction of local elected officials."[73]

The final version of Senate Bill 5 contained a two-tiered revenue cap. The Macks Creek cap, which had been lowered over time from 45 percent to 30 percent, was dropped again to 20 percent statewide. But municipalities in St. Louis County would have to meet a lower 12.5 percent revenue cap.[74]

The cities, of course, sued, and they won a temporary, pyrrhic victory. The Missouri Supreme Court ruled that the separate caps were unconstitutional, but it kept in place the 20 percent ceiling.[75] Over the next three years, municipal court revenue from traffic tickets dropped almost 40 percent statewide. Ferguson's traffic fine revenue dropped from $2 million a year to about $300,000.[76]

In December of 2018, ArchCity Defenders filed its latest class-action lawsuit, which targeted municipal court abuses related to court costs, this time against Edmundson, the city whose police chief had been caught promoting ticket quotas.[77] In court filings, the city denied allegations of any constitutional violations. The case is ongoing.

"We have an entire criminal legal system in this region and across the state that is wealth-based and criminalizes people daily for their poverty," Blake Strode, the executive director of ArchCity Defenders told me at the time.[78] "It may look slightly different from one jurisdiction to the next, but the fundamental dynamics are the same. In the case of Edmundson, there are thousands of largely poor, Black St. Louisans whose lives are still impacted to this day by the use of police, court and jail as an ATM machine for the city."

3

NO SALE OF JUSTICE

St. Louis, Missouri
November 2016

One of the key lessons of Ferguson, says Frank Vatterott, is that "the courts were charging too much money" to defendants. Vatterott is a St. Louis attorney and former municipal judge. He was a cog in the wheel of municipal courts and police departments in St. Louis County that were profiting on the backs of poor people. But he was also somebody who recognized some of the injustices in the system and had been waging a years-long battle against one specific court fee that, to him, symbolized the root of the problem. It was a $3 fee applied to most criminal court cases in Missouri that funds an additional retirement benefit for sheriffs.

The surcharge seems almost negligible. What's the big deal about $3? But who got the money—mostly rural sheriffs—and who lawmakers wanted to pay it—mostly poor people in Missouri's biggest cities—explains a lot about the nation's love affair with court fines and fees. By charging just $3 on every court case in Missouri, the sheriffs' retirement fund could raise millions of dollars a year. Take that one example and start spreading it around: $3 for sheriffs; $4 for prosecutors; $2 for clerks; another few bucks here and there for other pet projects of lawmakers. In nearly every state capitol in the country, one of these $3 fees gets added on to misdemeanor or traffic cases every year, generally to raise money for something that taxes applied broadly to the entire populace used to pay for. That's why this one $3 fee in Missouri—and the incredible efforts lawmakers deployed to collect it—holds a lesson for the nation.

On the day we first met, in the fall of 2016, Vatterott handed me a three-ring binder that was packed four inches thick with documents outlining his legal fight against the $3 sheriffs' retirement fee. In the binder was a section titled "No sale of justice."

The concept of not putting a barrier to justice between poor people and the courts is older than the American judicial system itself. In theory, it means that everybody has access to the courts; that justice is blind and doesn't discriminate between rich and poor. The concept harkens back to the Magna Carta, agreed to in 1215 between King John of England and barons who sought and demanded certain rights, including the right to not have to bribe a magistrate to have access to justice. "To no one will we sell, to no one will we deny or delay, right or justice," reads the fortieth clause of the Magna Carta.[1] It became an underlying principle of English, and then American, law that persists today. Vatterott, and other attorneys like him, believe that the rise of fines and fees in American courts creates an unconstitutional obstacle to justice, because of the unfair burden it places on poor people.

The still-raging battle over that $3 fee in Missouri helps explain how using court costs as a revenue generator became so attractive to lawmakers. The lengths that lawmakers and a state attorney general went to in order to get the charge implemented in Missouri's municipal courts adds important context to the rise of fines and fees across the nation. First: lawmakers know what they are doing. They know the municipal courts, where the bulk of the cases in the criminal justice system begin, are a cash cow. Second: they will use their power to force the courts to raise the revenue they need, going so far as to threaten the courts with their own budgets, if necessary.

In 1983, Missouri sheriffs went to the general assembly with a request. Even though they were part of the same taxpayer retirement system as most government employees, they wanted a separate retirement system established to supplement their pensions. Lawmakers weren't about to increase taxes to pay for this, and sheriffs didn't want to have to use their own income to fund the system, so the legislature passed House Bill 81, which created the Missouri Sheriffs' Retirement System, funded by a $3 charge added to every court case in the state.[2]

Within three years the system was up and running and started to pad retirement accounts.[3] Fast forward to 2010, after the Great Recession, and a problem arose. Like many public retirement systems across the country, the sheriffs' accounts took a hit when the stock market collapsed, losing about $5 million. It needed an infusion of money to become solvent.[4]

The sheriffs eyed the municipal courts, which were not charging the $3 surcharge because of a dispute about the language in the legislation that created the fee. The municipal courts are a gold mine because that's where all traffic cases start, and where most people in the state first encounter the judicial system.[5] Adding the charge to municipal cases would bring in about $3 million a year to the sheriffs.[6] In most rural counties, sheriffs are powerful political figures. They are first responders, law-and-order types. A nod from the local sheriff can guarantee an election for a local judge, or county commissioner, or state representative. County sheriffs have serious political clout.

But the sheriffs' plan hit a snag.

By 2010, some judges in Missouri had started to realize that rising court costs were becoming a problem.[7] The year after the Missouri General Assembly created the $3 surcharge, it added an additional $4 surcharge to fund a salary boost to a variety of other county officials, including clerks, assessors, recorders of deeds, treasurers, and, yes, sheriffs.[8] The analogy about boiling a frog comes to mind. Try to put a frog in boiling water and it will jump out. But put a frog in tepid water and slowly raise the temperature and the frog will die. Court fines and fees are similar. When you look at a person getting a $1,000 bill for a speeding ticket or possession of a marijuana pipe, it seems rather ridiculous. $15,000 for spending a year in jail? It's absurd. But what's a simple $3 charge to help fund a sheriff's salary? Or another $4 to pay all the people in the courthouse? It's just $7, right? Until it's $14, then $28, and so on. But that's for other lawmakers to figure out in another

term. Who is going to vote against paying sheriffs more money while
still being able to say they didn't raise taxes?

A taxpayer named Poole Harrison filed a lawsuit against the $4
charge, alleging that it was unconstitutional.[9] He argued that some
couldn't afford the rising costs, and that people using the courts
shouldn't be funding the salaries of county officials who have no connection to the judicial system.

In 1986, the same year the Missouri Sheriffs' Retirement System
started paying out benefits, the Missouri Supreme Court ruled in Harrison's favor. The judges determined that the increased salaries for various
county employees had nothing to do with the administration of justice.

"We, therefore, hold that the fees imposed in civil cases by S.B.
601 are unreasonable impediments to access to justice," the unanimous
court wrote, suggesting that the $4 surcharge was an unconstitutional
"sale of justice."[10] Of particular interest was a concurring opinion written by Judge Warren Welliver. In his opinion, Welliver, who was from
Boone County, noted that court costs in his county had been precip-
itously on the rise, going from $25 to $91 in civil cases in a matter of
fourteen years.

"I believe that access to the courts is being denied a large segment
of lower income Missourians because of increasing court costs. The now
approaching $100 court cost deposit in a circuit court civil case effec-
tively bars many lower income Missourians from asserting meritorious
claims in the court system," Welliver wrote. "Our own State of Missouri
ranks high among the states that should take a long hard look at their
entire courts costs structure. There should not be a $100 price tag on
access to justice."

For some of us, $100 doesn't seem like much of a barrier to justice.
But for Kendy Killman, Brooke Bergen, Sasha Darby, and countless
others, it can be the difference between living life—paying for food,
medical bills, and housing costs—and living life on the state's terms.

After the market collapse destroyed the sheriffs' retirement funds,
Republican state representative Kenny Jones, from the town of California, wrote a letter to Attorney General Chris Koster. Jones, a board

member of the retirement system and a former sheriff, asked the AG to issue an opinion as to whether the existing law applying the $3 surcharge already allowed it to be added to municipal court charges.[11] Koster, a Democrat, said that, while the question as to whether the original law was intended to include municipal courts along with all other courts in the state was "a close one," the surcharge should be applied in municipal courts. Attorney general opinions are not binding, however, and a key court official disagreed with Koster.

Greg Linhares was the head of the Office of State Courts Administrator, which is the administrative arm of the state's court system.[12] He was an expert on the issue of court costs. In fact, he sat on a committee of the national Conference of State Court Administrators that had been studying the issue of rising court costs around the country.[13] In 2011, the organization issued a white paper titled "Courts Are Not Revenue Centers" decrying the increasingly common practice of states using the courts to fund various government services.

"The need for governmental revenues must be carefully counterbalanced with the public's access to the courts. By increasing the financial burden of using the courts, excessive fees or miscellaneous charges tend to exclude citizens who have neither the monetary resources available to the wealthy nor the governmental subsidies for the poor," the report argued. "The proliferation of these fees and costs as chargeable fees and costs included in the judgment and sentence issued as part of the legal financial obligation of the defendant has recast the role of the court as a collection agency for executive branch services."

Linhares declined to advise the Missouri Supreme Court, which ultimately made the final decision on whether the surcharge would apply to municipal courts, to follow Koster's opinion.

Unable to get the court to apply the surcharge to municipal courts, Jones wrote Koster a second time, asking for an opinion again. When that didn't work, because Linhares stood his ground and was backed by the state's high court, a different state legislator wrote again, in 2013, asking for yet an additional opinion from the attorney general. The purpose in all these opinion letters was to put pressure on the Missouri

Supreme Court to apply the $3 fee to municipal courts. The letter was written during the legislative session in which Jones's son, Caleb, then serving in his father's former house seat, filed a bill changing the statute to specifically apply the $3 surcharge to municipal courts.

The bill went nowhere, in part because Vatterott rallied municipal judges to oppose it. But that didn't stop the sheriffs' retirement system.[14]

On Valentine's Day, in a senate budget hearing that was unrelated to the issue, Republican state senator Mike Parson, of Bolivar, pressed forward. Linhares was in the hearing to go through the annual process of presenting the details of the court's budget. But Parson, who would go on to become governor of Missouri, had another agenda.

"You're familiar with the sheriffs' retirement fund?" Parson, a former sheriff, asked Linhares.

"I've supported the courts when they've wanted raises, but yet you guys will not collect from the municipalities that fee," Parson said. "The attorney general has given two opinions on that already saying that it should be being collected. And yet we don't collect that and the courts have done nothing to help with that. It becomes a little frustrating to me as I keep supporting your agenda to a certain degree that we don't do that. That is going to be an issue to me and a burden to me if we don't change what we're doing on that. All I'm asking is to collect what should be collected, what I believe the statute says."

It was a threat. If the court didn't change its interpretation, its budget would be at the mercy of angry senators hungry to do the bidding of their local sheriffs. The judicial and legislative branches of government are independent of each other, but the legislature controls the purse strings.

The gambit worked.

At the time, attorney Bill Thompson was clerk of the Missouri Supreme Court.[15] Thompson, who was in the senate hearing room that day, ordered a review of the $3 surcharge. In August that year, the Missouri Supreme Court included it on its annual order listing various approved court charges that apply in all courts, including municipal ones.[16]

Many of the municipal judges, led by Vatterott, refused to back down.

Vatterott wrote an order for the city where he was a judge—Overland—that said he believed the application of the fee to municipal courts was an unconstitutional sale of justice, and he would not allow it to be charged in his court.[17] Several other municipal court judges issued similar orders.[18]

One of them was Judge Bryan Breckenridge, municipal judge in the southwest Missouri town of Nevada. "This Court finds that the imposition of the Sheriffs' Retirement Fund surcharge . . . would entail a sale of justice."[19]

Breckenridge is married to Judge Patricia Breckenridge, one of the members of the Missouri Supreme Court that had issued the order requiring the $3 charge to be collected.

About half of the 608 municipal courts in Missouri refused to collect the surcharge. Still, the Missouri Sheriffs' Retirement System ended up being flush with cash. Between 2012 and 2015, the fund showed a $10 million increase in assets.

Twice in coming years, Vatterott would sue to try to get the surcharge declared unconstitutional, but neither lawsuit made it to trial.[20] After he was cast into the public eye in 2014 because of his role representing municipal judges in St. Louis County, he became even more determined to do something about the $3 surcharge, which to him represented the scourge of rising court costs and fees in America.

In 2018, two Kansas City attorneys took up Vatterott's mantle, filing a lawsuit against the collection of the $3 fee on behalf of two clients who had to pay it after receiving speeding tickets. The case went to trial before Jackson County Circuit Judge Kevin Harrell in November 2019. During the trial, attorney Gerald McGonagle asked his client, Jerry Keller, a question that gets to the heart of the matter.

"Do you believe it's fair that you should pay a fee in Kansas City Municipal Court for a retired sheriff in a place like Mercer County?" McGonagle asked. Mercer County is a rural county about two hours north of Kansas City, whose sheriff is in the retirement fund that gets revenue from the $3 court fee.

Keller said he did not. The judge disagreed and ruled in favor of the sheriffs' retirement fund. The case was appealed to the Missouri Supreme Court. In a 6-0 decision issued on June 1, 2021, the court ruled that the $3 surcharge was unconstitutional. "Seven years of work," Vatterott texted me. "Justice!"

In nearly every year since the $3 surcharge was established, the Missouri Legislature has approved other court cost increases. One of the structural government realities that exacerbates this cash grab by state lawmakers is tied to the political movement led by Grover Norquist.

In some Republican-dominated states, where the "no new taxes" mantra is actually built into the constitution, turning to court fines and fees is the easy political choice for lawmakers starving for revenue.[21] Because the people who are paying the fines and fees have been convicted of crimes, they are easy to label as "criminals." A lawmaker who is against raising taxes and "tough on crime," can have their cake and eat it too: vote to increase court costs while campaigning on "no new taxes." Meanwhile, the local sheriff, prosecutor, and county commissioner, all beneficiaries of the backdoor revenue, will line up their support for the measure.[22] Cynical? It has occurred in every statehouse in America.

Oklahoma is a good example.

In 1992, voters passed SQ 640, a ballot initiative supported by the Oklahoma Taxpayers Union that requires any tax increase voted on by the legislature to receive a 75 percent supermajority, the most stringent in the country.[23] In practice, if not intent, it is a ban on the legislature's ability to raise taxes. The result, says Jim Roth, dean of the Oklahoma City University School of Law, is that lawmakers look to other forms of backdoor taxes for revenue, such as court fines and fees.

Roth, a former county commissioner in Oklahoma County, said the real-world result of SQ 640 "made decades of underfunding state government amplify problems in the criminal justice realm."

Between 2008 and 2012, district courts in Oklahoma suffered a 60 percent cut in state funding.[24] The rise in court fines and fees ran parallel.[25] Between 2014 and 2015 in Oklahoma County, for instance, the number of bench warrants issued for a failure to pay fines and fees increased from 1,000 a month to 4,000 a month.[26] This means that local governments are spending a significant amount of additional taxpayer money trying to round up poor people who owe court costs, but can't afford to pay them, in an attempt to balance the books. Those people end up in jail, which costs taxpayers even more money.

Also in 1992, the people of Colorado were doing the same thing. Voters passed the Taxpayer's Bill of Rights, or TABOR Amendment, which required statewide votes for tax increases and also limited the amount of revenue growth the legislature could approve each year, even when the economy was good.[27]

To the east, Missouri voters passed a similar provision called the Hancock Amendment in 1980, limiting the state's per capita tax rate to 1981 levels.[28] Missouri has become one of the lowest-taxed states in the country. To cover the difference, its court costs and fees have skyrocketed.[29]

The problem of out-of-control court debt has become so widespread, and so damaging to the lives of poor people, that for the first time, in 2019, the Federal Reserve Board included a survey of legal debt in its annual report on the "well-being of U.S. households." It was devastating: "Individuals whose families had outstanding legal expenses frequently were carrying other forms of debt as well. For instance, 43 percent of those whose family had legal debt also had outstanding medical debt," they found. "Those with outstanding legal fees were also disproportionately likely to have credit card debt and more likely to carry student loan debt—despite being less likely to have gone to college than those without unpaid legal debts."[30]

Unsurprisingly, the Federal Reserve Board found that people who earned less than $40,000 a year were significantly more likely to have outstanding court debt, and that such debt was disproportionately a burden on Blacks and Hispanics.

"Exposure to crime or the legal system correlates with lower levels of financial well-being. This was especially true among those who still had unpaid legal debts," said the report. "Fifty-three percent of those

whose family had outstanding legal debt were doing at least okay financially relative to over three-quarters of those without legal debt."

For the fairly small group of legal professionals who have been raising the issue of burdensome court costs and their effect on poor people
for years, this report by the Federal Reserve was a big deal.

"The Federal Reserve is the definitive authority on economic conditions in the country," said Lauren-Brooke Eisen, the director of the
justice program at the nonprofit Brennan Center for Justice in New
York. "The fact that they recognized that court costs and legal fees can
affect American households, and for years after they incur these debts,
is hugely significant."[31]

Norman, Oklahoma
November 2010

Kendy Killman didn't need the Federal Reserve Board to tell her
how much her outstanding court costs were having an effect on her
poverty. One fee that Killman received as part of her sentence was
a $40-per-month supervision fee to be paid to the district attorney.
When the first month's payment was due, she didn't have the money.
That amount is about 25 percent of her monthly income, but rarely does
a month go by when she actually has that amount in the bank, free to
use. So she didn't pay. Not that month or the months ahead. It was the
same dilemma faced by poor people every day. Food or medicine? Gas
or electric bill? Cable or air-conditioning?

About a year after she was sentenced, Killman got a call from her
oldest daughter, Meranda. Like her own mother, Killman had her first
child as a teenager. She has five children, each born between 1986 and
1991, including twin boys. Meranda was on the state's court system
online and plugged her mom's name into the search bar. There was a
warrant out for her arrest. It was for nonpayment of her court debt and
failure to perform community service.

"I couldn't even afford the damn $40 to get an attorney, but now I am expected to pay $100 a month? How am I going to do this?" Killman said.

Her debt kept increasing. The warrant comes with a new $50 fee, and another bond filing fee, and a clerk filing fee of $2.50.[32] Bench warrants generally aren't mailed to defendants. They exist in the state's database, and what often happens is that a person gets pulled over for speeding or some other infraction, and a police officer runs their name through the database and finds out they have a warrant out for their arrest.

Killman didn't want to wait for that to happen. So she just went to court and presented herself to the judge. The warrant was recalled, and she was told to come back in November. Killman still had to answer for not paying the fines and fees.

But she struggled to pay. From November until the following April, the bills came and she couldn't send money back. Two years had passed since her drive in a run-down car, just purchased for $400, that led to a questionable traffic stop, an even more questionable marijuana charge, and now this debt, which only went in one direction: up.

In April, Killman gathered every document that she could to explain her financial situation, from Bubba's diagnosis to copies of her federal disability check, her qualification for Section 8 housing and food stamps, anything that would explain that she couldn't afford a monthly charge of $40 to pay the district attorney for the privilege of being supervised on probation, let alone all the other costs that had been assigned her.

Killman stood before the judge and pleaded her case. It worked.

"Upon review of documentation, state determines that it would be an undue hardship for (defendant) to pay DA supervision (fees)," the judge wrote on a document given to Killman on April 26, 2011.

She thought she was free and clear of this nightmare.

"It is over," Killman said in the hallway of the Cleveland County Courthouse. "I was relieved. I took a breath and went home."

Killman was wrong. Her already two-year-long ordeal was just beginning.

4

....

FAILURE TO PAY

Columbia, South Carolina
March 2017

After making her first two payments, Sasha Darby fell behind. Unbe-knownst to her, as a result, a bench warrant had been issued for her ar-rest. Since bench warrants aren't mailed out, Darby had no idea. Darby had just found a new apartment after a couple of weeks of bouncing from one family member's home to the next. Effectively homeless, at least this meant she wouldn't have to sleep outside.

On March 28, she was at her mother's house, helping a family mem-ber who was being transported to a mental health facility. The police were there to assist—a routine task in such cases. One of the officers, however, happened to be the one who had issued the summons for Darby's assault. He ran her name and the warrant popped up: wanted for failure to pay her fines and fees in full. She owed $680.[1]

"I got handcuffed at my mother's house," Darby said. "Everything stopped in that moment."

She was taken to the Lexington County Jail. There, she was offered a choice: Pay what you owe or go to jail for twenty days. Like many people born into intergenerational poverty, Darby didn't know anybody who had that sort of cash around. Whatever money she had saved had just gone to her landlord as a deposit on the new apartment.

She chose jail. Or, more to the point, the system chose jail for her. Pregnant and alone, Darby was behind bars for the first time in her life.

This is the part of the judicial system that is invisible to most people who don't experience it. Darby had not committed another crime. She was working *with* the police to help a family member in need. But she was arrested and jailed because she couldn't afford to pay court costs that have been instituted by Lexington County as a revenue generator. Remember, all this stemmed from a spat with her roommate.

"I lost my job," Darby said. "I lost my apartment."

All over the country there are people like Darby living in poverty who do their time after pleading guilty or being convicted of minor crimes. And then they get a bill. Or they are offered time behind bars not as a punishment, but as an "alternative," because they can't afford the fine. As a result of their financial hardship they give up their freedom. There are no television shows about people like Darby, and yet in city and county jails across the country, there are thousands of people like her: the invisible victims of poverty criminalized in the name of justice.

The problem flies under the radar screens even for those directly involved in the judicial system. Jill Webb used to be one of those people. A defense attorney in Tulsa, Oklahoma, Webb worked for five years in the Tulsa County Public Defender's office. Over time, Webb and her fellow public defenders noticed that they kept seeing the same clients over and over again, back in jail, needing legal help. Webb was tasked with investigating why.

So she started spending time in the Tulsa County Jail, talking to clients represented by the public defenders. In one case, she was talking to an African American woman named Cynthia Graves, who had been in jail for nine days. She hadn't even seen the judge yet.

"What are you in for?" Webb asked.

"Failure to pay."

Webb started looking at the daily jail blotter, and frequently she would see the same three words: failure to pay. The Tulsa County Jail was full of people—most of them Black, many of them women—who were there for the same reason. Finally, it clicked. Webb had discovered a national crisis hiding in plain sight.

In retrospect, the reason was obvious. "I never thought about fines and fees because my clients didn't," Webb said. As is the case in most jurisdictions, most poor people don't actually end up going to trial for their various offenses.[2] After sitting behind bars for several days, maybe even a month or more, just waiting to meet their overworked public defender or go before a judge, defendants take the plea bargains offered by prosecutors. Now they're out, at least for a period of time, and get to go back to their lives. "They plead to just about anything to get out," Webb said. "The system is set up to make them fail."

In 2016, Tulsa County booked 1,163 people into its jail on failure-to-pay charges, in some cases as a stand-alone charge. On average, failure-to-pay defendants spent five days in jail that year. Doing so cost taxpayers $2 million more than officials brought in from the fines and fees themselves. Failure to pay was the fourth-most-cited offense in the Tulsa County jail.[3]

Farmington, Missouri
October 2018

In 2018, I spent months driving country roads between rural courthouses, from Farmington to Salem to Kingston, telling the stories of Missourians caught up in the criminalization of poverty. Each of their stories varied a bit: what they got arrested for, what their lives were like before going to jail, and how their experiences changed their outlook on life.

But one thing was the same: they were all poor.

My journey telling their stories would become the most important work I have ever produced as a journalist, winning me the 2019 Pulitzer Prize for Commentary.[4] It is those stories, those people, who drove me to write this book, to search out Killman and Darby and others like them across the country who have suffered in the name of justice.

The rest of this chapter introduces five of the people I met or wrote about in my travels across Missouri: Victoria Branson, Rob Hopple, William Everts, Cory Booth, and Amy Murr. Their stories, starting with an inability to pay fines and fees, highlight the depth of injustice inherent in the American judicial system. Unlike many of the victims of these schemes nationally—who are disproportionately people of color—all of them are white. They live in rural Missouri, which is overwhelmingly white. It is simply the nature of the local population.

The sheer number of people who are negatively affected by fines and fees imposed upon them primarily to help local governments raise money is a shock to the soul. As I wrote about each of them originally, I realized how each one of them, in their own way, brought people to an understanding of the injustice of these fines-and-fees schemes in slightly different ways. Some people identified with Branson because she was a grandmother. Others saw themselves in Booth's teenage indiscretions. Some were horrified at Everts's homelessness, caused at least in part by the criminal justice system.

I grew up in Colorado, but I have spent the past two decades practicing my craft in Missouri, my new home. It's where I met my wife, Marla, and where we raised our two children. It's a state that for much of its history has played a unique role in the nation, straddling north and south, urban and rural; serving as a kickoff point for Lewis and Clark's expedition, a Gateway to the West; and, in much of the twentieth century, being a bellwether presidential state.

Each of these Missourians, or their loved ones, trusted me with their stories, and those stories, not any journalistic jujitsu, caused lasting change in Missouri, because lawmakers, poverty advocates, and judges were moved to action. There are people just like them, but of all races and creeds, in nearly identical circumstances, in every state in the nation.

It was October 2018, and I was in rural St. Francois County, south of St. Louis, to meet Victoria Branson for the first time. I had written about her a year previously.[5] She had been at the women's prison in

Vandalia. While inside, she was a "pusher," the sort of detainee who does what she can to bring humanity to the daily grayness of life behind bars.[6] Branson would voluntarily "push" inmates who were wheelchair-bound, helping them move around their dim surroundings. The task offered a bit of normalcy. Before her stint inside, Branson worked at a nursing home caring for senior citizens—some bedridden, often near death. She went back there to work after she was released, and she was released, she says, because of something I wrote.

In late 2017, Circuit Court Judge Sandra Martinez sent Branson to prison because she was poor. That's not what the charge said, or the sentence, but the court record outlines a story that is all too common. For Martinez, this was part of a pattern. Twice in the past year, her decisions had been overturned by higher courts for using court costs as a precursor for putting people in jail.[7]

In one of those cases, the Missouri Court of Appeals crystalized what was happening to poor people in the name of justice.

"So, in this case we are left with a system in which all Missouri taxpayers have to pay for the salaries of judges, clerks, prosecutors, public defenders and probation officers to collect money from a grandmother on disability supporting her grandchildren in order to operate the St. Francois County jail," the court wrote.[8] "The amount of resources devoted to this task is astonishing."

In so many cases, such injustice continues unabated because nobody raises much of a stink. "My clients can't complain very much," says Amy Lowe, a public defender who represented one of the St. Francois County residents who had their cases overturned.[9] "It's very easy to dehumanize them and use them to raise money for government services."

Branson had owed child support to a dead man. Fourteen years ago, during a divorce, she paid $162 a month in support for her teen son, who was living with his father. Branson fell behind. She was charged with failure to pay child support. In Missouri, as in many states, falling behind on child support can lead to a criminal charge. In reality, the process often serves as a disincentive to collect child support, as the parents who owe the money end up losing income because of the legal system, making it less likely they can afford the child support they were behind on in the first place. Branson's case is even more extraordinary than that.

She pleaded guilty and was sentenced to four years in prison, but the sentence was suspended, or deferred. Not long after that, her husband killed himself. Her son moved home. With her husband gone and son back home, Branson figured her child support case was over.

Life went on. She moved away and ended up living with her boyfriend, Clifford Rickman, in southwest Missouri, on the opposite end of the state. After sixteen years, they broke up and Branson moved back to St. Francois County.

A local traffic stop turned up a bench warrant for Branson's arrest. She was jailed and couldn't afford the bail to be released.

For fourteen years, Martinez had been holding regular hearings on Branson's old child support case. Branson didn't know about them. Check any court file in rural Missouri and you're likely to find "mail returned" as an entry. Poor people often don't leave a change of address.

Martinez determined that Branson owed the court $5,000, nearly all of it not for child support but for Branson's time in jail and other court costs. She didn't have the money, so Martinez revoked her probation and sent her to prison.

"It's just not right for her to be in there," Rickman told me. He's remarried now, but he called me in the hope that somebody would take up Branson's case and get her out of jail. "The sentence the judge gave her was ridiculous. The boy's father has been dead for fourteen years. What good is it to put her in jail?"

Branson stopped by my table and poured me a tall glass of sweet tea. Christines is on Old Route 67, just down the road from Open Door Baptist Church. It's the sort of place that still had a smoking section; where the chairs and tables don't match and the daily special is going to have meat, potatoes, and gravy, always gravy. It's Branson's second job; she also works nights at a nursing home. She has long, red hair and green eyes. She was released from prison about a month after I wrote about her case.

"They called me in on the first of October and asked if I knew you," she told me. She was released a few days later.

If you're poor and Black and live in St. Louis or poor and white and live in St. Francois County or Dent County or Caldwell County—small farming communities that are bleeding population and use the courts to prop up sagging budgets—the story is often the same. In Missouri, poverty doesn't discriminate.

That's why in March 2016, the U.S. Justice Department sent a letter of guidance to all judges and court clerks in the country, reminding them of constitutional protections that are as old as the nation.

"Individuals may confront escalating debt; face repeated, unnecessary incarceration for nonpayment despite posing no danger to the community; lose their jobs; and become trapped in cycles of poverty that can be nearly impossible to escape," said the letter, which was signed by Vanita Gupta, the head of the department's Civil Rights Division, and Lisa Foster, who was then the director of the Office for Access to Justice.[10] "Furthermore, in addition to being unlawful, to the extent that these practices are geared not toward addressing public safety, but rather toward raising revenue, they can cast doubt on the impartiality of the tribunal and erode trust between local governments and their constituents."

In December 2017, Attorney General Jeff Sessions revoked that guidance, part of President Donald Trump's obsessive effort to erase the legacy of President Barack Obama.[11]

It was a few days after that when Branson had first texted me.

It was Christmas morning. I sat in my living room with my wife as we watched my two youngest children tear into their gifts. The fake yule log DVD was filling the television screen as holiday music played.

"Merry Christmas," the text said. At first, I assumed it was from one of my grown children. But I didn't recognize the number. I asked who was texting and Victoria Branson introduced herself to me for the

first time. I didn't even know she was out of prison. It's the text that
eventually brought me to St. Francois County.

The man at the table next to me at Christines is in his sixties. He wears
a sleeveless flannel shirt and has a 9mm semiautomatic Glock strapped
to his belt. This is open-carry country. Men have lost their jobs, maybe
even their farms, but they still have their guns. The union lead-mining
jobs are long gone.[12] The small factories that served the closed-down
Chrysler plant in St. Louis County are shuttered.[13]

People like Branson get by on minimum wage jobs—two of them
in her case—and hope they can satisfy the courts by making small payments when they can, $50 or $75 at a time.

The men at the corner table invite me over. This is a table like one
at every diner or coffee shop along an old country route in America.
A liar's table. The place where the regulars show up and shoot the shit.

They love Branson, so they decide they're OK with me.

There are people like her all over the hills and dales of St. Francois
County, they tell me, people who waste away in jail mostly because they
can't afford to buy their freedom. They get picked up for shoplifting,
drug possession—meth and opioids are the current rage—traffic offenses, and, yes, falling behind on child support.

They lose jobs, cars, houses, and children because of the financial burdens heaped upon them by judges who ignore constitutional
requirements to determine ability to pay. They crowd a county jail where
death comes far too often, or they get sent to prison. When they get
released, the bill is waiting for them, along with a monthly invitation
to stand before the judge or pay their monthly bill.

I would soon find out that the problem was much bigger than one
oft-overturned judge in St. Francois County. It was a problem all over
rural Missouri, in nearly every county in the state.

Kristen Brown emailed me shortly after I wrote about Branson to
tell me about her domestic partner of twenty years, Rob Hopple.[14] He
had spent six months in jail because he couldn't afford the ankle bracelet

Judge Martinez required him to purchase from one specific private probation company.

In some ways Hopple's case was much like Branson's: Same St. Francois County judge. Same prosecutor, Jerrod Mahurin, who had formerly worked for Martinez. For months, I put Hopple's story on the back burner. He was accused of exposing himself to a preteen girl who had spent the night with his daughter. He denied it. Brown denied it. An investigation by the state Child Abuse and Neglect Review Board determined no crime occurred.

Brown emailed me in early 2018, at the height of the #MeToo movement. I had written about several women who had been sexually assaulted or harassed. Believe women, I wrote, and I meant it.

But Hopple, who was forty-seven at the time, wasn't in jail because he was considered a danger to the girl or anybody else. After he was arrested, in November 2016, he posted bail. He's not public-defender poor, having worked steadily as a carpenter. Brown is a substitute teacher. Hopple hired a private attorney to help him fight the charges. One of the conditions of his jail release was that he wear an ankle monitor that cost about $300 a month.

Hopple lost his job after the arrest. Between the private probation bills and attorney bills, he had a hard time keeping up. But trial was set for April 2018, and he expected to win and get the episode behind him.

In April, Mahurin sought a delay. Hopple soon missed a payment on his ankle monitor and the private probation company sent a note to the court that Hopple had violated the conditions of his pretrial release, which are determined by the judge when somebody bails out of jail. That spurred a court hearing in front of Martinez, and before it took place, Hopple and Brown found another private probation company that charged less for ankle monitors. They went and bought one and had it turned on.

So in May, when he showed up for a hearing on his alleged violation, Hopple was wearing a monitor on each ankle. One worked. The other didn't. It wasn't good enough for Martinez. She sent him to the St. Francois County Jail. This time, the family didn't have enough money to bail him out.

In June, July, and September, court dates came and went. Mahurin kept asking for and receiving delays. Brown was convinced the prosecutor simply knew he couldn't win the case. But Hopple was stuck behind bars anyway.

"These people are absolutely destroying our lives," Brown emailed me in September. "I have never felt so helpless."

I wrote about Hopple's case that month.[15] In October I drove to Farmington for his scheduled trial. I was sitting at the coffee shop across from the courthouse on the square in the center of town when I got the news: The trial was delayed again. This time, with months of delays becoming problematic, Martinez set Hopple free.

Mahurin blamed me for the delay. He said my previous column about Hopple might poison the jury pool. He subpoenaed me for a deposition. That became a moot point when Mahurin lost the November election. So did Martinez. Hopple's next trial date in December was delayed, too. In 2019, the new prosecutor asked him to take a polygraph. He passed it and the charges were dropped.

Because he wasn't convicted, St. Francois County couldn't bill him for the six months he spent in jail there. Thank heavens for small favors. Hopple's case is an example of how local governments aren't the only bodies profiting off an abuse of the judicial system. Their partners in crime, so to speak, are the private probation companies that work hand in hand to keep local jails full.

The terms of probation, or of pretrial release, handed out by judges like Martinez and Brandi Baird are often significant and costly.[16] Most Missouri misdemeanor defendants have to pay for drug testing, even in cases in which they aren't charged with drug offenses. Miss a check-in for a drug screen? Probation violation. Fail a test? Violation.

The proliferation of private probation companies in Missouri started in 2008, after the Great Recession, when the state budget was tight.[17] The state cut the use of probation officers for misdemeanors to save money, and, in its place, private probation companies picked up the slack, contracting directly with cities and counties. Instead of the state funding the costs, the money comes from the defendants themselves, most of whom are poor.

The private, for-profit companies became the direct beneficiaries of the cycle of jail and probation, followed by debt, that is so common in Missouri courts.

"Private probation companies are trying to violate their clients," says Moberly businessman Jerry Swartz.[18] "That's their business model."

Swartz was charged with DWI in Ralls County in 2014. Judge David Mobley ordered Swartz to be monitored by an ankle bracelet that could detect alcohol use. The company Swartz paid was American Court Services, a private probation company that bought its building from the judge.

Swartz could afford to pay, but during his brief time in jail, he met many other defendants who told him stories of being tossed back in jail because they couldn't afford the ever-increasing private probation fees.

"When you add it all up, you are talking about an insurmountable hole for most people," Swartz says. "It's a cancer you can never get rid of once you get stuck in private probation."

That's what the nonprofit Human Rights Watch found in its 2018 report on private probation companies titled "Set Up to Fail."[19] The report examined private probation practices in Missouri, Florida, Kentucky, and Tennessee, and found numerous abuses where the drive for profit outweighed justice.

"The offender-funded system of justice is most burdensome and punitive for those who cannot afford its costs," the report finds. "When individuals are unable to pay, they face potential arrest, extended probation periods, and incarceration."

The report highlighted the case of a woman named Cindy Rodriguez, a fifty-three-year-old who lived in Murfreesboro, Tennessee. Like Brooke Bergen, she had originally been charged with misdemeanor shoplifting in 2014, the first time she had been arrested in her life.

She pleaded guilty and was placed on eleven months' probation, under the supervision of Providence Community Corrections, Inc., a private probation company. Rodriguez, who lives on disability payments because of chronic back pain, owed $578 in court costs. But she had to pay the private probation company a monthly fee of about $35, and then came the drug tests at $20 a pop.

One month, when she couldn't make a payment, the probation company reported her lack of payment as a violation of her conditions for release. Rodriguez was arrested and taken to the Rutherford County Jail.

A year into her probation she still owed $500.

This, Human Rights Watch found, is a common experience.

"In all four states researched for this report, if probationers cannot pay for the direct or indirect costs of probation, they face a number of legal consequences, including jail time," the researchers found. "The incarceration of people who do not pay fines and fees because they are genuinely unable to pay was outlawed in 1983 by the US Supreme Court, yet it remains a reality."

That 1983 case, *Bearden v. Georgia*, is a U.S. Supreme Court precedent that is supposed to make sure that ability-to-pay hearings take place in cases where incarceration is a possibility.[20] In the case's ruling, Justice Sandra Day O'Connor wrote that it was "fundamentally unfair" to send a man to prison because he couldn't afford to pay his court fines.

In 1980, Danny Bearden was a Tunnel Hill, Georgia, resident who got caught breaking into a trailer. He pleaded guilty to theft, burglary, and receiving stolen property. Bearden's prison sentence was deferred and he was put on probation and ordered to pay a $500 fine and $250 in restitution. The judge required Bearden to pay $100 that day, $100 the next day, and the $550 balance within four months. He borrowed $200 from his parents to make the first two payments.

Then, Bearden lost his job. He had a ninth-grade education and couldn't read. He tried to find another job but failed. Before his final payment was due in February 1981, Bearden called the probation office to let them know he was struggling to find work and wasn't going to be able to make the payment.

In May, the judge revoked Bearden's probation and sent him to prison. He was there two years to fill out the rest of his probation. His only probation violation was his failure to pay. He was sent to prison because he was poor.

"They're just poor people, okay? They got families and everything like that. They work a job. And even when they get behind in trying to pay, they go to jail," Bearden told National Public Radio in 2014 for a story that helped put the fines-and-fees issue on the national radar screen.[21] Bearden understood then that three decades after the U.S. Supreme Court said that people could not be put in jail for their inability to pay for fines and fees, judges were still finding ways to do precisely that.

Hamilton, Missouri
August 2001

Bearden could well have been describing the experience of William Everts, who lived in sparsely populated Caldwell County in northwest Missouri.[22]

"I'm such an idiot."

That's what Everts told the Hamilton police officer after he got caught stealing a computer from a church. It was August 24, 2001. Hamilton is a tiny town of about 1,700 people. It's an old railroad town, and the original home of James Cash Penney, who founded the eponymous retail chain. This is hog country, with wide-open spaces and massive confined-animal feeding operations, where you don't want to be caught downwind of a corporate farm.

Everts stole a computer from the Hamilton United Methodist Church. He had been at the church earlier in the day applying for food assistance for his family. While he was there, he spied the desktop computer and figured it might be easy to pilfer and sell for something. When the cops arrived at his house later in the day, he first denied stealing the computer. But when his girlfriend gave permission for the officers to open the trunk of her 2001 Ford Taurus, Everts fessed up.

"It's in there," he said. "I stole a computer from a church."

Everts was arrested and taken to the Caldwell County Jail. He would be there for thirty days because he couldn't afford bail.

He pleaded guilty to misdemeanor stealing of less than $500 and was sentenced by Associate Circuit Judge Jason Kanoy to time served. Then he got a bill. He owed the county $1,339.50.

Kanoy gave Everts until November to pay it.

It was an impossible task. So began a nearly decade-long journey in which Everts ended up homeless on the streets of Kansas City. Each month, Kanoy would schedule him for a hearing to pay some of his county debt, and when Everts, who had moved to Kansas City to try to find work, didn't show up, he'd issue a warrant for his arrest. At some point, if Everts got picked up in Kansas City for some petty offense, an officer would notice the warrant, and he'd be sent to Caldwell County. He'd spend a few more days in jail there and come out owing even more.

In 2015, Everts met Misty Robe. She was a volunteer with a homeless advocacy group that would make soup for people lacking shelter, and visit, feed, and clothe them when possible. When Everts told her about the money he owed in Caldwell County, and the monthly hearings he could never get to, Robe was disgusted.

So she wrote Kanoy a letter.

"Each time he is picked up for a warrant they will keep him for approximately a week and then charge him for that stay as well, adding to the already outstanding balance," Robe wrote. "As you can see this has been a thorn in his side for quite some time. My hope is to get it resolved once and for all so he can move forward with his life. He is open to negotiating a stay in jail to pay off his debt. Obviously, a no-charge stay."

What Robe was proposing is much how some county jails in Mississippi operate, as well as South Carolina, where Sasha Darby was jailed.

In those states, some counties will let poor people who can't afford their fines and fees spend extra time in jail to pay down their debt, creating a two-tiered system of justice, one for folks with money, and another for those without.[23]

In Alcorn County, Mississippi, for instance, $25 a day is knocked off debt for those who agree to be locked up instead of paying court fines and fees.[24] In some parts of Mississippi, there are restitution centers, where people who are incarcerated work for private employers—like a chicken processing plant—until their debts are paid down.[25] They are prisons operated by the government for the profit of the government and private business.

Kanoy didn't take Robe up on her offer. Until early 2019, the judge was still issuing warrants for Everts's arrest after holding his monthly payment review hearings. Robe doesn't understand it.

"To continually re-arrest somebody on a warrant just for failure to pay, at what point do you stop doing this?" Robe wonders. "William knows he's made poor choices and has to suffer the consequences. But he served his time."

Kanoy is the poster child in Missouri for judges who have decided that debt collection is job one. In 2017, for instance, Caldwell County collected more per capita in fines and fees than any other county in Missouri.[26] It wasn't a lot of money in aggregate—just $149,877—but it was $16.47 for every one of the 9,100 residents of the county.

And for the poor people who had to pay that debt? It weighed down their lives for years.

Breckenridge, Missouri
Summer 2007

Consider Cory Booth.

When he was seventeen, he stole a lawn mower.[27] Booth lived in Breckenridge, a town of 300 people just a few miles east of Hamilton. In the summer of 2007, he and his buddies saw a lawn mower sitting in a yard unattended. Booth took it. The owner filed a complaint, and the Caldwell County Sheriff's Office investigated. One of Booth's buddies fingered him. Eventually, after he had already returned the lawn mower, he confessed to the crime.

Booth was arrested and taken to the Caldwell County Jail, where he spent the night in a cell with a man being held by the feds on a felony bank robbery charge.

"I stayed awake all night," he said. "I was scared."

Booth pleaded guilty to the misdemeanor theft and Kanoy gave him a year in jail but suspended the sentence. As is common in nearly every rural county in Missouri, Booth would be supervised by a private probation company for two years. Booth had to pay a monthly charge to the company. He also had to pay for regular drug testing. Booth, at the time, was a pot smoker.

By November he had violated his probation by failing a drug test. He did seven days in jail and got his first board bill for jail time. A couple of months later, the same thing happened, and he did ten days behind bars. In November 2008, after another failed drug test, Kanoy sent Booth away for a year.

The only silver lining is that he let the teenager spend some of his sentence in rehab. There, Booth met his future wife. They've been married a decade and have five kids.

But hanging over their heads is the court debt Booth incurred, nearly all of it for room and board in jail, a bill that kept rising. By 2009, Booth owed $7,325.[28]

When I met him, in 2018, he had gotten his debt down to about $5,000, and he was still appearing before Kanoy month after month. "It's crazy," Booth says. "They make probation so hard so they can violate you. The system is the problem. It's a vicious circle. It's horrible."

Booth's story, like Bergen's, began to cut through the urban-rural divide that so often defines Missouri politics. Both Republicans and Democrats, from the city and the country, were outraged that a young man was being punished ten years after he stole a lawn mower when he was seventeen. Booth's problem wasn't that he kept stealing, it was simply that he couldn't pay his bill for jail time he probably never should have served.

One week when we talked before a court hearing, Booth was worried that Kanoy might lock him up again. He didn't have enough money to make a payment that day.

"I spent my judge money on medicine for the kids," Booth says. "It's a rob Peter to pay Paul situation, and Judge Kanoy is Paul."

Salem, Missouri
November 2018

I met Amy Murr the same day I met Bergen, who had first introduced us on Facebook.

Murr sat across from me at a table at JB Malone's bar and restaurant.

The bar is at the T intersection in Salem where Highway 72 runs south through Dent County and hits Highway 32. It sits on a hill overlooking the passing traffic at a crossroads in the middle of America.

Murr and Bergen had spent time in jail together, both on misdemeanors. Both were called before Judge Baird's courtroom month after month because they owed money for their jail bills.[29] The locals call them "board" bills, because they are for room and board. It sounds so much more civilized than a bill for jail, which is what it is.

Murr was like so many others in Dent County, a rural expanse of farmland and rolling hills surrounded by the Mark Twain National Forest in south-central Missouri, treated differently by a judicial system that hung like an albatross around the necks of those who are poor, or who have been caught up in the area's rampant drug culture. Murr has been both of those things.

She was arrested in February 2017 for violating an order of protection against her mother. Murr says she was just retrieving a television from the house that was hers, but she did violate the order. It wasn't her first arrest. She has several on her record. She was jailed on $5,000 cash bail and sat in the Dent County Jail for a couple of weeks before her public defender could get the bail reduced.

Then, while under pretrial supervision by a private probation company, she allegedly failed a drug test.[30] Back to jail. This time her bail was set at $10,000.

After three months in jail, she pleaded guilty to the misdemeanor and agreed to a sentence of time served.

In jurisdictions that charge for jail, "time served" is a misnomer. That's because Murr was still going to be called before Judge Baird's courtroom every month to make sure she made a payment on her jail debt, which had risen to more than $4,000 for the ninety-five days she sat behind bars.

So, like Bergen and the other former detainees in Dent County, she'd show up and pay what she could.

In July 2018, she was late to a hearing. Baird ordered her cuffed and sent to jail again, with another cash bail set at $5,000. Her defense attorney—who had become a pain in Baird's butt, filing motions taking her to task over actions he alleged were unconstitutional—tried to get Murr's bail reduced. Baird wouldn't budge.

That's when the bailiff, the same one who had tried to block me from a court hearing, paid Murr a visit in jail. If she'd fire David Simpson, her attorney, he said, Baird might let her go. Murr called Simpson and relayed the bailiff's offer.

"Fire me," the attorney said. Murr did. She was let out of jail. Murr immediately rehired Simpson, who filed a motion letting Baird have it.

"This court imposed and executed a sentence on Defendant one year ago . . . and Defendant completed her jail sentence on the same date," Simpson wrote in a motion he filed with Baird. "There is no statute or rule that permits a circuit court after it has imposed and executed a jail sentence to require the person who has served the jail sentence to appear in court for 'payment review hearings' in an attempt to collect the county sheriff's bill for the costs of the jail sentence."

Murr told me there are a lot of "wonderful women" in the Dent County Jail. Some have records, like she does. Many have no business being in jail. "I think they look at us like cattle," Murr says. "Put a number on us and stow us away in the jail. They have something against the weak and the poor." That's what Murr wanted to talk to me about this day, as we sat in a near-empty bar in the middle of the afternoon.

"Why are you doing this?" she asked me, with a syrupy drawl that accented her girl-next-door looks. Why was I writing about poor people, drug addicts, and county jail inmates, telling stories about people in rural towns all over the state who were having their civil rights trampled upon by local sheriffs and prosecutors and judges?

It's the simple indignity of it all, I told her.

Across the state, in rural counties where the courthouse on the square is still the center of community activity, people were being sent to jail mostly because they couldn't afford outrageous court costs in misdemeanor cases from shoplifting to being behind on child support. When they got out of jail, they often came home to broken lives, lost jobs and homes, separation from children, and even more financial difficulty. Then they got another bill: room and board for their time in the county lockup.

Judges then called the poor Missourians before the bench month after month, serving as debt collectors for county governments on pay-to-stay jail bills that would reach into the thousands of dollars. When they couldn't pay, or missed a court date, many of them were locked up again.

By way of answering Murr's question, I told her a story. In the mid-nineties, I got pulled over by a police officer in Arvada, Colorado, which, ironically, is where my oldest daughter now works in law enforcement.

My oldest son and I had been at his indoor soccer game. He would have been about twelve or thirteen at the time. After the game, I let him leave to spend the night with a teammate. Driving away from the soccer facility, and turning south to head to Littleton, where I lived, I saw the flashing red and blue lights behind me.

I pulled over. I handed over my license and registration, and the officer asked if I knew why she was pulling me over. I did not. It turns out, my registration tags had expired. I was going through a divorce from my first wife, and, well, that's one of those things that fell through the cracks during a disheveled period. It was my weekend with the kids, and my oldest daughter—the one who is now a cop—was at my apartment watching her little brother and sister.

The officer walked back to her car with my information. Soon, a second police cruiser showed up. Two officers slowly marched back to my car.

"Mr. Messenger, I'm going to need you to get out of your car, please. I'm placing you under arrest."

I got out of the car, was patted down and handcuffed. The officer placed her hand atop my head and lowered me into the back seat of her vehicle before asking me if I knew why I was being arrested.

Again, I had no clue.

There was a warrant out for my arrest. I had an outstanding speeding ticket from the town of Morrison that I had neglected to pay.

Morrison is the Macks Creek of Colorado.

It's a tiny little town in the foothills of Colorado, along Bear Creek, just west of the Hogback, that first line of hills that give way to the mountains. Morrison is most well-known for its proximity to two big tourist attractions, the Red Rocks Amphitheatre and Bandimere Speedway, both nationally renowned, one for rock concerts, the other for drag racing.[31]

Coming down Highway 74 from Evergreen, where I used to live, the speed limit is forty-five miles per hour. It drops to twenty-five as you enter Morrison, where you are sure to see (but not in time) a police officer sitting in one of the parking lots that fill up with tourists and sometimes Harley-Davidson motorcycles on the weekends.[32]

In 2017, Morrison raised about $1.2 million in fines and fees from traffic offenses. Nearly all that money is poured right back into its police department.[33] It's a self-replicating system. But for people who get those tickets and can't pay, it starts a cycle of debt, driver's license suspension, jail, and more debt. Colorado was one of many states cited by the American Civil Liberty Union's amicus brief in the 2019 *Timbs v. Indiana* case, in which the U.S. Supreme Court established that the constitution's protection against "excessive fines and fees" applies to states.[34]

"Since 2010, incarceration for unpaid fines and fees without pre-deprivation ability-to-pay hearings has been documented in at least fifteen states: Alabama, Arkansas, Colorado, Georgia, Louisiana, Maine, Michigan, Mississippi, Missouri, New Hampshire, Ohio, South Carolina, Tennessee, Texas, and Washington," the ACLU wrote.[35] "Those who are incarcerated for fines and fees they cannot afford suffer gravely."

I had been pulled over in Morrison for speeding maybe a year before the day I found myself cuffed in the back of the police car. The officer explained she was going to take me to the station to be booked. I'd need money for bail.

"How much do you have with you?" she asked. I was pretty sure I had $80 in cash in my wallet, sitting on the console in my car, where I left it when I grabbed my license and insurance information.

"That should do it," she said. She retrieved my wallet and took me to the Arvada police station. The officer snapped my mugshot and took my fingerprints. I sat in a tiny holding cell while she processed me.

An hour later, I paid my $80 and headed home.

That story, I told Murr, was one of the reasons I had committed myself to this cause. Were I poor and Black and in north St. Louis County, things could have turned out so much worse. Were I poor and white and in rural Dent County, my life could have been turned upside down.

But I didn't spend the weekend in jail. Social services didn't show up and take my children. My car was not impounded. I paid for my mistake and moved on.

Too many Americans in too many jurisdictions don't have that opportunity.

PART II

DEBTORS' PRISON

5

. . . .

PAY-TO-STAY

The story of how court debt becomes a crushing burden for people living in poverty often starts with a small mistake, the sort of thing many of us do when we are young. If we have parents who can afford an attorney, or we can afford bail, the mistake becomes just a blip on the radar screen of our lives. We write a check or swipe a credit card and move on. When the courts compound the mistake by emphasizing their role as debt collectors instead of keeping their focus on protecting public safety, little mistakes can transform themselves into what seems like a life sentence.

So it was for Leann Banderman, who, like Brooke Bergen, was a single mom in Salem, Missouri, struggling with poverty. In January 2016, she was arrested for shoplifting nail polish from the same Walmart as Bergen.[1] She was put in jail, with a cash bail set at $3,000, an amount she could only dream of paying. She sat behind bars for about thirty days, and then pleaded guilty in a plea bargain that sentenced her to time served.[2] Then she got the board bill: $1,400.

The nail polish was worth $24.29.

Nearly every one of Missouri's 114 counties charges such a bill for a stay behind bars, somewhere between $35 and $50 a day.[3] The bill is generally not charged in the urban areas, in St. Louis and Kansas City and Columbia.[4] Court officials in those cities suggest there are likely a couple of reasons for that disparity. First, the cities generally have larger tax bases from which to fund jails. Second, it's just not a practice that has caught on.

"It's horrible," says Gary Oxenhandler. He's a retired circuit court judge from Columbia, Missouri. "It's just not right," he says, to force poor people to pay for their time behind bars, and then send them back to jail when they can't afford to pay the bill. While nearly every state in the country has a statute that allows for such a charge, how it is applied varies wildly from city to county to state, says Lauren-Brooke Eisen, the director of the justice program at the New York–based Brennan Center for Justice.[5]

"Some individuals are leaving jails and prisons with a mountain of debt, much of it stemming from the fees they incurred behind bars, where a short telephone call home can cost as much as $20. These former inmates can face aggressive collection tactics, including additional fines, driver's license suspension, or, in some cases, re-incarceration. Often, former inmates must depend on family members to pay the bills or are forced to prioritize criminal justice debt over other pressing needs such as feeding, clothing, and housing family members who are reliant on their income. Some of these fees are collected while an inmate is incarcerated through deductions from the inmate's bank or commissary account. In some situations, however, the fees are collected through civil litigation aimed at a prisoner's assets or estate upon release. This debt can create a barrier to successful reentry," Eisen wrote in a 2015 report on inmate fees contributing to mass incarceration.[6]

In Minnesota, the application of the "pay-to-stay" bills would be worse if not for the work of law professor Brad Colbert.

Colbert, who teaches at the Mitchell Hamline School of Law in St. Paul,[7] filed a lawsuit against Minnesota's pay-to-stay law in 2008 on behalf of a client, Andrew Tyler Jones, who had been incarcerated in Olmsted County.[8]

Jones was charged in March 2004 with three counts of aggravated robbery. He was jailed and bail was set at $100,000. Jones was indigent and being represented by a public defender. He couldn't afford bail so he sat in jail. In November of that year, he pleaded guilty to the charges and was sent to state prison.

But while he was in prison, the sheriff of Olmsted County sent him a pay-to-stay bill of $7,150, $25 for each day he was held pretrial. In his lawsuit, Colbert argued that this was unconstitutional. The Minnesota law at the time required defendants to be "convicted" and "confined," before they could be charged for their time in the county lockup.

Jones had not been convicted during the time he was in Olmstead County. If he had financial resources, he wouldn't have been in jail at all, because he could have posted bail. Charging poor people for pretrial detention while folks who have money don't get such a bill violates their rights to both due process and equal protection under the law, Colbert argued. These are the rights guaranteed all Americans under the Fourteenth Amendment to the Constitution. Due process limits the ability of the government to trample on various other civil rights; equal protection protects against arbitrary discrimination.

"By charging indigent defendants who could not make bail and not charging wealthier defendants who made bail, the statute draws a distinction between indigent and non-indigent defendants," Colbert argued before the Minnesota Supreme Court.[9]

The court mostly agreed with Colbert, and in 2009 ruled that the pay-to-stay law as it was being applied violated the state statute, getting rid of a local government revenue source.[10]

Then the Minnesota legislature stepped in. The following year, lawmakers abrogated the court's decision, a process by which the state legislature, in effect, erases the case law and then passes a new one to take its place. The legislature clarified the law so that pay-to-stay bills could be collected, but only after sentencing.[11] "The charges may be assessed for any time for which the person receives credit for time served against the sentence imposed as a result of the conviction." The law also included a provision that a sheriff had to investigate a person's ability to pay before seeking to collect such a bill. Almost immediately, counties started collecting the pay-to-stay bills, and, Colbert said, it continues in a patchwork of mostly rural counties today.

Lauri Traub is the managing attorney for the public defender's office in Olmsted County, and she said the pay-to-stay bills are part of a larger trend in Minnesota (and the rest of the nation) where the clients least likely to be able to afford fines and fees and other court costs end up with massive bills they'll never be able to pay. There are booking fees, a fee to buy a padlock and shoes, fees for phone calls and emails, $20 a day to participate in work-release,[12] and a $900 fine for driving while intoxicated unless a defendant agrees to perform 90 hours of community service instead.

"Our clients can't afford $900. They're working two jobs if at all," Traub says.

While the judges in the state's two urban counties—Hennepin and Ramsey, home of Minneapolis and St. Paul—will regularly waive fines and fees for poor people, Traub says, that rarely happens in the rural counties.

"It's hard," Traub says. "The judges have always done it this way."

Unfortunately, such a reality leads to the occasional defeatist attitude for public defenders who have to appear before the same judges regularly, she said.

"After a while, when you make the argument over and over again, you start to think it's never going to happen," she said, and it is people living in poverty who pay the price. "When you start charging these very poor people, it's just a never-ending cycle. Seventy-five dollars to you and me is not the same as $75 to many of my clients."

The new law passed after Jones won his case is still not being properly followed, Colbert said.

In 2013 and 2014, for instance, Erik Christianson ended up in the Martin County Jail on a variety of petty charges.[13] Each time he left jail he received a pay-to-stay bill, ultimately totaling $7,625.

Christianson, who had been represented by the public defender, knew he couldn't afford to pay the bills. So he sent the sheriff of Martin County, Jeffrey Markquart, a letter requesting that the bills be waived.[14] When he didn't get a response to the first one, he sent two more. Markquart never responded to Christianson's letters. Meanwhile, the former defendant was being hounded by a collection agency for the bill.

Colbert filed a federal civil rights lawsuit against Markquart, declaring that by refusing to follow the Minnesota law and consider Christianson's ability to pay, his due process rights had been violated.

Markquart denied violating the law and sought a summary judgment ruling in his favor. He didn't get it. Instead, in July 2018, U.S. District Court Judge John R. Tunheim ruled in Christianson's favor and made it clear how by ignoring Christianson's letters, the sheriff did damage to the entire judiciary:

"Markquart's decision to ignore Christianson's letter accomplishes only one thing: it engenders a belief among citizens that our legal institutions cannot be trusted. Markquart was presented with a perceived violation of an individual's rights: He did not evaluate whether Christianson should have received a waiver. Markquart did not even respond to Christianson's complaint by stating why Christianson would not qualify for a waiver. He simply chose to ignore the perceived violation of Christianson's rights. All Markquart has done is lead Christianson and others to believe that Martin County does not care enough about the legal rights of its citizens to even respond to their concerns."[15]

As a result of the court case, Martin County stopped charging pay-to-stay fees.

Salem, Missouri
Early 2017

For her theft of mascara, Brooke Bergen had been sentenced to a year in jail and two years of probation. The jail sentence would be suspended, as long as she made it through probation unscathed.[16] That was never going to happen.

The probation was to be supervised by the private probation company MPPS. Among the ways the company makes its money is by doing random drug screenings of its clients, as ordered by the judge, even in cases that have nothing to do with drug use. Bergen, like so many of the people under the supervision of MPPS, was a drug addict. There was nothing new about this, and everyone involved in the case knew that.

In fact, anybody in the county who wanted to know it could easily access the information, because the practice of MPPS at the time—since changed after I reported the practice—was to post failed drug test data on the state court's public website.[17]

Two months into her supervised probation, Bergen was reported for a probation violation, for allegedly not answering a phone call for a random drug screen. Baird ordered her to jail for ten days, and Bergen received a bill for those days behind bars. Bergen remembers being in court and trying to explain what happened on the day she missed the phone call from MPPS.

"The judge wouldn't let me talk," she said.

A few months later, according to MPPS, Bergen failed a drug test.

It's worth noting that at the time, MPPS wasn't even required to follow any sort of national standard regarding quality of drug tests.[18] That changed in 2018 when state representative Justin Hill, a Republican from Lake St. Louis, pushed through a bill requiring private probation companies that perform drug testing to meet or exceed national standards.

Hill, a former police officer, had been alerted to the problem by a constituent named John DeFriese, whose son had been charged thousands of dollars in drug tests by another private probation company, Private Correctional Services. The company had reported that DeFriese's son failed the tests, which led to probation violations and jail time. But, suspicious of the results, DeFriese started spending his own money to send the tests to a private lab. Every test he sent came back negative.

"I couldn't believe this was happening," Hill told me.

His bill passed the house with only a single No vote. That came from state representative Jeff Pogue, a Republican from Salem, where MPPS is located. I called the company to ask Lisa Blackwell, who ran the company at the time, what she thought of the new law.

"I don't have nothing to say to you," she told me.

For clients of MPPS, to get the allegedly failed drug test sent to a certified lab costs about $80, which most don't have, particularly on top of the monthly probation fees they pay and outstanding board bills. After allegedly failing the drug test, Baird sent Bergen back to jail for fourteen more days. When she got out her jail board bill had climbed to $943.50, even after a couple of payments she had made. By the end of September 2017, MPPS filed yet another probation violation on Bergen. This time, the judge sent her away for a year.

"I lost hope," Bergen said. "I just gave up. They intended to put me back in there, and they did."

Bergen was in a modern-day version of a "debtors' prison." You might remember the phrase from the ArchCity Defenders lawsuit filed on behalf of Keilee Fant and other residents of Jennings and Ferguson who had been traipsed from jail to jail in north St. Louis County because they couldn't afford traffic tickets. Ask judges and prosecutors who are involved in sending poor people to jail because they owe court costs and they bristle at the use of the phrase. They argue they are sending people to jail because they missed court hearings, or violated pretrial conditions or probation, but at the core of all of these cases is a simple fact that prosecutors and judges cannot escape: if they weren't trying so hard to collect court costs and pay-to-stay bills, the poor people would not be sent back to jail.

There was a time, in the early days of the United States, when literal debtors' prisons were commonplace. People who owed others debt and couldn't pay would be sentenced to jail by judges and work off their debt over a period of time.[19] From before the country's official founding until the early 1800s, cities, colonies, and states around the nation had set up such facilities, many of them dungeon-like, to hold prisoners who had fallen behind on paying back their personal debts.

Manhattan had the "New Gaol" prison and Philadelphia had the Walnut Street Debtors' Prison. Those with connections, or access to financial resources, could get out fairly quickly. Two of the signatories on the Declaration of Independence—James Wilson and Robert Morris—both spent time in a debtors' prison. But much like today's criminal justice system, there were those who were poor who would labor for years in such awful conditions. Many would die there.

The system was borrowed from England, where debtors' prisons were often horrific places of child abuse, and were immortalized in the works of Charles Dickens.[20] Dickens wrote of soot-covered children who slaved away at London's Marshalsea Prison to work off their parents' debts. In real life, Dickens's father, John, had spent some time in that debtors' prison, and the effect on his life was clear, as the theme appears in many of his books.

In the U.S., after the War of 1812 contributed to a rise of the number of Americans and immigrants to the country who were in debt, the tide of public opinion turned against the practice of penalizing the poor in this way. The U.S. government banned imprisonment based on private debt in 1833. It was around the time federal bankruptcy law was beginning to take shape, and each state followed course.[21] Missouri added a constitutional prohibition of debtors' prisons in 1875.[22] Three different times in the twentieth century—including with the 1983 *Bearden* case—the U.S. Supreme Court reaffirmed the constitutional ban against putting people in prison over debt. But in many ways, as the cases of Brooke Bergen, Kendy Killman, and Sasha Darby establish, the practice continues, with judges and prosecutors finding contextual reasons to claim otherwise, but the truth is, there is no other way to frame this. Modern-day debtors' prisons exist and flourish all over the United States.

The Dent County Jail, which is in the basement of the courthouse, is like many jails in rural America, where shrinking tax bases have left counties without money for renovations. The place is so bad that it became a bit of a YouTube sensation as one of the worst county jails in America when the local weekly newspaper toured it with a camera and posted the video online.[23]

"For the women in Dent County jail, there are 2 cells which were originally intended to hold 4 people in each. At any given time there are 9 to 13 women in each cell. The mats cover the entire floor and some have their mats partially under the bunks or table, allowing only the top half of the person to be out," wrote Lashawn Casey, a detainee, in an email she sent me in 2018.[24] After I began writing about cases in the county, she wrote me and encouraged me to keep digging.

"Black mold grows freely on the ceiling, in corners and under the table," she wrote. "In the summer, the back wall sweats and puddles collect in corners and soak the blankets. This is where the women sit out their days reading, sleeping or talking. One day a week a TV is wheeled in to help break the monotony. Once or twice a month, if the jailor can find time, each inmate is allowed out of the cage for 15 minutes of sunshine and fresh air. Last month the female population outnumbered the male population, which is unprecedented in this county. I feel this is significant although I don't claim to know the cause. Perhaps women are less likely to get the money for bond or maybe they are just easier to manipulate."

They were single mothers who pleaded guilty to misdemeanors. Their stays in jail were extended by high bail and questionable violations of pretrial conditions. They received bills for their jail time completely disproportionate to their offenses. And months or years after they served their time, they were still being called before a Dent County judge to account for their debts.

The overcrowding was so bad, Casey told me, because so many of the women didn't belong there. She doesn't include herself in that category. Casey owns her crimes. She is a meth addict. For a while, she would deal drugs to feed her habit. During the time I was writing columns for the *Post-Dispatch*, Casey asked me not to use her name. It wouldn't help, she said. Focus on the women who really shouldn't have been in jail. Casey agreed to let me use her name for the purposes of this book. She's out of prison now, sober, working two jobs, and trying to rebuild her life.

There was one woman she remembers during her time in the Dent County Jail as indicative of how conditions in the jail deteriorated. The woman had bad eczema, and the condition was made worse because the water from the shower was so hot her skin couldn't handle the heat. So the woman didn't shower much, and as such, would often have dry skin just sloughing off her body. The cells for women were so crowded that conflict erupted often. One day, according to Casey, the woman with eczema got up and as she lifted her blanket, some dry skin fell into another woman's coffee. It took the intervention of several women to make sure there wasn't a fight.

"We had to beg for cleaning supplies," Casey said.

Almost immediately, Bergen's year in jail started making it harder for her to ever escape the pull of the criminal justice system in Dent County and its effect on her life and her ability to climb out of the depths of poverty. Her husband—they were still married though they didn't live together—took custody of their daughter and Bergen's son from another relationship. She was ordered to pay $277 a month in child support.

And what happened the first week she got out of jail?

Judge Baird scheduled her for a payment review hearing on her jail board bill, now more than $15,000 and rising. She would have to show up once a month to make a "substantial payment" the judge told her. What is "substantial" to somebody with very little income? In Bergen's mind, it was $100, a figure she could only get to by borrowing from friends. It was nowhere near enough to pay down the jail debt.

"It's a vicious cycle," Bergen told me. "They put all of this on you, and you can't get out. They made it impossible for me to get on with my life."

In many states across the country, the well-known phrase, "if you can't do the time, don't do the crime," loses all meaning when "time" becomes a life sentence because the defendant can't pay the costs foisted upon them. Wisconsin is a good example.

In 2011, Lamon Barnes was arrested and jailed in Brown County.[25] Barnes was notified of a $20-per-day bill for detention. On his own, he filed a federal lawsuit challenging the pay-to-stay statute, arguing that it shouldn't apply to pretrial detainees, that such a charge would be punitive before a conviction. He would go on to lose the case.

"There is no evidence that Brown County was motivated by a desire to punish pretrial detainees when it collected lock-up fees from them," wrote U.S. District Judge Lynn Adelman in his ruling.[26] "The policy appeared to be rationally related to the county's legitimate interest in 'effective management of the detention facility.'"

In other words, charging a backdoor tax to poor people is legal. Never mind that taxpayers are already paying for the jail through other taxes. In Wisconsin, at least twenty-three counties charge pay-to-stay fees. The story is the same in at least some counties in nearly every state, and in every region of the country:[27] Florida,[28] California,[29] Nevada, Colorado, Indiana,[30] and Ohio, just to name a few.[31]

One state, though—New Hampshire—recently ended its practice of seeking pay-to-stay payments from people who had been incarcerated in its state prisons.[32] The law had been on the books since 1996, but in 2019, Gov. Chris Sununu signed House Bill 518, which repealed it. The legislative debate had been spurred by a lawsuit filed by Eric Cable, who was sued by the state for about $120,000 in pay-to-stay bills after he had already served time on a negligent homicide charge. Represented by the American Civil Liberties Union, Cable countersued the state, claiming the attempt to recover charges for his time in prison was unconstitutional. In the end, the lawsuits were dismissed by both parties, but the ACLU sought a legislative remedy and succeeded in getting New Hampshire to repeal its pay-to-stay law, a first in the nation.

Lauren-Brooke Eisen, of the Brennan Center, agrees with Brad Colbert that such fees violate the due process and equal protection clauses in the Fourteenth Amendment, because they are so often applied disproportionately to people living in poverty, and specifically to people of color.

The more compelling argument that Eisen believes should be used to upend pay-to-stay fees, though, is that they violate the excessive fees clause in the Eighth Amendment. That clause says this: "excessive bail shall not be required, nor excessive fines imposed, nor cruel and unusual punishments inflicted."

Since it is generally poor people who have to pay them, pay-to-stay fees are inherently excessive. "There is a credible argument to be made that once society has determined to remove a group of individuals from the community, it is then 'excessive' and 'disproportionate' to charge them daily fees, booking fees, and even medical and other fees while their liberty is deprived and the justice system has already imposed a sentence for their crimes," Eisen writes.

There is a question as to whether pay-to-stay charges and other fines produce a noticeable public benefit. The Brennan Center estimates there are about $50 billion in uncollected court costs and fees nationwide, much of which will never serve its intended purpose, which is often to help pay for city or county government costs.[33] In fact, a 2019 study jointly produced by the conservative Texas Public Policy Foundation and the Brennan Center found that it often costs governments more money to try to collect court fines and fees than they bring in, meaning they are taking valuable resources away from other government services, such as public safety.[34] The study looked at several counties in Texas, Florida, and New Mexico, each states with a reputation for charging indigent defendants hundreds or thousands of dollars in court fines and fees.

Among the findings:

- "One New Mexico county spends at least $1.17 to collect every dollar of revenue it raises through fees and fines, meaning that it loses money through this system."
- "Judges rarely hold hearings to establish defendants' ability to pay. As a result, the burden of fees and fines falls largely on the poor, much like a regressive tax, and billions of dollars go unpaid each year. These mounting balances underscore our finding that fees and fines are an unreliable source of government revenue."
- "Jailing those unable to pay fees and fines is especially costly— sometimes as much as 115 percent of the amount collected— and generates no revenue."[35]

This is, in effect, what criminalizing poverty looks like. One of the longest active "debtors' prison" cases in Missouri explicitly shows this phenomenon in action.

Lake of the Ozarks, Missouri
Summer 2006

Alicyn Rapp had a bad breakup.[36]

It was 2006, and she was living with a boyfriend at the Lake of the Ozarks, the sprawling, man-made body of water created by a power-

producing dam in the central part of Missouri that has become a nationally known magnet for summer recreation. The Lake of the Ozarks
has more shoreline than California does, at about 1,150 miles, and its
various tucked-away coves in Camden, Benton, Miller, and Morgan
Counties draw about 5 million visitors for boating, fishing, swimming,
and other pursuits.

Rapp and her boyfriend lived above his window-tinting business. According to the police report, they got in a fight after she learned that he
had cheated on her. She stormed out of the apartment after smashing a
laptop.[37] She was charged with domestic violence and property damage.

By the time she knew about the charges, though, Rapp had already
hitched a ride back to St. Louis, where she grew up. She was a south-
side Catholic girl, attending St. Gabriel's and then Bishop DuBourg
High School. By the age of fourteen, Rapp was fighting addiction,
mostly to alcohol and meth. She has done three short stints in state
prison on drug possession charges. But it's one arrest—the one in Camden County—that has haunted her for most of her adult life.

After going through a couple of attorneys, Rapp pleaded guilty to
the charges in 2008, third-degree domestic violence and second-degree
property damage (both misdemeanors). She was sentenced to a year in
jail, which was suspended, and two years' probation. Her court costs and
fines totaled about $1,200.

By 2009, Rapp started to fall behind on her payments to the court,
and the cycle that would continue for more than a decade began. The
judge would order her to court to explain a missed payment. She was living in St. Louis—or in prison—and when she missed the court date in
Camden County, a warrant would be issued for her arrest. Rapp would
be picked up on a speeding ticket or some other offense, taken to jail,
and transported to Camden County, where she'd stay in jail for a few
days until the judge could see her. It happened in 2009, 2010, and 2012,
each time increasing the amount she owed the court because she would
then receive a pay-to-stay bill for her time in the county jail. At the Lake
of the Ozarks they had a name for this: "It's legendary," Rapp revealed.
"Come on vacation, leave on probation, come back on revocation."

We met for the first time in 2018 in a hole-in-the-wall bar in north St. Louis County. Rapp had read my columns on Bergen and other defendants who had been through Missouri's debtors' prison cycle and wanted to tell me about her case. Rapp's was the oldest case I wrote about.[38] Here's how important it is for the judges, sheriffs, and county commissioners in Camden County to collect their jail bills from people like Rapp:

In 2013, she was in the Chillicothe Correctional Center, a state prison, doing 120 days for meth possession. Rapp was tired of being behind bars. She was trying to turn her life around. She knew that once she did her time on state charges, she could escape the criminal justice system, but not in Camden County, where she was tethered to the courts, and jail, simply because she couldn't afford the ever-increasing costs coming her way.

So Rapp wrote the judge:

"I am writing you requesting time served in lieu of fines and/or jail time to run concurrent with my current sentence," Rapp wrote the Camden County Circuit Court. "I am trying to change my life and I would like a clean slate to start over."

The judge refused. Not unless she came up with the $1,639.70 she owed the court. She had paid when she could, but never enough.

When Rapp got out of prison, she was met by a Camden County sheriff's van, which took her back to the county jail. When she got out, her bill was higher: more "rent" for her time in jail, including the cost of the mileage for the van that brought her there. In 2017, Camden County took in more than $240,000 in pay-to-stay bills from people like Rapp, more than all but one county in Missouri.[39] Neighboring Laclede County collected about $20,000 more. According to Missouri court records, as of this writing, Rapp's case is still ongoing.

In January 2019, Camden County Judge Steve Jackson wrote this about the case: "In the case at bar, the Court believed Defendant's whereabouts to execute a warrant and obtain compliance with an appearance to resolve the issues of the case had been lost causing the Court to be inclined to dismiss. However, the State informs the Court today that since the last Court date, a journalist has written the State

by email and made note of a published article where the journalist in-
dicates communication with the Defendant who is living in St. Louis,
is aware of the unresolved case and it appears aware of the outstanding
warrant. The journalist has written the Court by email. The email appears to be an attempt of the journalist to influence the outcome of this
case with coercion or extortion by negative publicity."[40]

I'm not sure what email the court is referring to. I never emailed the
court. But I did write about Rapp's case.

"It's been 12 years, for God's sake," Rapp says. "I've lost jobs, my
house, cars, my children. I've done enough time. I've paid them enough
money. With this hanging over my head, I'm never going to get a clean
start. When is it going to stop?"

The last docket entry in her case was January 6, 2020.[41] "Case to remain pending," it says, hanging over Rapp like a permanent dark cloud.

Rapp and Bergen were hardly alone. There were hundreds, possibly
thousands, of defendants just like them in counties across Missouri,
stuck in this never-ending cycle of poverty and jail because they owed
money on jail board bills. The process that judges were using to collect
those bills was not allowed by state law, believed Matthew Mueller, the
young public defender who would eventually challenge the practice
before the Missouri Supreme Court. In 2018, he started his quest to go
about closing debtors' prisons in Missouri. One of his first stops was a
tiny courthouse in Mississippi County.

6

· · · · · · · · · · · · · · · · ·

THE KEY TO THE JAILHOUSE DOOR

Charleston, Missouri
August 2018

Tamara Tidwell stood before the judge and gave him a lesson in poverty.

It was August 2018, long after Circuit Court Judge David Andrew Dolan had sent Tidwell, who is white, to prison on a probation violation. On this day, Dolan and Tidwell weren't there to talk about guilt or innocence. Tidwell was guilty. She stole. She went to prison and served her time. Until, of course, the county charged her for the time she was in jail. When she couldn't afford to pay it, Dolan had her locked up again.[1] That's what they were here to talk about: money.

Tidwell lives in Anniston, a tiny blink-and-you'll-miss-it town in Mississippi County, one of the poorest counties in Missouri.[2] It's in the Bootheel, the southeast part of the state, where rich bottomland soil fed by the adjacent Mississippi River has long led to bumper crops of soybeans, winter wheat, corn, and cotton.[3] The courthouse is in Charleston, just eight and a half miles north along State Road 105. That doesn't seem very far, unless you live on $750 a month in federal disability payments, and you don't have a car.

Tidwell's attorney, Matthew Mueller, had filed a motion to "retax costs" in Tidwell's case.[4] Mueller was filing similar motions in courthouses across rural Missouri, arguing that judges were breaking the law by requiring people like Tidwell to show up month after month, long after their cases had been adjudicated, to pay board bills for their previous stays in jail. Dolan had been a judge in Mississippi and Scott Counties since 1992.[5] Before that he was the local prosecuting attorney. He didn't take kindly to Mueller questioning his methods. The case was simple, Mueller told Dolan.

When Tidwell had her probation revoked in 2014 and went to prison, the court taxed her costs—most of which consisted of a $920 bill for her pretrial time in jail, since she was unable to afford bail—to the state.[6] In Missouri, if an indigent defendant is convicted of a felony and goes to state prison, then the state picks up the court costs, including the room and board for time in the county jail. So, unlike most of the misdemeanor cases in this book, Tillman should not have received a pay-to-stay bill. Instead, the state received one. That the state pays for county jail costs when a prosecutor obtains a felony conviction creates a perverse incentive for prosecutors to overcharge defendants with more serious crimes. The system also puts counties at odds with the state legislature, because when budgets are tight, the state cuts its distributions for county jail expenses. That leaves counties looking for their pay-to-stay money anywhere they can get it.

Tidwell returned from prison to a surprise. Mississippi County sent her the same bill it had already sent to the state. She was supposed to show up in Dolan's court every month and make a payment or explain why she couldn't. Tidwell was diagnosed with a mental disability as a child. That's why she lives on Supplemental Security Income. She made one payment in 2017—$60—but missed other hearings and had been jailed by Dolan twice after warrants were issued for her arrest.

"I'm trying to figure out why she cannot come to court?" Dolan asked.

"I am disabled," she said. "No vehicle. No transportation."

Dolan wasn't satisfied.

"How did you get here today?"

"I called a ride."

"Okay," the judge said, "then you have transportation."

"Not all the time, sir, no. When you don't have money and you can't pay for the gas, then you run into complications."

In Mississippi County, being poor comes with lots of complications. More than 26 percent of the people there live below the federal poverty line for income, more than twice the rate in the rest of Missouri.[7] Only nearby Pemiscot County has a higher percentage of poor people.[8] When the Noranda aluminum mill in nearby New Madrid shut down in 2016, the loss of about nine hundred workers from several nearby counties left all sorts of mom-and-pop businesses in the lurch as their customers lost income.[9] Increased flooding from the Mississippi River, linked to a changing climate, has also contributed to the economic downturn.[10] There are only about 14,000 people in Mississippi County, and the poverty rate is high. Nearly half of the children live in poverty.[11] Tidwell has two children. They live with her mother. She sees them often. There is no public transportation in most places in rural Missouri. Without a car, getting to court once a month is a chore. But that wasn't good enough for the judge.

"How did you get here today? You called somebody?"

"Let's say the first of the month whenever I get paid, I have to pay them gas money, therefore, by the time my check does get here at the beginning of the month, I'm broke."

Mueller tried to get the judge back on topic.

"My overriding concern is having former clients of ours put in jail for not appearing in court for judicial proceedings directed at collecting costs," he said. "She is not charged with a crime or anything. It is just in collecting the court costs."

In the end, the judge ruled against Tidwell. She would not be getting her $60 back. She still owed the rest of her jail board bill. And she'd face even more jail time if she didn't keep showing up month after month until the debt was paid.

Dolan said, "She has got to come back and see me in October, like all the rest of those people."

Dolan's courtroom was full that day. For good measure, he chided Mueller for making the six-hour drive from Kansas City.

"I didn't know you had all of that free time," Dolan said. "The public defenders tell me they are so overworked."

Indeed they are. Missouri has the second-worst-funded public-defender system in the country.[12] Only Mississippi funds its system less than Missouri based on caseloads, according to the ACLU. Consider the case of Shondel Church, who is featured in the Brennan Center report that outlines the underfunding problems in Missouri and elsewhere.

In 2016, Church, who lived in Kansas City, was arrested for misdemeanor theft of a generator and toolbox in rural Lafayette County.[13] He couldn't afford the $5,000 cash bail set in his case.[14] He sat in jail for forty days before he even met with a public defender.

In the end, Church would spend 125 days in jail before pleading guilty—not because he didn't have a chance to beat the rap, but because he wanted out of jail. After he was released, he received a bill for $2,600. The next year, the American Civil Liberties Union and the Roderick and Solange MacArthur Justice Center filed a class-action lawsuit on behalf of Church and other defendants arguing that their right to counsel was being denied by the state's poor funding of the public-defender system.[15] The *Church* case was dismissed in 2020, but the ACLU and MacArthur Justice Center filed a similar lawsuit in state court. A judge in that case ruled in February 2021 that the Missouri legislature had to find a way to increase funding for the public defender's office.

"The State violates the Sixth Amendment . . . by charging an indigent defendant with a crime in which the State seeks the defendant's incarceration, and then delaying for weeks, months, and even more than a year before furnishing the defendant with an attorney," wrote Circuit Court Judge William E. Hickle.

This is the story that is repeated all over Missouri. Every step of the judicial process is designed to bury a defendant deeper into poverty.

"All of these indigent defendants are being set up for failure all over the country," says Lauren-Brooke Eisen.[16] "The under-resourcing has created a culture of case processing."

It was in this context that Michael Barrett, then the head of the

Missouri public-defender system, hired Mueller in November 2017 to be a one-man wrecking crew. Mueller's job was to break down this system. To find the cases where people were being jailed simply because they were poor, challenge the judges, and force the Missouri Supreme Court to set things right.

Mueller ended up on Barrett's radar screen for a simple reason: Judges and prosecutors were filing bar complaints against him. "Nothing eats at these rural judges like occupying a week on their calendar with a trial," Barrett says. And Mueller liked to take cases to trial.

The first complaint came from Hannibal, where Mueller initially worked as a public defender. The northeast Missouri river town, nestled along the banks of the Mississippi River, was made famous by the exploits of Tom Sawyer and Huckleberry Finn. The Mark Twain Boyhood Home and Museum is along Main Street, just a stone's throw from the river. Across the street is the Becky Thatcher House. The town is a visual tribute to the famous American author. The coffee shops, ice-cream joints, and bars have Twain-themed drinks.[17] Waterlogged by increasingly frequent floods, the town is a bit battered, though it still draws a crowd of tourists on a sunny summer weekend. Mueller arrived in March 2014, after his career took an important turn.

Mueller's father is an attorney. And his father before him. And one more generation, too. So what did Mueller do? He went to Washington University in St. Louis to get a degree in economics. He expected to follow that up with graduate school and a career in teaching and research. The pull of three previous generations proved too strong, though. He headed west, to Columbia, Missouri, where he graduated from the University of Missouri School of Law in 2013. Mueller landed a job at a civil collections firm, where he gained tremendous insight into debt collection practices in America. Working for banks and credit card companies, helping them squeeze a few more dollars out of people who owed them money, wasn't his cup of tea, though. So Mueller went to work in the low-paying Missouri public defender's office.

The job of a young public defender in a small town is often to go along to get along. First, there are just too many cases assigned to each public defender because of the aforementioned lack of statewide funding. Then there are the political difficulties. With a locally elected sheriff, prosecutor. and judge all generally sharing the same tough-on-crime philosophy, a low-paid, just-out-of-law-school public defender often finds his or her most successful path to get their clients out of jail with plea bargains that avoid the trouble of a trial.

"As they see it," Mueller says of the prosecutor and judge, "the system works best when cases are processed quickly, that is, no contested hearings, no trials and no substantial motions practice. The system prefers that the rights of criminal defendants are waived and that guilty pleas are entered. This is no secret."

Mueller didn't play by the preexisting rules. He filed motions for bond reduction and discovery. He sought hearings to argue the finer points of law. He set out to defend his clients, most of whom were charged with low-end drug possession, with robust arguments and demands for jury trials.

"The local prosecutors and judges did not take kindly to this," he said.

The local prosecutor filed a complaint with the Missouri Bar Association.

Most attorneys want to avoid bar complaints. The worst ones— based on dishonesty, financial shenanigans with a client's money, or malpractice—can lead to a suspension of one's license to practice law.[18] Most are dismissed, but not without some effort.[19] Mueller was accused of engaging in a "motion practice," meaning he was, it seems, practicing too much law. The complaint was dismissed. The prosecutor wrote Barrett and tried to get Mueller moved to another office. It didn't work. The second complaint was like the first, this time from a judge accusing Mueller of seeking too many jury trials. The judge who filed the complaint, Mueller says, was not wrong. No rural court could handle the scheduling nightmare of taking every single case it files to trial. That was part of Mueller's reason for filing so many aggressive motions on cases. He saw case after case filed with flimsy evidence in which guilty pleas were the result of high bail and aggressive charging by prosecutors, as compared to good police work and strong evidence. When you put a poor person in jail and pleading guilty is the only way to get back to their kids, their jobs, their home, that's a strong incentive.

Mueller wanted prosecutors to make their cases. He wanted his clients to have their rights—all of them—protected. And he wanted judges to be on his side when it came to protecting those rights.

"The basic assumption is that most criminal cases will result in a guilty plea. The judges operate under this assumption. Their only job is to make sure the person has an attorney when this happens," Mueller said. "I came in and upset that entire system."

After a little more than a year in Hannibal, Mueller ended up in the Columbia public defender's office. There, he got assigned more serious cases, the sorts of felony cases—murders and shootings and sexual assaults—that he could take to trial. In his first year he took fourteen cases to trial, and he won most of them.

"I was hooked."

Just as in Hannibal, though, he quickly moved on, this time to the Commitment Defense Unit, which represents clients accused of being sexually violent predators. Nearly all those cases go to jury trials, and that's where Mueller wanted to be, in front of a judge or jury, using every tool at his disposal to represent his clients. Even the best attorney, though, loses nearly all those cases, and so did Mueller. In Missouri, the Sexually Violent Predators Act makes it next to impossible for a defendant to win; most end up spending their entire lives post-conviction behind bars.[20]

Soon the head of the public defender's office, Barrett, approached Mueller with an offer.

Go back to your roots, Barrett said. File motions on old cases in front of judges across rural Missouri, where indigent clients were being forced back to jail simply because they were poor, and get cases to the appeals courts and the Missouri Supreme Court to undo decades of injustice.

Mueller was living in Kansas City, so he started focusing on cases there, mostly in Platte County, and he attacked the part of the system that was key to the entire scheme: high cash bail amounts that kept people in jail on minor offenses before they had ever been found guilty.

In Missouri, Barrett said, "If you were held on pretrial bond in jail, the likelihood that you'd get a sentence of incarceration after a plea or trial was three times higher than if you were able to post bail." This is the lynchpin of the criminalization of poverty in the American judicial system, a misapplication of the constitutional purposes of bail to create a dual system of justice, one for people with money, one for those without. That makes the application of bail punitive before a defendant has been found guilty of a crime, and it leads to devastating consequences for the people stuck behind bars. They lose jobs, cars, homes, and their children. And that's just the beginning.

In most states, the reality of having an underfunded public defender's office means defendants are in jail even longer because they can't even get an attorney to file a bond reduction hearing based on their inability to pay. Prosecutors take advantage of this, offering to release defendants on time served if only they will plead guilty.[21] With few public defenders willing to buck the system in the way Mueller did, defendants take the deal, and they get out of jail, only to be handed a bill for their time behind bars, a monthly charge to pay to a private probation company, and the likelihood that they will return, not for re-offending, but for missing a court hearing, or failing a drug test, or simply being unable to pay down their court costs and fees.

It's a cycle that is nearly impossible for a person with nothing to break.

That's the argument made by the Institute for Constitutional Advocacy and Protection in an amicus brief filed on one of the debtors' prison cases Mueller eventually argued before the Missouri Supreme Court:

"Indigent defendants sentenced to a jail term in Missouri are, in effect, punished with two separate sentences," reads the brief, which was also signed by the Fines and Fees Justice Center, the Roderick and Solange MacArthur Justice Center, Fair and Just Prosecution, and the conservative Show-Me Institute. "First they serve the court-ordered jail time. Second, once the jail time is completed, they must pay for the expense of each day of their incarceration, a debt that often amounts to hundreds or even thousands of dollars. This debt—frequently referred to as a 'jail board bill'—is often insurmountable for indigent individuals, causes incalculable harm and follows them for years. Even worse, numerous courts across Missouri require individuals laboring under the cloud of jail debt to report to court for monthly show-cause hearings—on the legally unsupportable theory that jail debt can be taxed as 'court costs'—to either make payment or explain why they cannot."[22]

Cassi Licata knows this cycle far too well.

In August 2018, Ray County Circuit Court Judge Kevin Walden scheduled her for a payment review hearing. A few years earlier, in 2012, Licata, who is white, had fled her home in that western Missouri county to seek protection in a domestic violence shelter in Oklahoma.[23] During the time that she was there, the man she was hiding from, her child's father, was awarded custody. Licata ended up being charged with felony interference of custody. She fought the charge, lost, and ended up in jail for nine months. Eventually, the conviction was overturned, and in a plea bargain, the charge was reverted to a misdemeanor. But, having already served her time in jail, Licata was presented with a jail and medical bill of more than $22,000, an amount she could most certainly not afford to pay.[24] Walden scheduled her for monthly hearings to make payments or explain why she couldn't. In August, she missed one. Licata was seven months into a high-risk pregnancy and her doctor told her not to travel. When the warrant was issued for her arrest, Licata sent a letter from two different doctors to the judge. But the warrant remained in effect. On January 3, 2019, Licata was arrested. Bail was set at $1,500. She couldn't afford it, so she was locked up.

It's cases like Licata's that led the ArchCity Defenders, a nonprofit law firm in St. Louis, to file a lawsuit in federal court alleging that judges were violating the civil rights of poor defendants by using bail as a punitive action rather than for its intended purpose, which was to ensure that a defendant shows up for court, or, in extreme cases, to protect society from a potentially violent criminal. Licata was the victim—not perpetrator—of violence.

That lawsuit alleges that bail policies in St. Louis "imprison people on unaffordable money bail, deny them even the most basic procedural protections, and violate their fundamental constitutional right to pretrial liberty and their equal protection right not to be detained because of their poverty."[25] Such lawsuits have been filed in multiple states and have led to bail reforms throughout the country, most famously in New York, which in 2019 eliminated the use of cash bail for most misdemeanor and nonviolent felony charges.[26]

The New York reforms were expected to reduce jail populations by about 40 percent—mostly people being held pretrial on misdemeanors or nonviolent felonies. But almost immediately after the new law went into effect there was pushback, particularly from the police union and some tough-on-crime district attorneys.[27]

Three months after the law took effect, the legislature amended it, giving more discretion to judges to impose cash bail in some circumstances.[28] In Missouri, the supreme court implemented some bail reforms that same year, issuing new court rules just a few days after the ArchCity Defenders' lawsuit was filed, reiterating the need for judges to hold ability-to-pay hearings for every defendant, and making sure that poor defendants had the same opportunity to be released from jail pretrial as those with more resources.[29]

For reformers like Tampa, Florida, prosecutor Andrew Warren, these changes to how bail has been abused by the judicial system were a long time coming. "The bail system doesn't actually follow the law," Warren said. "We detain people for inability to pay hundreds of times a day. It's done that way because it's a fast-food industry."[30]

Indeed, in courtrooms across the country, there are often law days that have people lined up around the courthouse like cars outside a McDonald's around dinnertime. They take off half a day from their minimum wage jobs to get a chance to stand in front of a judge for a few minutes, often without an attorney, to answer on minor charges. Sometimes they get a go-directly-to-jail card, or they have to wait a month until they can speak with a public defender.

Those who can't afford bail are more likely to end up in jail for a long period of time before they've ever been convicted of a crime. And that process, a growing chorus of reformers are saying, does nothing to make communities safer.[31]

In fact, it might do more harm than good.

That was the result of a 2013 study funded by the Laura and John Arnold Foundation that looked at recidivism rates in Kentucky by defendants who were held for long periods of time pretrial, and those who were released on a summons.[32]

The study found strong evidence that those who were held in jail on cash bail that they couldn't afford were more likely to re-offend than those who were released and could return to jobs and family. The study is referenced by an amicus brief filed by the Texas Public Policy Foundation in the St. Louis bail lawsuit.[33]

"St. Louis's bail system makes the community weaker by depriving citizens of community ties and the means to support themselves by increasing the likelihood of future criminal activity," the foundation wrote in its legal brief. Referencing the 2013 study, the foundation wrote:

"Low-risk defendants held for two to three days were 40 percent more likely to commit new crimes before trial than those held for no more than 24 hours. And low-risk defendants detained for 31 days or more were 74 percent more likely to commit new crimes before trial."

In his new job, Mueller's landmark debtors' prison cases involved two men, George Richey and John Wright. Like many of the rural Missouri defendants Mueller represented, Richey and Wright are white. Nationally, the criminalization of poverty tends to affect people of color disproportionally, but outside of the state's urban areas in Kansas City and St. Louis, the victims in homogeneous rural Missouri are mostly white. Wright lives in Higginsville, a small town of about 4,700 people located in rural Lafayette County.[34] To get there, you turn north at the Pilot truck stop on Interstate 70 just east of Kansas City. If you get to the Confederate cemetery, you've gone too far. In 2016, Wright didn't pay for a cab ride.[35] He doesn't drive, the result of a traumatic brain injury he suffered when he was nineteen. Sometimes he forgets things. Wright was charged with a misdemeanor. He was jailed with cash bail set at $5,000. Wright couldn't afford bail, so he sat in jail. After spending about three months in jail, he pleaded guilty and was sentenced to time served. When he got out, the county gave him a bill for $1,300.

A law charging for jail time has existed in Missouri since at least the late 1800s,[36] but there was a time when a man like Wright wouldn't have received a bill. The 1909 version of the Missouri law that allows counties to charge for jail time, for instance, included an exception for "insolvent prisoners." The law also seemed to take a more compassionate view of jail time, allowing inmates to bring in their own food and bedding to keep costs down and make them more comfortable.[37]

Those historic versions of the law rekindle an image of the fictional town of Mayberry from the 1960s television sitcom *The Andy Griffith Show*, where the town drunk, Otis, would meander into the jail on his own to sleep off a bender, and Aunt Bee would bring him a home-cooked meal once he sobered up.[38] Sometimes, Otis would use his own key to let himself into the jail. This is actually a concept rooted in the system of American justice, as Mueller would argue in one of his cases.

"The defendant must have the keys to the jailhouse door," Mueller said. What he means is that the defendant must have an opportunity to argue that their bail is too high. They must have an opportunity to have access to an attorney who can seek to free them from confinement. The system doesn't allow a judge to simply lock somebody up and throw away the key. Missouri's law no longer includes an exception for defendants who can't afford to pay,[39] and as Mueller traveled the state filing appeals in cases where poor people were jailed over their inability to pay such bills, he found that many judges weren't taking the time to hold ability-to-pay hearings before they set bail.

Lafayette County Associate Circuit Court Judge Kelly Rose scheduled

Wright to come to court every month after his release to report on the $1,300 he owed.[40] Thirteen times he showed up and paid about $380 total toward his jail bill. Wright knew that if he missed a hearing, or stopped making payments, he would end up in jail again.

That's precisely what happened to Richey.

In 2015, the Warrensburg man was arrested for violating an order of protection.[41] It's a misdemeanor, but like Wright, he faced a bail he couldn't afford and sat in jail for ninety days. Richey pleaded guilty and was sentenced to time served.[42] His bill for room and board while in jail was $3,158. When Richey hadn't made any payments on the bill by the end of the year, St. Clair County Associate Circuit Court Judge Jerry Rellihan issued a warrant for his arrest.

Richey spent sixty-five more days behind bars in early 2016. By then his jail board bill was more than $5,000. Month after month Rellihan ordered him to the courthouse in Appleton City, a town of about 1,100 people southeast of Kansas City. Richey didn't have transportation to make the trip every month, so he moved to Appleton City, where he mostly lived out of a suitcase.[43] Like Wright, his only source of income was about $600 a month in federal disability payments.

The Wright and Richey cases were just two of dozens Mueller filed in courts all across Missouri between 2017 and 2019. In each case the young public defender was arguing that the court system was violating Missouri law by holding rural defendants in jail mostly because they were poor.[44] He called it a modern-day debtors' prison scheme and there's no other way to describe it. He lost nearly all the cases he filed at the circuit court level, going up against judges like Dolan and Rose, but that was expected. Then he appealed, hoping to get the cases ultimately before the Missouri Supreme Court. The Wright and Richey cases were the vehicles that upended the system.

Mueller faced a receptive Missouri Supreme Court in early 2019 that for nearly five years had been focused on one time or another on the persistent problem of courts being used as debt collectors.[45] It started shortly after August 9, 2014, when Michael Brown was killed by a police officer in Ferguson.[46]

In the months after Brown's death, the Missouri Supreme Court was presented with evidence of the failure of the judiciary: municipal courts nickel-and-diming indigent defendants to no end, jailing them because they couldn't afford the fines, violating their civil rights repeatedly, and exacerbating their desperate financial situations in an attempt to raise money to prop up cash-strapped governments.[47] Broken taillight? Get a ticket. Can't afford it? A warrant is issued for your arrest. Don't show up to court? Time for jail. Cities built their budgets around this source of revenue, and cops were threatened with their jobs if they didn't meet quotas.[48]

The victims of those municipal court schemes were mostly poor and Black.[49] George Richey, Brooke Bergen, Victoria Branson, Cory Booth, and other rural victims of the jail board bill scheme were mostly poor and white.

In 2015, Mary Russell was the chief justice of the Missouri Supreme Court, and in her annual speech to the Missouri Legislature, just months after the streets of Ferguson and St. Louis had erupted in protest, she addressed the fundamental unfairness of what was happening in the courts:

"Courts should primarily exist to help people resolve their legal disputes. If they serve, instead, as revenue generators for the municipality that selects and pays the court staff and judges—this creates at least a perception, if not a reality, of diminished judicial impartiality," Russell said. "It is important to ensure that municipal divisions throughout the state are driven not by economics, but by notions of fairness under the rule of law. The Supreme Court is ready to work with you to ensure that people who appear in municipal courts are treated fairly and with respect."[50]

That year, the Missouri Supreme Court issued new rules to limit municipal court abuses, including one requiring ability-to-pay hearings.[51] And the Missouri Legislature passed the law that would limit the amount of revenue a city could depend upon from traffic tickets.[52] The law required regular audits to make sure cities complied.

By early 2019, when Mueller's appeals on Wright and Richey made it to the Missouri Supreme Court, Russell was no longer the chief justice, but she was still on the court.[53] She and the other two women on the seven-person court—Patricia Breckenridge and Laura Denvir Stith—seemed particularly bothered by the scheme to put poor Missourians back in jail because they couldn't afford the initial bill for jail time.

In the supreme court cases, Mueller channeled the spirit of Edward Crawford. In the 2014 Ferguson protests, Crawford was the man captured in my colleague Robert Cohen's Pulitzer Prize–winning photo that became the most visceral and iconic photo of that moment in history.[54] Wearing a T-shirt emblazoned with a U.S. flag, Crawford, a Black man with long dreadlocks, grabbed a burning tear gas canister that had been shot by police near some protesters and children. He tossed it back, and the photo, for many, became a visual representation of the Black Lives Matter movement, a metaphor for our times.[55]

As he stood before the seven black-robed judges of the Missouri Supreme Court, Mueller looked out of place. Thirty years old, tall, and thin, this was his first time arguing before the high court.[56] He was not much older than the two rows of law school students from Mueller's alma mater, the University of Missouri School of Law, sitting in the back of the courtroom. Their presence was a dead giveaway that something important was about to happen.

Mueller wore a dark suit, had mussed black hair and a permanent smile. Despite being six-foot-one, he had to look up to the judges in their black-leather chairs behind the raised and polished wood-paneled bench. Mueller's girlfriend and parents sat in attendance. Here, Mueller was lobbing a legal bomb right back at the court, asking the justices to rein in county judges who were trampling the rights of rural Missouri citizens. The Missouri Supreme Court didn't duck. Instead, it handed Mueller the biggest win of his young career. Russell wrote the unanimous decision that declared the debtors' prison scheme in rural Missouri would come to an end.[57]

"The courts should not have required them to repeatedly appear to account for debts the courts could not legally designate as court costs, and, in Richey's case, the circuit court should not have sent him back to jail for failing to make those payments," Russell wrote for the court in March 2019.[58]

A key to the case was that the Missouri Legislature had not codified jail board bills as court costs per se, meaning that while counties could charge them, they couldn't use the court system to try to collect. Repercussions for those who could not afford to pay them could be civil, such as the interception of a tax refund, but not criminal, such as another stay in jail.[59]

Bergen could no longer be threatened with jail because she owed the court a bill. The same was true for Richey and Wright and thousands of Missourians like them.

"I feel like I can breathe again," one similarly situated defendant told me after the court ruling. The legal cloud of tear gas that had been choking the poor in Missouri was lifted.

In a bit of serendipitous timing, the ruling came a month after a unanimous U.S. Supreme Court ruled in the *Timbs v. Indiana* case that the Eighth Amendment protections against excessive fines also apply to states.[60] "Protection against excessive punitive economic sanctions secured by the Clause is, to repeat, both 'fundamental to our scheme of ordered liberty' and 'deeply rooted in this Nation's history and tradition,'" wrote Supreme Court Justice Ruth Bader Ginsburg in a ruling that has significant potential to upend the nation's addiction to court fines and fees.

Both unanimous rulings were resounding victories for ending the criminalization of poverty. The decisions reverberated from coast to coast in courtrooms and capitols where judges and lawmakers are working to reform the criminal justice system so that those lacking financial resources don't have their civil rights trampled as the courts work overtime to keep them in a state of distress.

For some, though, people like Bergen and Richey, the damage has already been done, and continues to this day. The court ruled that Richey shouldn't have been put in jail for failing to pay his previous jail bill, and the rest of the bill he owed was wiped out, but he didn't get his money back.[61] A few months after the decision that will forever be attached to his name was issued, he was back in jail.[62] Judge Rellihan sentenced him to be there for two years on a probation violation that stemmed

from a misdemeanor peace disturbance. Richey, like the television character Otis, gets himself into trouble when he's drinking.

Before he headed back to jail, Richey packed his belongings into a
storage unit. His son neglected to pay the bill.

"I have nothing," Richey told me in a phone call from the St. Clair
County Jail.

Richey will end up with another bill for jail time, this one bigger
than the one that landed him before the Missouri Supreme Court.
More than 50 percent of the detainees in Missouri prisons are there on
probation or parole violations.[63] Often, as in Richey's current case, one
of the probation violations is failure to pay.[64] Missouri is not alone. In
Idaho, Wisconsin, Missouri, and Arkansas, more than 50 percent of the
prison population is there on what the Justice Center of the Council of
State Governments calls "supervisory violations," the most prolific of
which is failure to pay. Thirteen states owe a third or more of their prison
populations to a violation similar to what landed Richey back in jail.[65]

One step forward, two steps back.

In August of 2019, attorney Michael-John Voss, one of the Arch-
City Defenders attorneys, drove four hours across the Missouri landscape to visit Richey in jail. ArchCity Defenders is the law firm that
helped bring attention to municipal court abuses after Brown's death
in 2014 by filing class-action civil lawsuits against multiple cities in the
St. Louis region, including Ferguson.

Voss and his crew are taking up where Mueller left off, looking for
a civil opportunity to recoup the money collected from indigent defendants illegally by the court system that is supposed to exist to protect
their rights. Other, similar lawsuits are making their way through the
court system in Missouri, in part spurred by the Richey decision. It's
the latest front in the battle to protect poor people from judicial abuses
in Missouri and the nation.

"The same kind of abuses of due process are happening at the circuit
court level that we've seen in the municipal courts," Voss says. "The legal
system works a certain way for people with money. It works a certain
way for people without money. It's designed that way."[66]

7

. . . .

JUDGES VS. JUDGES

Kingston, Missouri
March 2019

Associate Circuit Court Judge Jason Kanoy had a full docket scheduled of the precise sorts of payment review hearings that the state's highest court had said he could no longer hold.

"There has been a development," Kanoy announced as one of the thirty-one defendants scheduled to be there that day stood before him.[1]

The wooden planks on the second floor of the historic courthouse in Kingston creaked as the man, a painter by trade, shifted his weight back and forth on his feet.[2] He wasn't in a comfortable place. He couldn't make the payment on his pay-to-stay bill. He was there to explain to Kanoy that work was hard to find in the rural county where jobs were scarce.

The painter had no clue that a group of black-robed judges had decided just forty-eight hours previously that there was no need for him to stand before Kanoy. His bill could go to collection, but the state could no longer threaten him with a return visit to jail if he couldn't afford to pay it.[3] It had been two days since the Missouri Supreme Court had ruled unanimously that judges could not force defendants back to the courtroom month after month, threatening more jail time if payments on pay-to-stay jail bills could not be made.

Kanoy didn't tell him that.

"There are a pile of cases where people owe us money," Kanoy said. "And I have to review them all."[4]

Before court that day, Michael Barrett, the head of the public defender's office, and I met for lunch at the Red Rooster Cafe, a hole-in-the-wall diner in Polo, about ten minutes south of the courthouse on Highway 13. We joked that we'd better be careful driving that day. There's nothing the local sheriff would probably like more than to have a reason to cite either of us with an expensive ticket that might add to the Caldwell County coffers.

Polo is the town where Nicholas T. McNab, who is white, lived as a kid. In 2008, when he was seventeen, he and some of his buddies broke into a ballfield concession stand and stole some candy bars, some taffy, and some beef jerky.[5] It was a teenage prank by some kids who were up to no good.

McNab was put in jail with his cash bail set at $10,000. He spent eight days in jail, pleaded guilty to misdemeanor stealing, and was sentenced to time served, a sixty-day jail sentence that was suspended, and two years' probation.[6]

Almost two years later, right before his probation was scheduled to end, the private probation company supervising him gave him a drug test. McNab failed the test. He went to jail on a probation violation.

By the time he got out of jail, he owed $2,000 in pay-to-stay bills. A decade later, when I started writing about Kanoy, the poster child in Missouri for collecting such bills, McNab was still being scheduled for monthly payment review hearings.

It's a shame, says Jim Rust, a local attorney who had represented McNab on a misdemeanor pot possession case.

"This kid is not a criminal," Rust says of McNab. "He's a small-town guy trying to get by."[7]

Rust calls the payment review hearings a form of double jeopardy, with defendants who live in poverty punished over and over for the same crime.

"This kind of thing happens a lot around here," Rust says. "It's not just Judge Kanoy. This stuff has got to stop."

That's what the Missouri Supreme Court said with its historic and unanimous ruling in March 2019.

But it didn't stop. Not in every courtroom.

The reason that Kanoy had scheduled more than two dozen people to appear in his courtroom that day was the same in every case: money.[8] They all owed Caldwell County money, mostly for pay-to-stay bills for jail time already served. Now that the Missouri Supreme Court had up-ended the extrajudicial process that allowed him to collect $16.47 for each of the 9,100 people living in his county, more per capita than any county in Missouri, Kanoy needed to "review" things, he said in court. So rather than cancel the hearings, he set new ones a month out, re-quiring the defendants to come back again after he figured out how he was going to respond to the court's ruling. Kanoy was stalling, or out-right ignoring the Missouri Supreme Court ruling, Barrett thought, and pushing hearings back so he could figure out how to make sure his collections weren't impeded.

One of the defendants in the courtroom that day was Jason Sharp, whom I had written about a few months earlier. Sharp knew about the Missouri Supreme Court ruling. We had regularly messaged each other on Facebook since I first wrote about his case. But he also knew he had to show up in Kanoy's courtroom that day or face the possibility of more time in jail.

There was a warrant out for his arrest.[9]

Sharp's journey with Kanoy started in 2012 when he fell $350 behind in child support.[10] Like many states, Missouri criminalizes the failure to pay child support. It's a Catch-22. Men like Sharp and women like Victoria Branson should pay their child support. But when economics forces people to fall behind, putting them in jail doesn't exactly help mothers or fathers—after all, now they are separated from their children. Like suspending driver's licenses, the action has a self-defeating purpose, says St. Louis attorney Stephanie Lummus.[11] In 2018, she sued the state of Missouri over its practice of suspending driver's licenses of people who fall behind in child support, arguing it was being done in an unconstitutional fashion without due process.

"We're hamstringing the very people who we want to go out and get a job," Lummus says.

When Sharp fell behind in child support, Kanoy issued a warrant for his arrest. He was picked up after a traffic stop and jailed. Sharp was there for thirty days because he couldn't afford bail. He pleaded guilty to misdemeanor failure to support and was sentenced to time served. He received two years of probation, which was supervised by a private probation company. A couple of months into it, he was behind in his payments for his pay-to-stay jail bill of about $1,500. Also, he hadn't yet found a job, a requirement of his probation.

"I was trying to find a job," Sharp told me. "But the whole time you're paying these costs, you have to go to court every month."

Kanoy found him guilty of violating his probation. Keep in mind, Sharp had paid back the child support payments. But now Sharp owed money for his time in jail. Twice in the next few years Sharp would fall behind or miss a date in court and go back to jail for a few days. The bill amount continued to climb.

So here he was in 2019, still having to appear before Kanoy, even after the Missouri Supreme Court said the scheme that demanded his presence was illegal.

"It's going to take a while to sift through things," Kanoy told Sharp. "Our little chats won't be happening anymore."

But for Sharp, and the others who showed up in Kanoy's court on that day, the "little chats" weren't over. Kanoy scheduled Sharp to come back in May, and most of the other defendants as well.[12] Most had been paying what they could afford, a bit at a time, for years, but Kanoy applied most of those payments to the jail board bills first, meaning many still owed for other fines and fees that could be used to require them to appear in court, even if the rest of the jail board bill had to be sent to civil collections.

Think of it this way: For defendants like Sharp, their original bill included things like the $3 fee for sheriffs' retirements, and other various small fines and fees. But if they could never pay enough to make the largest part of that bill—the pay-to-stay bill—disappear, then those other charges still existed and could be used as a pretense to force another court appearance.

After court, Michael Barrett and Matthew Mueller met with Sharp and exchanged phone numbers. The two public defenders were going to keep an eye on Kanoy. "He should have canceled all these hearings," Barrett said.

The next day, the head of the public defender's office sent a letter to Kanoy, reminding him of the Missouri Supreme Court decision. "Stop using your court to leverage the freedom of poor persons in exchange for revenue for Caldwell County," Barrett wrote.

In some ways, judges like Kanoy don't answer to their state's supreme court. They answer to the voters. Like the majority of judges in Missouri, Kanoy is elected every four years through local elections.[13] The members of the Missouri Supreme Court and the state's appeals courts and circuit courts in its biggest cities, however, are appointed through the Missouri Nonpartisan Court Plan, known colloquially around the country as the "Missouri Plan."[14] This dichotomy, with different judges in the state being selected or elected through different means, creates a political obstacle to various forms of criminal justice reform. For Mueller, judges hold the key to undoing the criminalization of poverty as much or more than prosecutors or even police.

"Most criminal defense attorneys are quick to say that the injustice in our system rests with the police and the prosecutors," Mueller says. "I disagree. For the most part, I think the prosecutors and the police do their job fairly well. There are exceptions, of course, but generally, these are decent people doing their job as best they can. For me, the injustices in our criminal justice system rest with the judges."

That is why, Mueller says, that Judge David Andrew Dolan, for instance, reacted to him with such disdain during the *Tidwell* case, and why judges like Brandi Baird in Dent County and Sandra Martinez in St. Francois County and Kanoy in Caldwell County were so quick to dismiss his appeals of their decisions to send people to jail because they were poor.

"I was not filing a motion saying the police conducted an unlawful search of my client, or claiming that the prosecutor failed to disclose certain evidence," Mueller says. "I came into [Dolan's] courtroom and told him that he can't jail poor people over board bills. I told him that he was doing things incorrectly. Many people just assume that judges are without fault. They assume that if some injustice happened that it was at the hands of the police or the prosecutor. But this is not always the case. We have to be vigilant of our judges, too."

In that regard, understanding how judges obtain their posts, and keep them, is key to understanding how the criminalization of poverty happens under their watch.

There was a time in Missouri when all judges were elected. But Tom Pendergast changed that.[15] From 1925 to 1939, Pendergast was the political boss of Kansas City. The son of Irish immigrants, Pendergast was the youngest of nine children, born in 1872 in St. Joseph, Missouri, to Michael and Mary Reidy Pendergast. Tom would follow his older brother James, who had moved to Kansas City for a series of jobs and had become the owner of the American House, a hotel and saloon in the West Bottoms, near the Missouri River.[16] At the turn of the century, this was where the working poor and immigrants toiled in difficult industrial jobs, from meatpacking plants to rail yards and warehouses. They were Black, white, and brown and all mostly lacked much money.

Pendergast would become both their champion and their corruptor, and they would become the early base of the Pendergast political machine. Like his brother James, Tom Pendergast got himself elected as an alderman in Kansas City, and he controlled votes for Democrats with small favors here and there, at the ward and city level. But he was much more ambitious than his brother. Pendergast figured if he could control enough ward and local votes, then soon the statewide politicians would come calling. He built an empire tied to saloons, the concrete business, gambling, and union construction workers, with everybody taking a little bit off the top in the contracts that would come their way in exchange for some votes on election day.

Through his handpicked city manager in Kansas City, Henry McElroy, Pendergast controlled millions in taxpayer funds, some of it federal pass-through money intended to help put people to work during the Great Depression.[17] McElroy would use that money to hire Pendergast workers, who would pass much of the cash on to the machine and do little actual work.

In 1932, Pendergast's machine helped coordinate the election of Guy Park, a former judge, as governor of Missouri. Soon Pendergast was filling the state government with appointments friendly to his machine and securing state contracts for friends who made sure he got a cut. All it took at times was a simple letter from Pendergast to the governor.

"My dear Governor," Pendergast wrote to Park on May 8, 1934, "this will introduce you to Mr. Herman Fram, who is connected with our organization here in Kansas City. Mr. Fram is desirous of securing some business from the State, and anything you can do for him will be appreciated by me."[18]

Before long, Pendergast was even packing the courts with judges who were loyal to him, and that was a step too far for some of Missouri's leaders. When the Missouri Supreme Court ruled that Kansas City could take local control of its police department—which had been under state control since the Civil War—McElroy made sure the department answered to him and followed a simple rule: leave Pendergast alone.[19]

By 1937, the state's legal community was aghast at the potential for Pendergast to even control the courts. So a group of about eighty of them—Democrats and Republicans—met in the middle of the state, at the Tiger Hotel in Columbia, to plot a new plan forward. Among the attendees were some of the most prominent attorneys in the state, including the scion of a family that maintains national prominence today: Rush Hudson Limbaugh Sr.[20]

Limbaugh, the grandfather of the famous conservative radio personality, was a Cape Girardeau attorney and former state representative who was active in Democratic politics. The attorneys created the Missouri Institute for the Administration of Justice, and they proposed selecting the state's top judges through a merit selection process, rather than by election, to make sure that judges maintained a high quality and certain level of political independence.

The attorneys gathered enough signatures statewide to place the constitutional question on the ballot on November 5, 1940. The initiative passed, and the Missouri Nonpartisan Court Plan was born, the first in the nation in which at least some judges—in St. Louis, Kansas City, and the appellate courts—would be selected by merit.

The Missouri Plan works like this:

When there is an open position for a judge, attorneys apply to a judicial commission, which is made up of attorneys, citizens, and gubernatorial appointments whose terms are staggered so one governor can't have too much influence. The judicial commission interviews the applicants and scores them based on merit.[21] When the plan was originally conceived this part of the process was done in secret, but in the mid-2000s, under the leadership of then Missouri Supreme Court justice William Ray Price, it was opened to the public.[22]

The judicial commission then sends a list of the top-three finalists to the governor, who picks the judge from that list. The judge must stand for a retention election before voters after one year, a sort of up or down vote on the judge, without an opponent. If he or she is retained, the judge then stands for a retention election once a term, which is six years for circuit judges and twelve years for appellate judges.[23]

The plan doesn't eliminate politics entirely from the selection process. Historically, Republican governors received panels that had at least one judge of a similar political persuasion, and the same for Democrats. But the plan makes it significantly less likely for one corrupt machine politician like Pendergast to either control the appointment or sway a local election.

Since the adoption of the Missouri Plan by voters in 1940, the idea of merit selection of judges spread across the country. Thirty-eight states have adopted some sort of similar plan for at least some of their judges, particularly at the appellate level.[24]

"In the appellate courts, the nonpartisan plan has largely shielded judges from being identified as partisans," says former Missouri Supreme Court justice Michael Wolff, the retired dean emeritus of the St. Louis

University School of Law. "It helps shield appellate judges because they sit in groups of three on the court of appeals and almost always in groups of seven on the Supreme Court. If you walked down the street and asked the first twenty people to name a single Missouri Supreme Court judge, you would understand just how anonymous they are."

Such anonymity is not the case in rural Missouri courts, where the judges run in partisan elections. Some politicians who oppose the Missouri Plan point to the familiarity with local judges that voters develop as a reason why such elections are preferable. But such elections also offer explanation as to why a scheme like charging for board bills and putting people who can't afford to pay them back in jail lasted for so long. It's no coincidence that the judges in the biggest cities in Missouri, appointed under the nonpartisan plan, don't charge or collect board bills.

In small towns like Salem or Farmington, where the courthouse is the center of town, local elections focus, generally, on four key figures who work in those stately buildings: the sheriff, the prosecutor, the county commissioner, and the judge. All four figures are a key part of the process that too often leads to fines and fees being used as precursors for jail time among people who cannot afford to pay them.

"Local judges are sensitive to their local voters and other local officials," Wolff says. "So with board bills, the judges may have been trying to keep county commissioners happy because the commissioners set the court's budget for everything except judicial and some clerk and juvenile officer salaries. And some locally elected judges are just mean peckerheads who are perhaps representative of their constituents. And sometimes if a judge is soft on crime, the judge may find that a local prosecutor runs against the judge. Andrew Jackson, the original Trumpist, led the movement to elect judges in this country. Most countries are more sane."

In France, for instance, judges must pass through a gauntlet of merit selection procedures, and then go to a special school for judges, before they join the bench. Most industrialized countries have some sort of similar merit selection process. Other than the U.S., only Japan and Switzerland, among major industrialized countries, have judicial elections.[25]

Former Oregon Supreme Court justice Hans Linde lamented this reality in a 1988 speech: "To the rest of the world," he said, "American adherence to judicial elections is as incomprehensible as our rejection of the metric system."[26]

Lisa Foster, the former California judge, sees the dichotomy between how local judges are elected and how those are selected on the Missouri Supreme Court at play in the Richey and Wright cases. More broadly, in every board bill case brought to local courts by Mueller, the locally elected judges ruled against the public defender, protecting a system in which the judge acts as tax collector. But the Missouri Supreme Court ruling was unanimous and clear in its verdict that the scheme was illegal.

"Elected judges face subtle and overt pressures—particularly at the municipal court level," Foster says. "The subtle pressure comes from the mere knowledge that their job and their clerk or other staff's jobs may well depend on how much money they are able to raise through fines and fees. It can manifest throughout the process from conviction through the imposition and then collection of fines and fees. The overt pressure is obviously a situation like Ferguson, which I suspect continues to exist in many of the towns that depend heavily on fines and fees for general revenue. That, by the way, is the reason I think this is more pronounced in rural communities—they are revenue starved and tend to depend on court debt to survive."

California's system is a hybrid of the Missouri Plan. Appellate judges are nominated by the governor and then confirmed by a judicial commission.[27] Appellate judges then stand for reelection in twelve-year terms. Judges at the superior level, as Foster was, run for nonpartisan election, though as a practical matter, they, too, are generally appointed first by the governor.

That's because judges often retire before their terms are up, then the governor appoints a replacement. In California, the governor sends potential appointments to the judicial commission for evaluation, and they are rated as qualified or unqualified.[28] The judges then stand for election only if they are challenged by another attorney.[29]

In South Carolina, most judges are elected by the general assembly after they are first approved by a judicial merit selection commission.[30] That's not the case for judges at the municipal and county level. County "magistrates," who hear many misdemeanor cases like the one that snagged Sasha Darby in the judicial system, don't even have to be attorneys. At one point, all they needed was a high school degree, though that has since been changed to a four-year college degree.[31] Magistrates are appointed by the governor and confirmed by the senate. Municipal judges are appointed by city councils.[32]

If it were up to Foster, there would be no judicial elections at all, including the retention elections called for in the Missouri Plan.

"I hate judicial elections," Foster says. "First, elections cost money, and most judges rely on lawyers—the lawyers who appear in front of them—for money. It's unseemly. Second, even in a system like California's, the fact of election can influence decisions. The best example I can give is the death penalty. Juries are required to recommend a sentence in death penalty cases, but the judge can accept or reject that recommendation. I know of only one case in California where a judge rejected the death penalty recommendation."

When it comes to judicial elections, they giveth and they taketh away. Such is the case with Judge Martinez of St. Francois County and Judge Baird of Dent County, two who became synonymous with putting people in jail because they couldn't afford their court costs. Baird was first appointed as an associate circuit judge in Dent County in 2011, by Governor Jay Nixon, a Democrat.[33] Like many rural judges, Baird got her start in politics, having worked for the speaker of the house as a legislative assistant before being appointed to an open prosecuting attorney position and then winning election for that job in 2010. Like in California, the quickest path to becoming a judge in Missouri is often through a gubernatorial appointment. Often, but not always, that judge then cruises to electoral victory.

So it was for Baird until 2018.

That was the year she became the subject of a series of my columns for putting people in jail because they couldn't afford to pay their board bills. While the *Post-Dispatch* doesn't have wide circulation in Dent County or the other counties of the Forty-Second Judicial Circuit, the local newspaper, the *Salem News*, also started covering the controversy.[34]

"The public defender and ACLU only look at these matters from one perspective," Baird told the *Salem News* a couple of weeks before the election.[35] "However, the judges have to view it more broadly and consider all sides. I examine each of these cases carefully, based upon the facts and fairly apply the law for the people of Dent County . . . those who repeatedly commit crimes help pay for the time served for crimes they commit."

Baird would lose her election that November to Republican Nathan Kelsaw.[36] Truth be told, her party affiliation likely had more to do with her loss than her work exacerbating the practice of modern-day debtors' prisons. Like many rural counties, Dent used to be full of conservative Democrats, many of them tied to union manufacturing jobs. But as factories closed and those jobs dried up, the political winds shifted.[37] A look at the electoral map in Missouri in the 2016 presidential election shows nearly the entire state a deep red, with most counties, including Dent, overwhelmingly voting for Donald Trump for president and down-ballot Republicans throughout.[38] Two years later, Baird switched parties and ran for judge again, this time as a Republican.[39] But she lost in the primary.

For critics of the Missouri Plan, this is how judges should be elected, in partisan votes where the people closest to the judges get to decide. That was the argument in 2012, the latest attempt by opponents to the merit selection of judges to change the rules in Missouri.[40]

That year, a group called Better Courts for Missouri successfully got the Missouri Legislature—with a supermajority of Republicans in both the house and the senate—to put an initiative on the ballot to insert more politics into the merit selection process, allowing the governor in particular to have more freedom to choose judges in Missouri's biggest cities and the appellate courts.

The effort was founded by a Missouri billionaire named David Humphreys, whose family owns a roofing company called TAMKO. That company had faced numerous lawsuits across the country alleging that its roofing shingles were defective. TAMKO lost some of the lawsuits and was ordered to pay consumers millions of dollars in damages.[41] While Humphreys's spokesman for the effort to upend the Missouri Plan—lobbyist James Harris—talked a good game about the changes to the merit selection plan being about preserving an "impartial" court, attorneys in the state, and ultimately voters, saw through the ruse and overwhelmingly defeated the proposal at the ballot box.[42] In fact, Missouri went the other way, bringing merit selection to Greene County, home of the growing city of Springfield.[43] Despite pressure from national conservative groups like the Federalist Society—which asserts tremendous political pressure in the confirmation process of U.S. Supreme Court justices—no state that has adopted a merit selection process has ever gone back on it, despite various attempts like the one in Missouri in 2012.

Attorney John Johnston, who was president of the Missouri Bar when Better Courts was trying to dilute the merit selection process, believes that's because voters generally trust the judicial branch of government more than other branches.[44]

"People are happy with the justice system," Johnston says.

But that can change when money gets pumped into the process and turns judges into politicians. That's what happened in Iowa in 2010. Since 1962, the Midwestern state has followed its version of the Missouri Plan, in which the governor appoints members to the Iowa Supreme Court from a panel selected on merit from a judicial commission.[45] Until 2010, every Iowa Supreme Court justice who had stood for a retention election had won.[46] There was no campaign spending on any of those elections.[47]

Then, in 2009, Iowa became the first Midwestern state to legalize gay marriage, after a unanimous state supreme court overturned as unconstitutional a law that defined marriage as only between a man and a woman.[48] Almost immediately, national outside interest groups descended on Iowa to make the 2010 retention vote of three of the Iowa justices a national referendum on gay marriage.

Money talks. More than $1.4 million in outside money was spent on negative television ads to convince voters to turn out their judges, and that's what happened for the first time in the state's history.[49] The amount of outside money was even higher in neighboring Illinois. Such campaign spending in judicial races is common in Ohio and Michigan, states that have partisan elections for top judicial openings. Millions of dollars are spent on such campaigns, nearly all of it from outside groups trying to influence the selection of judges. In the same year that Iowa had three judges lose retention elections, more than $9 million was spent on supreme court elections in Michigan, more than $5 million in Pennsylvania, and more than $4 million in Ohio. Alabama and Illinois checked in at $3.5 million each, massive amounts of money for judicial elections, spent by either the attorneys who appear before the judges or political parties or outside groups seeking to bend the judiciary to their particular belief system. It's the sort of spending that Foster and other advocates of judicial independence find obscene, because they believe it reduces voters' faith in the judiciary: judges should be viewed as referees calling balls and strikes based on the law, not bending the law to their political preferences or, worse, the views of their campaign donors.

After losing their election in 2010, the three Iowa Supreme Court justices who were not retained issued a statement criticizing the "unprecedented attack by out-of-state special interest groups," and suggested that such attacks would reduce the faith people have in an independent judiciary.[50]

"Ultimately, however, the preservation of our state's fair and impartial courts will require more than the integrity and fortitude of individual judges, it will require the steadfast support of the people," the justices wrote.

The judges who tend to have the most interaction with citizens are found at the lowest level of the judicial system, such as in municipal or county court. That is where some of the worst abuses are as they relate to the criminalization of poverty. Most of those judges are either elected or appointed by partisan politicians who have budgets to balance.

In January 2015, Mary Russell, the Missouri Supreme Court chief justice, addressed the ongoing problem in municipal courts in her annual address to the Missouri Legislature. It was just a few months after the uprising in Ferguson, and state lawmakers and other political leaders were gaining an understanding that an underlying cause of the unrest was a municipal court system that was being used as a revenue generator for cash-strapped cities.[51]

This undermines faith in the judicial system, and must stop, Russell said.

"Municipal divisions play an important role in enforcing local laws, and they handle more than two-thirds of all cases filed in our state courts. For many people, the municipal divisions are the first and only contact they have with the court system. And, as we all know, first impressions can be lasting impressions."

In many municipalities in the St. Louis area, the judges were law partners with the city attorney, or sometimes served a similar role for another neighboring city, tying a few big law firms into the revenue-generating business in multiple cities throughout the region.[52]

But at least they were all attorneys.

That's not the case in South Carolina among the lower-end judges who hear the majority of misdemeanor cases in that state. There a special sort of judge called a "magistrate" hears such cases, from minor assaults to shoplifting and petty theft, the sorts of cases brought by police and sheriffs' departments answering to mayors who depend on the fines and fees from those cases to make budgets balance.[53]

Those magistrates are political appointees of the governor with the approval of the senate, where the jobs are mostly handed out as political plums to the well-connected. The results can be horrendous in courtrooms all over South Carolina, where magistrates handle 800,000 cases a year.

In November 2019, reporter Joseph Cranney of the *Post and Courier*, with the help of the ProPublica Local Reporting Network, examined the use of magistrates in county courts in South Carolina and uncovered a trail of abuse and violations of civil rights, most of it in the name of profit for the counties that preyed on poor people caught up in the convoluted web of justice.[54]

"Welcome to the magistrate courts of South Carolina, where citizens often must fend for themselves before judges lacking formal training in the law and whose errors can result in punishing consequences for defendants," Cranney wrote. "These courtrooms, the busiest in the state, dispose of hundreds of thousands of misdemeanor criminal cases and civil disputes each year. They are overseen by political appointees, selected through a process that often places connections over qualifications. It's a system that's unlike any other in the country, and one that has provided fertile ground for incompetence, corruption and other abuse."[55]

Among the most shocking findings in the report:

- "Nearly three-quarters of the state's magistrates lack a legal degree and couldn't represent someone in a court of law."
- "A loophole in state law has allowed a quarter of South Carolina's magistrates to remain on the bench after their terms expired, letting them escape the scrutiny of a reappointment process. One controversial magistrate continues to hold court two decades after her four-year term ended."
- "In 12 of the state's 46 counties, magistrate appointments are decided by a single senator who can stock the courts with hand-picked candidates."
- "More than a dozen sitting magistrates have been disciplined for misconduct by the state's judicial watchdog, but they aren't required to disclose their offenses when seeking a new term. Even the governor, who is supposed to act as a check on nominees, is kept in the dark before signing off on their reappointments. This has allowed judges who misapplied the law or abused their positions to slide through, no questions asked."[56]

Most of the men and women who come before such magistrates do so without attorneys, and they waive away multiple rights as the magistrate encourages them to push cases through quickly. They agree to plead guilty to charges even when they likely have a defense, and they end up with fines worth hundreds or thousands of dollars that, if they can't pay, will bury them for years.[57] In 2016, one of the most compelling victims of this South Carolina judicial scheme was Sasha Darby.

PART III

....

PATH TO FREEDOM

8

THE COURTHOUSE

Columbia, South Carolina
April 2017

Sasha Darby woke up in agony. She was staying on a friend's couch because she had nowhere else to go. She walked out of jail after twenty days behind bars in Lexington County to find out she had been evicted, and she had lost her job. Darby was four months pregnant with her second child and she knew something was wrong.

"I was in pain," she said. "Extreme pain."

She went to the bathtub, turned the water on, and writhed in agony. She would have a miscarriage. To this day, she blames her loss on the criminal justice system. This loss, and her time in jail, reveal a gap in the general public's understanding of how things work—particularly for those on the margins—when they interact with the local courts, and the entire infrastructure that sets them up to fail.

"I will always wonder what could have happened in my life," Darby says. "I just don't know."

After the miscarriage, Darby's friends took her to the Daybreak LifeCare Center, a facility that offers health care and shelter services to pregnant women in Columbia, South Carolina. "I still had blood on me," Darby said. "They sent me to the hospital."

That's where she met Nusrat Choudhury, who at the time was the deputy director of the ACLU's racial justice program. She is now legal

director of the ACLU of Illinois.[1] For months, Choudhury and a host
of other attorneys and volunteers had been court watching in Lexington County, recording civil rights violations, most perpetrated by
magistrates who were untrained in the law, some of whom weren't even
attorneys. She had heard about Darby's case and her being jailed over
an inability to pay court debt, and she wanted to talk to her. Choudhury
was horrified by what Darby had been through, her existing poverty
exacerbated by the criminal justice system not because she was a criminal, but because she didn't have $680 in court fines. As punishment she
would be jailed for three weeks and she would become homeless, lose
her job, and lose her baby.[2]

"There were no services for someone in her situation," Choudhury
said.

In June 2017, the ACLU filed a federal civil rights lawsuit in Lexington County against the magistrates, the sheriff, and the head of
the public defender's office, alleging that the South Carolina county
operation was a "modern-day debtors' prison" and that the victims were
mostly people of color who happened to be living in poverty.[3]

"Impoverished people are routinely arrested and incarcerated for
their inability to pay fines and fees imposed by the County's magistrate
courts in traffic and misdemeanor criminal cases," the lawsuit alleges.
"Each year, hundreds, if not more than one thousand, of the poorest
residents of the County and its surrounding areas are deprived of their
liberty in the Lexington County Detention Center ('Detention Center') for weeks and even months at a time for no reason other than
their poverty and in violation of their most basic constitutional rights."
Choudhury calls Lexington County "one of the most draconian debtors' prisons we've ever seen."[4]

The lawsuit alleges that defendants aren't offered an ability-to-pay
hearing in cases where incarceration is a possibility, and often don't
have access to legal representation, rights guaranteed to all American
citizens by the Fourteenth and Sixth Amendments to the U.S. Constitution.[5] Four of Choudhury's clients are single women, three of them

Black, one Hispanic. All were jailed because they fell behind in paying astronomical court fees that stemmed from traffic stops or misdemeanor crimes. Darby's twenty-day jail stay was tied for the shortest of all the women who joined the lawsuit as plaintiffs.

Twanda Brown spent fifty-seven days in jail over her inability to pay a $1,900 court debt that stemmed from a traffic stop. She was pulled over for not having a light over her license plate, and then ticketed also for driving on a suspended license. Amy Palacios spent twenty days in jail over $647. Cayeshia Johnson spent fifty-five days in jail after a traffic stop because she couldn't afford $1,287 in fines.

Lexington County and the various defendants, including the magistrate in Darby's case, have denied in court records that any of the defendants' constitutional rights were violated.

The story is the same from South Carolina to Missouri to Oklahoma. The courts have been hijacked by a tax-collection scheme that regularly violates the rights of indigent defendants, and those actions have devastating consequences for poor people.

After she lost her baby, Darby moved back to the Boston area, where she still lives. Her lawsuit is pending.

Tulsa, Oklahoma
April 2017

Thousands of miles to the west, in Oklahoma, Jill Webb, the public defender, and another Tulsa attorney, Dan Smolen, were collecting defendants to file a similar class-action lawsuit against Oklahoma for operating debtors' prisons.[6] They did so in November 2017 on behalf of Ira Wilkins, a homeless man who had been arrested multiple times on failure to pay charges.

The lawsuit was filed against the Oklahoma Sheriffs' Association, every sheriff in the state, and a company called Aberdeen Enterprizes II, Inc., a private, for-profit corporation that contracts with the sheriffs to collect unpaid court debts.[7] In court records, the defendants denied any violation of the plaintiffs' constitutional rights and sought dismissal of the lawsuit.

Webb has a confession to make. She and Smolen didn't really know what they were doing. This was her first-ever civil lawsuit. Like Matthew Mueller in Missouri, Webb became a bit of an outcast in the state court system just for bringing attention to what she believes is a completely unconstitutional and amoral scheme in which poor people were regularly being jailed and having their lives upended not because they were criminals but because they couldn't afford the backdoor taxes being thrust upon those least likely to be able to pay them. "I couldn't see all that, and not do something about it," Webb said.

The lawsuit drew headlines all over the state—and nationwide.[8] One of the people watching was Kendy Killman. She saw a story online that mentioned the lawsuit and looked it up. It had been nearly six years since she walked out of the Cleveland County Courthouse thinking she had properly paid her debt to society for a misdemeanor charge that probably never should have been filed.

By 2012, Killman was still getting a bill for court costs from Cleveland County for $1,115. It turns out, the only fee that had been erased in court was the monthly fee due to the prosecutor's office. The rest of the fines and fees were still in place, and they increased every time she missed a payment and a new warrant for her arrest was issued. It happened in 2012 and again in 2015.[9] Each time, Killman would be arrested, taken to court, cuffed to a bench for a couple of hours, then freed when she made a payment of $25. One time she even made a payment of $100, the highest one she can remember making.

In 2015, Cleveland County sold Killman's court debt to Aberdeen Enterprizes II.[10] Aberdeen adds about a 30 percent surcharge to the court debt it collects and passes some of that money to the Oklahoma Sheriffs' Association. It's a good money-making scheme for the non-profit association that supports county sheriffs in the state. In 2015, for instance, its agreement with Aberdeen earned it more than $800,000 in revenue.[11]

Aberdeen has aggressive collection techniques. Specifically, threatening former defendants (or people who thought they were former defendants) with jail time if they don't come up with the money to pay the court fines and fees.[12] That's what happened to Killman several times, including just a couple of months before she read the story in the *Tulsa World* about the lawsuit against Aberdeen and the sheriffs. One time, in 2012, knowing she had a warrant out for her arrest, Killman just went to court and sat in Judge Steve Stice's courtroom. She knew the drill. Stice would start his docket at about nine in the morning and it would last until noon or so. Then Killman would go up to the bench and tell Stice why she was there.

"I got this bad feeling right in the pit of my stomach," Killman said. "I tell him why I am there and he looks up my case."

Stice told her that he saw in the record where the probation fees and community service hours had been dropped but that she still had to pay her fines.

"He looked at me and smiled—one of those, 'oh, silly girl, you don't know anything' kind of smiles—and said he didn't have the ability to drop my fines and court costs."

It didn't matter that a year earlier Stice had determined Killman was under financial duress, enough to drop some minor fines, but not most of them. Nothing had changed in her situation. She still had no money to pay. But the court still wanted its money. Stice dropped the warrant and sent her on her way.

"I walked out of his courtroom and had a seat on the bench and just cried for a good ten minutes," Killman said.

There was a time early in her case when Killman thought she had caught a break by landing Stice as a judge. He was a former contract public defender, unlike so many judges who move to the bench after being prosecutors. Perhaps he would be more empathetic, she hoped.

Stice owns property in downtown Norman that rents office space to Oklahoma Court Services, Inc., a private probation company that supervises some of the very people that come through Stice's court. The private, for-profit company pays Stice more than $2,000 in rent per month, the *Oklahoman* newspaper reported in 2013, and the judge sends defendants who appear before him in aggravated drunk driving cases to the company, where they have to pay for expensive alcohol monitors and defensive-driving classes. The local prosecutor, who supervises the vast majority of the defendants on probation in cases before Stice, has objected to the practice of sending the drunk-driving cases to a private probation company, in part because of the loss of fees paid to his office. "I'd have to stop prosecution in lots of cases if I didn't have that money," district attorney Greg Mashburn told the *Oklahoman* at the time. "Right now, it's aggravated DUIs. What is it tomorrow?"[13]

"I have followed the rules," Stice told the *Oklahoman*. "I have followed every rule that there is. I have disclosed everything to everyone. It's on my ethics reports. I'm not the only judge that owns real estate."[14]

Killman thought she was following the rules too, but it didn't work out too well for her. In 2015, another warrant was issued for her arrest. This time, Killman did something she hadn't done before. She asked her family for help. Her birthday was coming up, and she asked her mom, kids, whomever could come up with a few bucks, to donate to her court costs in place of any birthday gifts they had planned to give her. A week after her forty-sixth birthday, she paid $100 to the court, and her warrant was recalled. By 2017, her court costs bill was up to more than $1,600, even after she had paid about $800 through the years, from the original fines and fees of $1,100.

As she read the story about the lawsuit, she saw herself. She was in every way like the plaintiffs, who had suffered the consequences of what the lawsuit called "an extortion scheme in which the Defendants have conspired to extract as much money as possible from indigent people through a pattern of illegal and unconscionable behavior." Killman called Smolen and Webb to tell them about her case. She wasn't the only one. "We were flooded with calls," Webb said. Webb came to realize she had underestimated how bad the problem was, in both the cities of Tulsa and Oklahoma City, where the primary victims were people of color, and in rural counties throughout the state, and the college town of Norman, where Killman lived.

Soon, Webb and Smolen had help from some heavy hitters.

Two Washington, D.C., based nonprofits, the Civil Rights Corps and Georgetown University's Institute for Constitutional Advocacy and Protection, offered their services to Webb and Smolen to help elevate the importance of what could be a groundbreaking national civil rights lawsuit.

The Civil Rights Corps, a nonprofit dedicated primarily to ending the criminalization of poverty, was founded by attorney Alec Karakatsanis in 2016.[15] Since its founding it has filed civil rights lawsuits against debtors' prison practices, against illegal bail procedures, and in opposition to driver's license suspensions over failure to pay court costs in several states, including Oklahoma, Missouri, Texas, California, Florida, Alabama, Pennsylvania, and Michigan.[16]

A 2008 graduate of Harvard Law School, Karakatsanis founded his first nonprofit—Equal Justice Under Law—in 2014 with fellow Harvard graduate Phil Telfeyan. Their first lawsuit stemmed from a court-watching visit in Montgomery, Alabama, when Karakatsanis sat in a courtroom with sixty-seven defendants, all there because they owed money to the court system from various fines and fees.[17]

"All of them were African American; not a single one of them [was] accused of a crime," Karakatsanis would later write in *Time* magazine about the experience. "They were all in jail because they owed money to the city of Montgomery for unpaid traffic tickets."

Karakatsanis and local attorneys Joseph McGuire and Matthew Swerdlin would file a federal civil rights lawsuit that March alleging that the city violated multiple civil rights of the various defendants by failing to hold ability-to-pay hearings or making sure defendants had the right to counsel, then jailing some of them, forcing them to work off their court debt behind bars.[18]

"The treatment of Sharnalle Mitchell, Lorenzo Brown, Tito Williams, Courtney Tubbs, and each of the other Plaintiffs reveals systemic illegality perpetrated by the City of Montgomery against some of its poorest people. The City of Montgomery, as a matter of policy and practice, engages in the same conduct against many other human beings on a daily basis, unlawfully jailing people if they are too poor to pay debts from traffic tickets and the associated fees, costs, and surcharges that the City increasingly levies," the lawsuit alleged. "In the year 2014, these practices have no place in our society."

Indeed, they didn't. As a result of a settlement in the case, the city of Montgomery agreed to hold ability-to-pay hearings for indigent defendants and stopped jailing defendants over their inability to pay court fines and fees.

But the practices persist throughout the country.

This lawsuit was filed five months before the Ferguson unrest brought the practice of jailing poor people over their failure to pay traffic tickets into the national consciousness. Both Equal Justice Under Law and the Civil Rights Corps would later join with the St. Louis-based ArchCity Defenders in filing federal civil rights lawsuits in Jennings and Ferguson alleging similar violations of constitutional rights as in the Montgomery lawsuit.[19] During the protests in Ferguson, Karakatsanis spent part of his time sleeping on a couch of one of the ArchCity Defenders' founders—Thomas Harvey—as they prepared civil rights lawsuits and tried to keep protesters out of jail.

The upstart nonprofits, along with a civil rights stalwart—the American Civil Liberties Union—began a persistent march across the country, fueled in part by activists on the ground, bringing attention from state to state about the ever-increasing reliance of local governments on fines and fees charged to poor people in traffic and misdemeanor cases, with collection practices that created modern-day debtors' prisons. Killman joined the Oklahoma lawsuit that was refiled and expanded with multiple defendants in early 2018. The lawsuit lays out the extortion scheme in Oklahoma that is commonplace in many other states as well.

"Plaintiffs are impoverished individuals who have been saddled with court debts without any inquiry into their ability to pay and who have had debt-collection arrest warrants sought and issued against them for no reason other than that they are too poor to pay these court debts. Notwithstanding Plaintiffs' repeated pleas of financial hardship, it is the practice of Aberdeen, Inc. to repeatedly threaten Plaintiffs, and other impoverished court debtors who make up the proposed class, to make payments that they cannot afford; to coerce them with threats of arrest if they do not pay; and, with the assistance of the Defendant Judges who issue the arrest warrants sought by Aberdeen, Inc. and the Defendant Sheriffs who execute them, to have Plaintiffs actually arrested and detained solely for nonpayment. The unflagging aim of this enterprise is to squeeze as much money out of impoverished court debtors as possible.

"Through these extortionate practices, Aberdeen, Inc. has collected—and all Defendants have reaped the benefits of—tens of millions of dollars in payments from the poorest individuals in Oklahoma. This money has provided millions of dollars to Aberdeen, Inc., millions of dollars to the Sheriffs' Association, and tens of millions of dollars to the Oklahoma court system to pay for judicial salaries and other essential expenses of the district courts and court clerks' offices. To generate these payments, Defendants have subjected Plaintiffs and proposed class members to arrest, prolonged detention, and illegal threats. Plaintiffs and proposed class members have been separated from their families and friends; lost their jobs and driver's licenses; and sacrificed the basic necessities of life, including groceries, clothing, and shelter as a result of Defendants' conduct."[20]

For Killman, the court debt that had been hounding her and producing endless warrants for her arrest years after her traffic stop came to a head in early 2018, not long after she joined the lawsuit. It started with an arrest; not hers, but that of her grown, disabled stepson, Bubba, in Oklahoma City, just north of Norman. Because he has severely low IQ and had a diagnosed mental disability, Killman knew she had to get to the jail to help take care of her son. But she also knew there was a warrant out for her arrest because of her court fines, and she knew she would be arrested as soon as she stepped into the jail building.

So she called Smolen for advice. He told her he would send an attorney, David Bross, to go with her to court and get her warrant taken care of before she headed to Oklahoma City to see her son, who had been admitted to a special mental health court. A few days later, Killman,

Bross, and a *New York Times* reporter and photographer in town to do a story on fines and fees walked into the Cleveland County Jail as Killman turned herself in. "It was like *The Grapes of Wrath*," Killman said, referencing the classic John Steinbeck novel about the Joad family escaping poverty in Oklahoma during the Dust Bowl.[21] Indeed, Killman didn't escape poverty that day, but soon she would get rid of the court debt that had been hanging around her neck like an albatross for nine years.

That day Killman sat in a jail waiting room for five hours. She never saw a judge, but a hearing was set and she was released. She came back in September, with Bross, for the hearing before Stice, but the judge rescheduled court that day, and she was supposed to come back in November.

This later day started like so many others in Cleveland County Court, and yet something miraculous was about to happen. Stice calls the first person up; it is somebody who is there because they couldn't pay their fines and fees. The judge asks them to sit in the jury box and says he'll get to them later. The next person is called up; they are there for the same reason. Stice asks the court how many people are there because they owe fines. Killman and about half the courtroom raise their hands.

"The judge stood up, looked at all of us, and said, 'I am not doing this today,' and he walked out," Killman said. Stice asked everybody to go to the clerk one by one to make some sort of payment arrangements. Bross would have none of it. He explained he came all the way from Tulsa for the third time in three months and he wanted to see the judge.

Stice tried to offer to cut the fines in half, and Killman and Bross balked. They explained their long, nine-year journey to the judge, who moments ago appeared frustrated that his entire docket was there so he could collect a debt. And with a wave of his hand, Killman's debt was gone. Stice suspended it.

"We left that courtroom and haven't been back," she said. "No more hiding. No more worrying about going to jail. I think about those people in court with all the familiar faces, and I know they are struggling with the same things I was, and I feel bad for them."

I asked Webb if she thought that judges, sheriffs, and lawmakers just didn't understand the realities of a single mom trying to live on a minimum wage job or, as Killman does, on federal disability payments. She thinks the problem is more devious than a simple failure to understand.

"I think some of them purposely want to punish the poor," Webb said. "I think they just really believe that if you make things difficult on poor people, they won't be poor anymore. Some of them just hate poor people."

Both the Oklahoma and South Carolina federal lawsuits have been in a stalling pattern for a couple of years as the governments being sued over alleged civil rights violations defend themselves and seek dismissal of the legal actions. In seeking dismissal of the Lexington County case, attorneys for the county called the debtors' prison allegation "erroneous" and defended the jail sentences as a legal "alternative" to financial penalties. U.S. Senior District Judge Margaret B. Seymour denied the motion for summary judgment filed by Lexington County and the case continues.[22] In Oklahoma, the story is similar, with the various defendants arguing the case should be dismissed because the law enforcement entities that have been sued, and the private, for-profit collection agency working on their behalf, are protected under a legal doctrine called qualified immunity.[23]

That's the concept developed by the U.S. Supreme Court that came under attack in 2020 during the rise of the "defund police" movement following the death of George Floyd in Minnesota. Floyd was a forty-six-year-old Black man who had been stopped by police investigating an alleged counterfeit $20 bill. They cuffed Floyd's hands behind his back and held him to the ground while one officer knelt on his neck for more than nine minutes. Floyd would soon be declared dead, and his death, caught on cell phone video, would spark national outrage and protests. Part of the debate would turn to the concept of qualified immunity, which makes it difficult for police officers, or the cities they work for, to be held liable in cases of alleged brutality.

Under qualified immunity, a law enforcement officer or agency can only be sued for civil rights violations if the specific allegation has been found by the court previously to be clearly illegal.[24] The concept of qualified immunity has gotten so broad, say activists and many defense attorneys, that it has become almost impossible to hold police officers or their departments accountable in cases of police brutality.[25] The legal concept means this: If a federal court has not previously found certain law enforcement conduct to be an egregious civil rights violation, then police officers, or sheriffs, and their employers are protected from being held accountable. In effect, they are immune from lawsuit.[26] The same concept is being used to try to protect governmental bodies from any accountability in cases where poor people are being sent to jail over their inability to pay various court costs.[27]

The federal judge in the Oklahoma case dismissed the case in March 2021, ruling in favor of the defendants that there was no federal jurisdiction to decide the issue.

"The Court is aware of a number of efforts in other states to change the fee-based funding of their court systems and the difficulties it presents to low-income defendants," wrote U.S. District Judge Terence C. Kern. "However noble or well-intentioned Plaintiffs goals may be, the structure and funding of the Oklahoma criminal justice system is controlled by the State's legislative and executive branches."[28]

The plaintiffs in the Oklahoma case have appealed Kern's ruling.

If either the Killman case in Oklahoma or the Darby case in South Carolina end up with a settlement, or make their way to trial, the various fines-and-fee schemes throughout the country could fall like a house of cards. In the meantime, as did the Missouri case against debtors' prisons brought by Mueller, other lawsuits targeting the criminalization of poverty are succeeding and having a positive effect on policies in multiple states. Two of the most important ones were in the State of Tennessee, both brought by the Civil Rights Corps and other legal partners. The first was filed by Karakatsanis in 2015 against Rutherford County and the private, for-profit probation company the county had contracted with, Providence Community Corrections.[29] The county is southeast of Nashville and its biggest city is Murfreesboro.[30] The complaint, filed on behalf of Cindy Rodriguez and other indigent people like her, reads like so many other of the similar lawsuits being filed in other places, referring to the scheme by which county governments and private probation companies jail poor people over their inability to pay court costs as "extortion."[31]

"The crux of this scheme is a conspiracy to funnel misdemeanor probation cases in which court debts are owed to a private company, which then extorts money out of individuals who have no ability to pay court costs, let alone private fees," the lawsuit alleged. "The private company, whose goal is to maximize its own profits, acts as a 'probation officer' to collect those debts—as well as to assess and collect its own additional and substantial fees and surcharges—through repeated and continuous threats to arrest, revoke, and imprison individuals who are indigent and disabled if they do not pay. As a result of this extortion enterprise, the Plaintiffs and others similarly situated have lost their housing, lost jobs, lost cars, undergone humiliating physical intrusions on their bodies, suffered severe medical injuries, sold their own blood plasma, sacrificed food and clothing for their vulnerable children, and/or diverted their low-income disability checks—all in order to pay private 'supervision fees.' They have languished year after year on recurring terms of 'user-funded' probation under constant threats to their physical well-being, and they have been repeatedly jailed because of their poverty. This cycle of ever-increasing debts, threats, and imprisonment has left the Plaintiffs and thousands of people like them in Rutherford County trapped in a culture of fear and panic."

In 2018, the lawsuit settled for $14.3 million, money the county and Providence Community Corrections had to pay to the victims of the scheme whose civil rights had regularly been violated. As part of the settlement, the defendants denied any violations of constitutional rights, but Rutherford County agreed not to contract with any private probation companies in the future, and to a number of changes of policy to protect indigent defendants. [32]

Later that same year, in July, a federal judge ruled that Tennessee could no longer suspend driver's licenses for failure to pay court costs, a massive problem in dozens of states. The lawsuit that led to that ruling was filed in 2017 by the Civil Rights Corps, the National Center for Law and Economic Justice, nonprofit Just City, and the Memphis law firm of Baker, Donelson, Bearman, Caldwell & Berkowitz. [33]

"If a person has no resources to pay a debt, he cannot be threatened or cajoled into paying it; he may, however, become able to pay it in the future. But taking his driver's license away sabotages that prospect," wrote U.S. District Judge Aleta Trauger, who called the suspension process "powerfully counterproductive." [34]

In the five years preceding the lawsuit, Tennessee had suspended nearly 250,000 driver's licenses over failure to pay traffic ticket costs, [35] and another 140,000 driver's licenses over court costs. For poor people, of course, a suspended license makes it less likely a person can get to work, and more likely they will risk arrest by violating the law in order to get to work out of necessity. Neither of those actions serve as an incentive for the state to get money it may be owed. Because the suspensions happened without any due process, they were unconstitutional, Trauger wrote. As a result, the suspensions were temporarily halted and more than 100,000 Tennesseans were given an opportunity to get their driving privileges reinstated without the need to pay down the debt in return.

But in May 2020, the plaintiffs received bad news: a related case, this one specifically about traffic-related debt, was overturned. The U.S. Court of Appeals for the Sixth Circuit ruled that Trauger's preliminary injunction against the Tennessee law could not stand, because a controlling case in the circuit, *Fowler v. Benson*, a similar case in Michigan, had been found constitutional by the same court previously. [36] In some bitter irony, the judges in the appeals court agreed that the suspension of driver's licenses for unpaid traffic debt was bad policy, and likely unconstitutional, but the judges said their hands were tied.

"Stripping people of their driver's licenses because of their inability to pay is not only cruel and unwise, it is unconstitutional. I regret that, until a change comes from the en banc or the Supreme Court, Fowler forecloses us from rectifying this injustice," the court wrote.

Despite the loss in Tennessee, the various law firms working on this issue are hoping that eventually they will get a case before the U.S. Supreme Court to overturn the ruling in the *Fowler* case. Several other similar lawsuits have been filed in other states, including Missouri,[37] South Carolina, Pennsylvania, Oregon, California, and Texas. A national coalition called Free to Drive has started pushing for state lawmakers to end driver's license suspensions over unpaid court debt The coalition is having an effect, with legislation filed in more than a dozen states.[38]

The reality facing the passel of attorneys and activists who have made the eradication of illegal fines and fees in the court system their cause, however, is that the job can't truly be finished without the help of state legislatures. Those are the bodies that created the statutes that both allowed the massive rise in court fines and fees as backdoor taxes, and the ones with the power to pass new laws to makes sure their states aren't creating a whole new generation of poor people who get introduced to the concept of debtors' prison.

In Missouri in 2019, a Republican lawmaker named Bruce DeGroot realized he needed to be part of the solution. While the Missouri Supreme Court was considering the case that would ultimately lead to a unanimous decision to make it illegal to jail people over an inability to pay jail board bills, DeGroot filed a bill that would put similar language into state law.[39] The debate, and the result, points to a path forward for the rest of the nation.

9

....

THE CAPITOL

Jefferson City, Missouri
February 2018

In one word, state representative Mark Ellebracht defined the debtors' prison scheme playing out in nearly every rural county in Missouri: "Extortion."[1]

That's what the Democrat from Liberty, Missouri, called the process of judges requiring indigent defendants to come back to court month after month and threatening them with more jail time for sentences they had already served if they didn't come up with money to pay rent on that previous time behind bars. To be clear, this is what the civil rights attorneys and Ellebracht mean when they use that word: Extortion is the act of trying to obtain something through force or a threat. When judges, prosecutors, and sheriffs, sometimes on behalf of the county commissions that fix their budgets, use the threat of jail time to try to obtain money from poor people, that's extortion, Ellebracht argued to the House Special Committee on Criminal Justice, chaired by state Republican representative Shamed Dogan, of Ballwin.[2]

Extortion is the same word that appears multiple times in the various civil rights lawsuits being filed across the country seeking to upend the criminalization of poverty in America by forcing the criminal justice system to start protecting the civil rights of poor people. That's why Ellebracht was testifying in a basement hearing room in the Missouri Capitol on a February morning in 2018, in favor of a bill he was cosponsoring with Bruce DeGroot, a Republican from Chesterfield, a western suburb of St. Louis.[3] Both men are lawyers who had toiled in some of the courtrooms where putting poor people in jail because they can't afford to pay for various forms of court debt has long been standard practice. Their aim with House Bill 192 was to bring an end to that practice.

DeGroot happens to be my state representative. He filed his bill after reading my columns on the debtors' prison scheme being executed by judges in rural Missouri.[4] DeGroot and I make for an odd partnership.[5] He's a conservative Republican. I've always fancied myself a political independent, true to my western roots in Colorado where I grew up. Of course, in the era of Trump, when the Republican Party moved so far right as to make it unrecognizable to the party that elected George W. Bush to the White House, I increasingly found myself supporting progressive causes further to the left of the political spectrum.

I had voted for Bush twice before voting for Barack Obama twice. In the era in which DeGroot served, there were few Republicans I could imagine earning my vote, including him. It was in that environment that he called me, in early December 2018, as I was traversing the state of Missouri, writing about injustice in rural courts, with poor people who had committed minor crimes as the primary victims.

"I grew up poor," DeGroot told me in that initial phone call. We were both hesitant, not just because of our perceived political differences, but because of how critically I had written about him. I had filed one column about poverty that had DeGroot on the wrong side of the issue. It was about a year earlier, and he was sponsoring a bill that would make it easier for third-party debt collectors to win court cases against people who had fallen behind paying their bills.[6]

As an attorney, DeGroot had worked for some of these big debt companies. They create limited liability companies that buy up old, defaulted debt, like from credit card companies and rent-to-own companies that end up with unpaid debt from people who are unlikely to ever have the money to get caught up. Those companies file bulk lawsuits and end up winning judgments against the debtors, many of whom never receive notices or go to court, or they receive a notice but don't recognize the company trying to collect the debt.[7] People remember owing money to JCPenney, but not to Cavalry SPV I, LLC. The bill DeGroot was sponsoring that year would make it easier for companies to collect the debt without having to go through the process of verifying that it was actually owed.[8]

"It's a very dangerous bill," St. Louis attorney Jim Daher told me at the time.[9] The bill was part of a growing trend in Missouri and national politics that created a Democratic and Republican split every year in the legislature. On one side was the U.S. Chamber of Commerce, in effect an arm of the national Republican Party, pushing so-called tort reform bills to tilt the civil liability playing field toward big business and away from consumers.[10] On the other side were the trial lawyers who represented consumers hurt by bad corporate actors and who sometimes won big class-action lawsuits against large corporations.[11]

Traditionally, the Chamber of Commerce donated mostly to Republicans, and trial lawyers funded Democrats. The proxy battle plays out in the Missouri Legislature nearly every year. That year, as in most, I was on the side of consumers. DeGroot was on the side of the big corporations. But it wasn't always this way. That was the point of my column. Just five years earlier, before he was a state representative, before he started working for big debt-collection companies, DeGroot was an attorney who represented poor people who were battling against those very companies. He testified against the very bill he was now sponsoring.[12]

"This is a bad bill," DeGroot had written on the witness form he signed when he testified against it. In fact, just a couple of years after that bill failed, the federal Consumer Financial Protection Bureau would fine a couple of the nation's largest third-party debt collectors for their inaccurate debt collection practices, ordering them to refund about $60 million to consumers.[13] Now DeGroot was on the other side. It was hypocrisy of the highest order, I thought. DeGroot, of course, disagreed. So when he called me a year later, I was suspicious. It turns out, so was he.

"It was hard calling you," DeGroot told me later. "In my job, the media is not friendly. But having read a few of your columns on debtors' prisons, I knew that you were right. I knew I had to act."

As I was writing about Brooke Bergen, stuck in jail for a year after allegedly shoplifting an $8 tube of mascara from Walmart,[14] or Cory Booth, still being required to go to court once a month a decade after he served his time for stealing a lawn mower when he was seventeen, DeGroot saw himself.

DeGroot was born in 1963 in Sioux Falls, South Dakota, the son of Harold and Patricia DeGroot. "My father was an alcoholic and couldn't hold a job," DeGroot said. His parents divorced when he was four; Mom was only twenty-five, with three children under the age of five. "She had no job, no education, no family support, she didn't even know how to drive a car." DeGroot has vivid memories of being poor, he says, and knowing that his family was living in a state of relative poverty. Never enough at Christmas. Hand-me-down clothing. No vacations. Food stamps until he was in high school.

"One of the most memorable things I recall was the monthly ordeal of receiving my free lunch card," DeGroot said. "The teacher would call all the kids who had money to pay for their cards to come up to her desk, and she would accept the $10 to pay for their lunch card for the month. She would then call the kids who received free lunches, only two or three of us, and make a big production of giving us our pink cards. As a ten- or eleven-year-old this was humiliating beyond imagination. I lived in constant fear of being identified as being poor."

DeGroot's mom convinced a banker to loan her enough money to put her through respiratory therapy school, and she completed her training and ended up with a job at Sioux Valley Hospital, until she retired at sixty-five. She never made more than $30,000 a year when Bruce was growing up, but her work ethic rubbed off on him, he says.

DeGroot, who says in his official Missouri House biography that he is a descendant of Buffalo Bill, would go on to graduate from the

University of South Dakota. He then graduated from the St. Louis University School of Law.[15] As a young lawyer, he would regularly find himself in a rural courtroom on what some of the judges call "law day," when the courtroom would fill up with arraignments, traffic-ticket cases, and, of course, payment review hearings.

"In some jurisdictions, particularly rural ones, the criminal and civil dockets are held on the same day before the same judge," DeGroot said. "To me, the process was eerily familiar. The bailiff would call the defendant to rise and stand before the judge. The judge would then announce to the defendant, and those present in the courtroom, the amount the defendant owed and asked if that amount could be satisfied today, and, if not, why not? I could not help but notice the similarity to my pink lunch card days. I noticed the embarrassment of the defendants as they had to explain to the judge, and those in the courtroom, why they needed more time. Both young and seasoned attorneys are conditioned to this process in rural communities."

More often than not, though, lawyers don't say anything during these proceedings. It's how the system is set up. If the attorneys don't represent the particular client, they can't step up and argue on their behalf that various due-process rights are being violated. Some of it is simply related to the parochialism of the local court system. No attorney who represents clients regularly before a particular judge wants to end up on their bad side, particularly a young attorney early in their career, which often is the case for the public defenders who represent the clients discussed throughout this book.

Matthew Mueller offers the perfect example of that, with judges and prosecutors filing bar complaints against him the moment he started upsetting the status quo. As DeGroot started working on his legislation, I put him in touch with Mueller and with Michael Barrett, the head of the public defender system.

Then I called both men myself with a request: Watch the bill carefully. As a journalist, I was walking a fine line. Columnists clearly advocate for positions, at times, and there was no doubt I was pushing hard in my series of columns for some serious criminal justice reform in Missouri. But it was unusual for me to be having off-the-record conversations with lawmakers sponsoring specific legislation, and offering suggestions based on my reporting on where the bill would be most effective. I stayed out of the politics, but to say I was deeply invested in the result of the bill sponsored by DeGroot and Ellebracht would be an understatement.

The first hearing that early February morning was a success. Nobody testified against the bill.[16] A wide coalition from all along the political spectrum supported it: the ACLU, the public defender's office, the Missouri Catholic Conference, Americans for Prosperity. All offered overwhelming support, as did members of Dogan's committee, from both parties.[17]

"It is profoundly unfair for people to be incarcerated simply for the inability to pay," said Jeanette Mott Oxford, representing Empower Missouri, a nonprofit that advocates for policies that primarily help reduce poverty.

Early in the hearing, DeGroot let his colleagues know where he'd ultimately like to see this debate go. "I'd be open to an amendment that you can't charge people for jail," he said. DeGroot and Ellebracht had discussed trying to ban board bills altogether. Simply charging people for a stay in a jail that taxpayers are already paying for makes no sense, DeGroot said. Advocates like Lauren-Brooke Eisen of the Brennan Center have long agreed. It's almost double taxation, and it creates a two-tiered justice system, as poor people almost always spend more time in jail pretrial, often because they can't afford bail, thus increasing their board bills.[18]

But the two Missouri lawmakers didn't think such a bill could pass because sheriffs, county commissioners, and prosecutors would all likely protest the loss of revenue. With the Missouri Supreme Court headed toward a decision on the same topic, the lawmakers didn't want to go through the motions this legislative session, only to have to be back at it the next year. They thought they had the momentum and support to pass the bill. So they limited the bill's scope to just making sure that people can't be rejailed because they couldn't afford to pay their board bill. Instead, the proposed new law would allow a sheriff to seek a civil collection of the bill.

DeGroot's bill would pass out of the committee the next week. The week after that, the U.S. Supreme Court ruling on the *Timbs* case written by Justice Ruth Bader Ginsburg would provide even more momentum for the national campaign against excessive fines. The decision involved a man in Indiana, Tyson Timbs, whose $42,000 Land Rover had been seized by the state in a drug case. The vehicle was worth more than four times the maximum fine under Indiana law for Timbs's drug conviction. Indiana's supreme court had ruled the seizure—common in states throughout the country in drug cases—was legal because the U.S. Constitution's Eighth Amendment protection against excessive fines had not previously been applied to states. For the first time, the U.S. Supreme Court said it did, and the justices were unanimous in their decision.[19]

"For good reason, the protection against excessive fines has been a constant shield throughout Anglo-American history," Ginsburg wrote. "Exorbitant tolls undermine other constitutional liberties. Excessive fines can be used, for example, to retaliate against or chill the speech of political enemies . . . Even absent a political motive, fines may be employed in a measure out of accord with the penal goals of retribution and deterrence."[20]

By unanimously applying the Eighth Amendment protection against excessive fines and fees to the states, the U.S. Supreme Court gave a massive boost to various legal efforts around the country that were battling the criminalization of poverty.[21]

Dogan, a Republican, opened his hearing with a big smile that day. Stopping unconstitutional asset forfeiture was an issue he believed strongly in, and that morning, his committee would pass a bill he sponsored trying to limit such forfeitures in Missouri, where state law enforcement agencies would piggyback with federal agencies to make such forfeitures in drug cases and end up with a windfall that would often go into the growing militarization of local police departments, with tiny sheriffs' departments and municipal police forces buying armored vehicles, helicopters, and other military-grade gear with their ill-gotten bounties.[22]

That day, the committee passed Dogan's bill as well as a bill sponsored by Justin Hill, the Lake St. Louis Republican, which sought to rein in the copious amount of drug testing being performed by private, for-profit probation companies in misdemeanor cases. This was an attempt to protect people like Bergen, for whom a drug addiction might lead to a probation violation on a charge that had nothing to do with drug abuse.[23]

Barrett testified before the committee that day, and he talked about the importance of the *Timbs* decision. All these elements of what he called "policing for profit" work together, he said. "Too often, these fines and fees keep [defendants] in the criminal justice system long after their time has been served," Barrett said.[24] Later, DeGroot's bill would clear another legislative barrier, passing the rules committee so it was available for floor debate in the house.[25] DeGroot would have to wait until May, after the Missouri Supreme Court had issued its own unanimous ruling on the debtors' prison issue, for that debate to take place.

"I've seen these situations play out," DeGroot told his fellow lawmakers on the house floor as he introduced his bill as a way to end debtors' prisons in Missouri. The term might seem harsh to some, the representative said, but in practice, that's what was happening in rural counties throughout the state. "What happens is you have to bring some money to the judge and pay part of your debt. If you don't show up a warrant goes out for your arrest and you are placed back in jail, thereby increasing the amount that you owe to the court even more. About four or five months ago, one of my constituents, a journalist from the *St. Louis Post-Dispatch*, Tony Messenger, started writing a series of articles about these situations in our rural courts. There are some pretty outlandish stories."

Then he brought up Bergen. Like so many people I've talked to since I started writing about people put in jail over their inability to pay court costs or board bills, Bergen's story is often the one that perhaps best helped him see the incredible injustice placed on poor people in American courts.

For some it is simply the absurdity of the math, comparing the alleged theft of an $8 tube of mascara to the more than $15,000 she would end up owing the court. DeGroot raised this stark difference during the debate on the bill. For others it's the year in jail, which seems ridiculous on its face, or the private probation company that she had to pay monthly fees to that contributed to putting her back in jail over and over again.

There's another factor that attracted me to Bergen's story: like Clint Eastwood, I like my characters flawed. Think of some of Eastwood's biggest films, the ones he directed, like *Mystic River* or *A Perfect World* or *Gran Torino*.[26] The good guys almost always have character flaws that make them unlikable, and the bad guys end up being sympathetic, like Kevin Costner's escaped prisoner character in *A Perfect World*.

If the criminal justice system worked only for those people without flaws, who didn't make mistakes, who didn't battle drug addiction or occasionally make bad decisions, then what is the point of all the civil rights guaranteed in the U.S. Constitution? Do they apply to all of us, even in our weakest moments, or not?

Because he experienced poverty himself, and had represented his share of Brooke Bergens, DeGroot could empathize with the people who were being hauled off to debtors' prison as a result of a flawed system that penalized them unjustly and without any regard for who they are and what they're dealing with as people.

"She now owes close to $15,000. We've put her in a position where she can't succeed," DeGroot said during debate of his bill. "She can't get out of the system, ever. What this bill does is simply do away with that system."

DeGroot's high school–aged son was in the gallery to watch the debate that day. This was something special, something different from the other bills DeGroot sponsored, he said. "This may be the best thing I've ever done with my law degree."

The bill would pass the house overwhelmingly. But when it came back from the senate, DeGroot and Ellebracht had a difficult decision to make. Sen. Mike Cunningham, a Republican from rural Rogersville, in the southwest part of the state, inserted an amendment that in some ways was contradictory to the theme of the bill. Cunningham's amendment would add a $10 fee to any summons served by a special process server, with that money to go to a supplemental fund that would increase deputy sheriff salaries.[27]

It was a classic "screw the Lou" amendment, DeGroot said. In the Missouri Legislature, there is a rural-urban divide, with the rural interests generally having the most power, and St. Louis interests often at odds with the rest of the state. In this case, sheriffs already had such a fee in state law, but in St. Louis, with the busiest courts in the state, the majority of summons issued in civil cases were served by private companies. Those extra costs would now get passed through to various clients, and that money would go to supplement salaries of deputies in areas where lawmakers were averse to raising taxes. It was the same old fines-and-fees scheme, though the costs weren't going to be paid as directly by poor people as, say, board bills were. DeGroot and Ellebracht both hated the amendment. But fighting it would jeopardize the entire bill. So they compromised for political expediency, however difficult it was on its face. The bill passed and was signed into law by Gov. Mike Parson on July 9, 2019.[28]

In Minnesota, state representative John Lesch wasn't having as much success. Lesch is an attorney in St. Paul, and a member of the Minnesota Democratic-Farmer-Labor Party. A member of the legislature since 2003, Lesch had for years been trying to pass legislation to reduce the effect of fines and fees in the court system on the lives of poor people. As both a former prosecutor and defense attorney he had seen firsthand the cycle of criminalization that often started with a simple traffic ticket. Fines and fees had been on the rise in Minnesota since the Great Recession, as they were in most states. "We kept on adding fees, as budgets got tight," Lesch said. For fifteen years, Lesch had tried and failed to pass a bill that would make it clear in state law that every defendant must have an ability-to-pay hearing, including in traffic cases, and that there would be an opportunity for judges to waive such fees if a defendant clearly couldn't afford them.[29]

Minnesota lawmakers passed a $25 state surcharge to be applied to all traffic and criminal cases in 1998, but it has since tripled that surcharge, and added many others, including an additional $12 fee for all traffic cases.[30] One of Lesch's bills to reduce the criminalization of poverty almost made it to the finish line in 2018. With the support of Nick Zerwas, the Republican from rural Elk River, a bill that would end the suspension of driver's licenses of people who couldn't afford to pay their court debt almost became law.[31]

For both Lesch and Zerwas, like the growing coalition of folks in the Free to Drive movement, it was simple common sense that if you took away a poor person's driver's license because they couldn't afford court debt, the state actually made it less likely they could pay that debt, and more likely they would lose a job and be driven deeper into poverty.

"How ridiculous is the idea that we take away a person's ability to work because they haven't made enough money to pay a fine or fee?" Zerwas said during a 2019 panel discussion at a Cash Register Justice seminar in New York that I attended.[32] "This is an issue that crosses all political boundaries and goes to common sense." That argument almost carried the day in 2018. The driver's license suspension bill passed, but it got rolled into an omnibus bill 1,000 pages long that contained numerous other topics. Minnesota governor Mark Dayton vetoed the bill, unrelated to the driver's license suspension issue, but the proposal backed by Lesch and Zerwas died anyway.[33]

Lesch, who is the chairman of the public safety committee, continues to be hopeful that his two bills will gain traction. In 2020, the spread of COVID-19 shut down progress on most bills, particularly any that might cost local governments revenue, as his bills would. But his partner on the issue from the other side of the aisle, Zerwas, has left the legislature, and he's been replaced by a former deputy sheriff who is significantly less supportive of the issues than Zerwas was. So, for Lesch, it's back to the drawing board.

But while the driver's license suspension bill was failing in Minnesota, similar measures were finding success in other states, some of them dominated by Republicans, others by Democrats.

It is still the law in thirty-five states and the District of Columbia that driver's licenses can be suspended—in some cases it is mandatory—for failure to pay court costs. But the number used to be higher.[34] In 2016, Vermont became one of the first states to repeal such suspensions for at least some court fines and fees.[35] Maine followed in 2017, as did California. In 2019, Texas and Montana followed suit, and in 2020, Oregon and New York passed similar laws.[36] In early 2021, Illinois joined the movement.

In 2017, amid pressure from the Southern Poverty Law Center and the MacArthur Justice Center, two nonprofits advocating for an end to wealth-based driver's license suspension, bureaucrats in Mississippi didn't even wait for lawmakers to act. Instead, presented with empirical evidence that they were violating the civil rights of people whose licenses were being suspended for an inability to pay court fines, the Mississippi Department of Public Safety suspended the practice.[37]

A letter from Assistant Attorney General Harold E. Pizzetta III formalized the arrangement, and the state began the process of reinstating the driver's licenses of about 100,000 Mississippians.[38] Two years later the state legislature passed the Criminal Justice Reform Act and formalized the change in state policy by putting it into law.[39]

"If Mississippi can do it," said Lisa Foster, of the Fines and Fees Justice Center, "everybody can do it."

That's the goal of a new piece of legislation introduced in Congress in 2020. Two members of the U.S. Senate, Democrat Chris Coons of Delaware and Republican Roger Wicker of Mississippi, introduced their federal Driving for Opportunity Act, which would offer incentives for states to stop debt-based driver's license suspensions.[40] Nationally, about 11 million people have lost their driver's licenses from debt-related suspensions.[41]

"At a time when the COVID-19 pandemic has made it even harder for Americans to pay their bills and care for their families, taking away someone's driver's license can make it nearly impossible to hold down a job and therefore pay back their debts," Coons said in introducing the legislation.[42]

Indeed, a 2007 New Jersey study found that only about 6 percent of drivers lost their licenses for driving-related issues. Most were suspensions related to unpaid court fees, or back child support, or other similar debt related issues. About 42 percent of the people who got their licenses suspended lost their jobs, and nearly half of those folks couldn't find another job.[43] The whole process is just "counterintuitive," Zerwas said. The evidence in at least one state that stopped suspending driver's licenses for failure to pay helps prove that point, says Foster. In the year after California changed its law on driver's license suspension, collection of court fines and fees actually went up by nearly 9 percent.[44]

"More people paid on time after they stopped suspending driver's licenses," Foster said. "There's a reason for that. People were working."

This is also one of the concepts behind the bail reform legislation that is making its way slowly through various states. Besides trying to make sure judges are protecting the civil rights of defendants and not applying bail punitively to keep poor people in jail pretrial, there is a strong argument to be made that getting such defendants out of jail and back with their families and allowing them to keep their jobs does more to improve the local community than locking people up who are presumed innocent.

Since 2017, that has been the status quo in New Jersey, one of the first states to significantly reduce the criminal justice system's reliance on cash bail, or, as Alec Karakatsanis of the Civil Rights Corps likes to call it, wealth-based detention.[45] If the threat of further jail time for failure to pay fines and fees is how the judicial system keeps poor people tethered to the courts, cash bail is how they get reeled in. In both cases, people who have little financial means face additional jail time—either without a conviction, or after having already served their time—simply because they don't have enough money to buy their freedom.

In 2013, lawmakers in New Jersey decided to do something about this. A state commission found that the way cash bail was being applied in New Jersey was regularly keeping poor people locked up in jail on minor offenses because they couldn't afford to buy their freedom, while wealthier people facing more serious charges that could make them a danger to the community were regularly set free because they could pay a bail bondsman enough to be released.[46]

The commission found that 73 percent of the people in jail in New Jersey were there on "pretrial" detention, meaning they hadn't been convicted of anything yet; and 12 percent of those people were there because they couldn't afford $2,500 in bail or less.[47] It's no wonder. According to a 2018 Federal Reserve study, nearly 30 percent of Americans would have to borrow money if they ended up with a $400 unexpected expense.[48] That's the reality of what paycheck to paycheck looks like for millions of Americans, and it's why so many of them languish in the country's jails simply because they have been charged with an offense, even, sometimes, very minor traffic offenses.

The findings in New Jersey mirrored the cash bail practices in nearly every state in America. The commission created bipartisan support for a move away from a cash bail system, and in 2016, more than 60 percent of New Jersey voters passed the constitutional amendment, which all but erased cash bail as a detention method in the state.[49]

Under the new system, judges can detain people determined to be a danger to society without bail, or they can release pretrial defendants on various conditions, such as refraining from alcohol or drugs, having a GPS monitor, or a curfew. In the first year of the new law, the state's jail population dropped by more than 20 percent, and crime fell.[50] In November 2018, attorneys Christopher Porrino and Elie Honig wrote an analysis of the New Jersey bail reforms that suggested it should be a model for the country, in part because the biggest beneficiaries were the indigent defendants who previously were jailed for being poor.

"In 1964 Attorney General Robert Kennedy testified before Congress that the 'problem, simply stated, is: The rich man and the poor man do not receive equal justice in our courts. And in no area is this more evident than in the matter of bail . . . Bail has become a vehicle for systematic injustice,'" the attorneys wrote. "We as a country have known this truth for over five decades. Now, New Jersey has shown that bail reform truly does work. The road map is available for everyone else to follow. We call on all other states to join us in creating the fairer and more just bail system that Kennedy envisioned so many years ago."[51]

The simple truth of the cash bail system in the U.S. is that the reality on the ground—that it is used to keep poor people locked up pretrial as a strategy to force guilty pleas—is different from what the average American might think it is, if they get their understanding from one of the television shows like *Dog the Bounty Hunter* that glorify the bail bondsman as somebody keeping America safe by tracking down escaped felons.[52]

The next two states engaged in serious reform efforts came from both coasts, New York in the east and California in the west. Bail reform advocates celebrated big victories in both states and then watched as they were put on hold or somewhat reversed. The California bail reforms were driven by a lawsuit filed on behalf of sixty-three-year-old Kenneth Humphrey by the Civil Rights Corps.[53] Humphrey, who is Black, is a retired San Francisco shipyard laborer who in 2017 was charged with a residential robbery. Humphrey was accused of stealing $7 from another man. His bail was set at $600,000. The high bail had a punitive effect of holding Humphrey pretrial, with no conviction. There was no ability-to-pay hearing.[54] Civil Rights Corp sued, saying the action violated his Fourteenth Amendment rights to due process and equal protection under the law, as well as his Eighth Amendment right to protection against excessive fees.[55]

In 2018, the California Court of Appeals agreed with Humphrey and his attorneys.[56] The bail process that was regularly being followed in California was violating the state's constitution. The court knew that its ruling would upend the system of justice as practiced in the state for decades, but it forced a serious statewide discussion about how to change the bail system so that poor people were no longer regularly abused by the system.

"We are not blind to the practical problems our ruling may present," the appeals court wrote. "The timelines within which bail determinations must be made are short, and judicial officers and pretrial service agencies are already burdened by limited resources. But the problem this case presents does not result from the sudden application of a new

and unexpected judicial duty; it stems instead from the enduring un-
willingness of our society, including the courts to correct a deformity in
our criminal justice system that close observers have long considered a
blight on the system."[57]

In effect, the court ruled that California's cash bail system was unconstitutional. It urged the legislature to get to work,[58] and it did, passing a
law in 2018 pushed by Gov. Jerry Brown, which got rid of money bail, and
led to most nonviolent misdemeanor defendants' release from jail.[59] It's
a plan Brown had advocated for as far back as 1979, during his first run
as the state's governor, when he said in his State of the State address that
California's bail system was an unconstitutional "tax on poor people."[60]

"Thousands and thousands of people languish in the jails of this
state even though they have been convicted of no crime. Their only
crime is that they cannot make the bail that our present law requires,"
Brown said decades ago.[61] It took more than forty years for the legislature and the courts to catch up to his way of thinking.

But the problem was far from solved. The ACLU pulled its support
from the new law in its final version because it gave local judges too
much discretion to use controversial algorithms to determine community risk that still could lead to the jailing of too many poor people for
the wrong reasons. Then the state's bail industry successfully placed a
referendum on the November 2020 ballot to try to undo the legislative
reforms.[62] California voters defeated Proposition 25, meaning the legislative bail reforms did not become law.

Meanwhile, the California Supreme Court hadn't yet ruled on the
Humphrey case, which was appealed again. The California bail reforms
were in a state of flux, frozen in time, awaiting final court action.[63] That
action came in March 2021, when a unanimous California Supreme
Court ruled in favor of Humphrey.

"The common practice of conditioning freedom solely on whether
an arrestee can afford bail is unconstitutional," Justice Mariano-
Florentino Cuéllar wrote for the court, ruling that existing bail practices violated both state and federal protections. The ruling didn't erase
cash bail in California, but it required ability-to-pay hearings and gave

strong guidance to judges that they could no longer keep defendants locked up simply because they couldn't afford bail.

New York experienced a similar roller coaster. In 2019, the state legislature passed criminal justice reforms that would have eliminated cash bail in 90 percent of cases, which would have led to at least a 40 percent reduction in jail population in the state, advocates for the reforms argued. The pushback, from tough-on-crime police unions and prosecutors, as well as the bail bond industry, which stood to lose its cash cow, was immediate and powerful. Critics of the new rules argued with little evidence that it was leading to an increase in crime.[64]

By April 2020, the legislature dialed back the reforms, keeping some of them in place but giving judges more discretion to apply cash bail in some cases.[65] Two steps forward, one back: that's the dance that is taking place in courts and state capitals all across the country when it comes to the criminalization of poverty. The forces fighting for the status quo, from the bail bond industry to private probation companies and law-and-order sheriffs and police departments, are politically powerful. Michael Milton has seen the progress and pushback up close. He's the Missouri advocacy director and site manager for the national nonprofit Bail Project, which raises money to help pay the cash bails of poor people who are otherwise locked up on pretrial detention, mostly because they can't afford bail.[66] St. Louis was one of the first sites for the project, which is now operating in cities across the country. The pushback narrative is simple: once there is one person the Bail Project helps get released who then reoffends—never mind the statistics about the overwhelming success of people returned to their families and jobs—the law enforcement community garners front-page headlines about the "danger" of releasing people from jail.[67]

"Unfortunately, it isn't just the tough-on-crime folks that's pushing back but also 'progressives' that walk backward every time someone does violence. I think we can continue to push bail reform down the field if we uplift a more full argument for eliminating cash bail—that people should be released without bail and they must be supported thoroughly once they have," Milton said.

It's that support once a poor person is released from jail on a pretrial detention, especially if they lost housing or jobs while in jail, that can make all the difference in the world. Finding the revenue to help people in that situation, getting drug or alcohol treatment, accessing transportation or job training, that is at the core of the "defund the police" movement, shifting resources from a system that was created to lock people up to one that works to rebuild communities, keep families together, and reduce the incentives for crime.[68]

In 2020, the Bail Project released a report titled "After Cash Bail" that focused on the sorts of investments that cities and states will need to make to transform the concept of pretrial justice so that the world after cash bail can be successful. Nearly all the recommendations focus on relieving poverty, helping people obtain the services and job training they need to create more vibrant communities.[69] That's the sort of future that legislators could be imagining as they rethink the American justice system, but first they have to get off the roller coaster of passing reforms and then backing down before they have an opportunity to succeed.

Less than one year after Missouri lawmakers tackled the debtors' prison scheme long perpetrated in its rural counties, one state senator tried to undo DeGroot's bill.[70] The reason? Money.

"I have a small county in my district that is going to have to lay off a deputy," said Sen. Bill White, a Republican from Joplin. "There's a lot more flexibility to collect money if board bills are classified as court costs."

In the closing weeks of the 2020 legislative session, which had been upended because of the coronavirus pandemic, White slipped an amendment onto an omnibus crime bill that would have completely undone DeGroot's work from the year before, as well as reversed the Missouri Supreme Court decision in the Richey and Wright cases. White's amendment would have changed the law to classify board bills as court costs, like other fines and fees, which would have meant judges could go back to threatening jail time for indigent defendants who couldn't afford to pay for their involuntary stays in jail. DeGroot was livid when he found out. A staff member in the office of Eric Schmitt, the attorney general, had noticed the amendment, which was added with no debate. It was not filed as a stand-alone bill, so the issue received no legislative hearings in either the house or the senate. "They snuck it in when nobody was looking," DeGroot told me. I wrote a column about the sneaky attempt to undo a vote that had been over-whelmingly bipartisan just a year earlier. Shortly thereafter, the offending amendment was stripped from the crime bill in the house.[71]

But it will return. The sheriffs want "their" money. That is the frustrating element of the criminal justice reform movement on so many fronts, for many of the advocates working to change laws state by state, whether it's bail, debtors' prisons, private probation companies or driver's license suspensions. As happened in New York and California, once voters or lawmakers decide to protect poor people from civil rights violations regarding cash bail, the bail bonds industry, and the tough-on-crime political machine, fight back and try to take back lost ground.[72]

In Minnesota, for instance, progress made on the driver's license suspension issue in 2018 receded a year later.[73] Similarly, Missouri politicians are facing pushback on positive developments in protecting poor people from undue harm at the hands of the judiciary. The advocates for using the judicial system to extract wealth from the poor have deep pockets and strong lobbies. Poor people often have few people to speak up for them in the hallowed halls of state legislatures.

That's why Karakatsanis, in his book, *Usual Cruelty*, laments elements of the criminal justice reform movement, because many of the bureaucrats who at least outwardly endorse some of its concepts don't want to actually do the heavy lifting of emptying the nation's jails of the mostly poor people who don't belong there.[74]

"The emerging 'criminal justice reform' consensus is superficial and deceptive," Karakatsanis writes. "It is superficial because most proposed 'reforms' would still leave the United States as the greatest incarcerator in the world. It is deceptive because those who want largely to preserve the current punishment bureaucracy—by making just enough tweaks to protect its perceived legitimacy—must obfuscate the difference between changes that will transform the system and tweaks that will curb only its most grotesque flourishes."[75]

That so many of the "tweaks" that have been made in part because of the lawsuits filed by Karakatsanis and others are facing pressure to be reversed serves as a clarion call that not enough is being done to reform the clear abuses of the American justice system, the victims of which are poor, and, too often, people of color.[76]

My own experience in Missouri validates this fear. Several of the people I wrote about in these pages—George Richey, Lashawn Casey, Brooke Bergen, and Leann Banderman—ended up back in jail or prison even after both the state supreme court and the Missouri Legislature determined that they and people like them were being put back in jail illegally.[77] But each of them had records, and old demons resurfaced, and local officials found a way to put them back behind bars. During much of the time I was writing this book, Bergen was in state prison for driving on a suspended driver's license. Though hardly the sort of crime that makes her a danger to society, she was locked up again, a human in a cage, in part because her previous record was used to give her ever harsher punishment for her relatively minor infractions. She was released in January 2021, only to get home to Dent County and find out she faced a new drug charge that apparently emanated from an incident before she was sent to prison.

Bergen would never get the chance to defend herself from those allegations. As soon as she got home to Dent County, she posted pictures on Facebook of her with her two children. They were smiling. I sent her a message, telling her I hoped to visit in a few days.

"That would be nice," she wrote. "I'll keep you posted."

Eight days later she was dead, at the age of thirty-two, unable to escape the grips of her addiction. There was irony in Bergen's funeral. It was held at Wilson Mortuary on Missouri Highway 32, directly across the street from the Walmart where Bergen's shoplifting landed her in Dent County jail for a year.

She never recovered from that year. Blame the drugs, blame her own bad decisions, or blame the criminal justice system, it is all part of the milieu that ended her life too young. "You are more than your addiction," read a friend of Bergen's at her funeral, from a poem the friend wrote. "You are more than your shame."

I'm not sure the same can be said about the state of America's criminal justice system. Its shame is apparent in the disrupted lives, and the deaths, of those the system works overtime to bury in poverty, in the name of justice.

More than any other issue I've written about in my career, the abuse of poor people by the judicial system so that municipal and county governments—and some private companies—can profit has drawn massive, bipartisan support from lawmakers and readers who otherwise might not care about the politics of criminal justice reform. The tweaks, or baby steps, are moving the country in a better direction, albeit more slowly than any of the advocates for change desire, and not fast enough to save the lives of those drowning in its wake.

There was a Catholic priest who throughout 2018 and 2019 would write me emails every time I wrote about a new county that was keeping a poor person in jail because they couldn't afford to pay their board bill. He would ask me for the names of the local judge and prosecutor and the county commissioners, and then he would email each explaining that he planned to avoid traveling in their counties. Even if the priest didn't understand the intricacies of the legal system, he did understand the realities that face people living in poverty every day, and he wouldn't stand for it.

The priest gave me hope. Perhaps, one day, enough citizens will join hands to give the reformers the political power they need to implement the sorts of reforms that will strike a match to the current wealth-based realities of the American judicial system, burn it down, and in its place rebuild a fairer and more truthful version of justice for all.

10

THE KOCH BROTHERS MEET THE ACLU

Jeremy Cady and I met on the plush green grass in front of the Missouri Capitol. It was the spring of 2009, and a group of capitol staffers, reporters, and even the occasional elected official would kick a soccer ball around on a rectangular section of lawn that more often than not went unused except for during the occasional political gathering. Thomas Jefferson cast a shadow as we played. The thirteen-foot bronze statue of the nation's third president, sculpted in 1926 by artist James Earle Fraser, stands guard before the capitol in Jefferson's namesake city.[1]

We'd set a few orange cones out to mark boundaries and goals, with the sidewalk nearest the Capitol's grand stairway serving as out of bounds. In the shadow of the 437-foot-long building, with its exterior made of limestone from Carthage, Missouri, and its 134 Roman-style columns, it was as though we were playing in a glorious one-sided coliseum, built just for us atop a bluff overlooking the Missouri River.[2] Once a week or so, we'd play three-on-three, or four-on-four, depending on how many would show up. Cady and I generally guarded each other because we were both big, slow, and, well, generally lacking in superior soccer skill.

Cady was a Republican staff member in the house. I was a capital correspondent for the *Post-Dispatch*, having come to the state's largest newspaper after a stint as editorial page editor of the *Springfield News-Leader* in southwest Missouri. Like many people who worked in

Jefferson City, I lived in Columbia, home to the University of Missouri, and made the half-hour drive to the capitol each day.

The soccer games were a blast until sometime later that year, when the speaker of the house, or one of his underlings, ran us off the public grounds. This was a space normally reserved for more dignified events, such as inaugurations or political rallies, like the day Republican vice-presidential candidate Sarah Palin packed the capitol grounds with thousands of onlookers. That was the day before Barack Obama was elected president.[3] Cady would eventually leave state government and go to work for Americans for Prosperity, a libertarian political organization funded by the Koch Brothers.[4]

Charles and David Koch inherited their father's Wichita, Kansas–based chemical and energy company, Koch Industries, and turned it into a behemoth worth hundreds of billions of dollars.[5] The two men, lifelong libertarians, committed billions of dollars into a vast network of political action committees that in the past couple of decades has moved the American political landscape, and particularly the Republican Party, to the right.[6] The largest and most powerful of these organizations is Americans for Prosperity, which has become best known for its sustained attacks on public-sector labor unions and its successful blocking of climate change legislation.[7]

Nine years removed from those soccer games on the capitol lawn, in December 2018, Cady emailed me and asked if I'd be interested in speaking about the debtors' prison columns I was writing at an Americans for Prosperity event in St. Charles County.[8] In the traditional context of the political spectrum, this would have been seen by some as akin to inviting Democrat Hillary Clinton to keynote a Lincoln Days GOP dinner in rural Missouri. To say the least, we were strange bedfellows. Until that point in my career, any of my writing on the Koch Brothers or Americans for Prosperity was hardly positive.

Here's how I described Cady's invitation in a sarcastic email I wrote later to a former Republican lawmaker:

"Tonight I'm giving a talk at an Americans for Prosperity meeting," I wrote to former representative Matt Bartle, an attorney in Kansas

City. "Yes, the *Post-Dispatch* pinko-commie columnist hanging out with Koch Brothers–funded conservatives. And tomorrow one of the AFP guys is speaking at a panel in St. Louis sponsored by Empower Missouri, a generally pretty liberal group. Criminal justice reform has found its sweet spot!"

For the record, I'm not a pinko-commie, though I've been accused of worse.

But in Missouri, long before President Trump referred to the press as the "enemy of the people," or CNN as "fake news,"[9] Republicans had a catchy but derisive name for my employer: the Post-Disgrace, a clever shorthand to patronize the paper as too liberal, mostly due to the reputation of the editorial page, which I once led. Like many cities, St. Louis was long a two-daily-newspaper town. The *Globe-Democrat* was more conservative. The *Post-Dispatch* more liberal. Reporters for the two newspapers would battle for scoops while the editorial pages would take pot shots from their respective office spaces, which were, for a time anyway, across the street from each other. The *Globe-Democrat* closed in 1986.[10] To this day, the sorts of folks who refer to my employer as the Post-Disgrace lament its passing.

The *Post-Dispatch* editorial page is guided by ideas first set out by the newspaper's founder, Joseph Pulitzer.[11] The scion of one of the nation's most heralded newspaper families spoke the words that would become the newspaper's platform on April 10, 2007. The words are printed each day on the editorial page of the *Post-Dispatch*:

"I know that my retirement will make no difference in its cardinal principles, that it will always fight for progress and reform, never tolerate injustice or corruption, always fight demagogues of all parties, never belong to any party, always oppose privileged classes and public plunderers, never lack sympathy with the poor, always remain devoted to the public welfare, never be satisfied with merely printing news, always be drastically independent, never be afraid to attack wrong, whether by predatory plutocracy or by predatory poverty."[12]

These words still serve as my writing guidepost, particularly the encouragement to "never lack sympathy with the poor," and to "never be afraid to attack wrong, whether by predatory plutocracy or by predatory poverty."

I was writing to Bartle with a purpose. Around the same time I was invited to speak to the AFP group, Missouri governor Mike Parson, a Republican, had proposed closing a state prison.[13] It was a move contemplated by several governors in the past as Missouri struggled to deal with its ever-increasing corrections budget, in a state prison system that at the time had a population of more than 32,000 inmates.[14]

Several years earlier, in 2010, Bartle had unsuccessfully made the same proposal.

It was after the Great Recession, and Missouri, like most states, saw its revenues plummet.[15] By 2010, without federal aid to come from the American Recovery and Reinvestment Act, Missouri faced a $1 billion shortfall.[16] To respond to the shortfall, the senate's leader at the time, Republican Charlie Shields, had a unique idea. He called it Reboot Missouri. Shields shut down regular senate business for a day so that lawmakers, lobbyists, and citizens could do something that rarely happens under Missouri's capitol dome: talk to each other.[17]

Perhaps freed by the fact that he was in his last term as leader of the senate, soon to be forced out because of Missouri's legislative term limits, Shields briefly created an atmosphere of thoughtfulness and bipartisan cooperation.

All too often, legislative hearings are staged affairs, with bills sent to friendly committees, where chairmen guide them to a predetermined solution, with votes meant to put opponents on the record before upcoming primaries. This was different. It was a breath of fresh air. Leaders worked together on a common goal as Missouri faced down economic disaster. Shields appointed a bunch of senators to hold brainstorming sessions in different parts of the senate.[18] There were no Robert's Rules of Order; no grand speeches. This was a good old-fashioned talking-and-listening session, seeking real solutions amid the enveloping turmoil. This was the Missouri described by Willard Duncan Vandiver, a

U.S. congressman from the state at the turn of the twentieth century. It is Vandiver who is widely credited with coming up with the "show-me" phrase that would become Missouri's motto.[19]

"I come from a state that raises corn and cotton and cockleburs and Democrats, and frothy eloquence neither convinces nor satisfies me," Vandiver said during a naval banquet in 1899. "I am from Missouri. You have got to show me."[20]

Bartle, a thin, bespectacled attorney, is a conservative in the William F. Buckley mode, which is to say he's intellectual about his limited-government beliefs, as compared to the neoconservatism of the Trump era, which is whatever the twice-impeached former president said it was on a given day.[21]

Bartle rolled up his sleeves, took his jacket off, and scribbled notes on an oversized pad of paper on an easel.[22] Sitting in the first-floor senate conference room that day were supreme court justices, lobbyists, public defenders, prosecutors, and senators of both parties. They talked about rising costs and the inability for the state to afford to continue to put more people in prison.

Missouri's incarceration rate of 859 people per 100,000 of total population had been steadily climbing since the late 1970s, making it the tenth highest such rate in the nation.[23] The corrections budget had shown a similar rise: Between 2001 and 2008, for instance, the corrections budget rose 65 percent, eating up an increasing percentage of the state's budget.[24] If the Missouri budget were a pie, the piece dedicated to the state's prisons was getting larger year after year, while the piece for the state's colleges and universities, for instance, was turned into a sliver of its former self.

In this atmosphere, Bartle whipped through pages of notes made with an oversized Sharpie and came to a simple conclusion: Missouri was putting too many people in jail. There was no way to fix the state's budget problems without closing a prison.

"We got swept up in it," Bartle told me, reminiscing. "One thing was clear—we were all agreed it was time to rethink criminal justice and incarceration. Both the right and the left thought so."

One of the people in that brainstorming session was Missouri Supreme Court justice William Ray Price, who, like Bartle, is a conservative Republican. That year, in his address to the legislature, Price made the conservative case for criminal justice reform:

"I could quote different statistics and relationships to you all morning, but the simple fact is, we are spending unbelievable sums of money to incarcerate nonviolent offenders, and our prison population of new offenders is going up, not down—with a recidivism rate that guarantees this cycle will continue to worsen at a faster and faster pace, eating tens of millions of dollars in the process," Price said. "Missouri cannot afford to spend this much money without getting results."[25]

Price's colleague Judge Michael Wolff was also in the room. Wolff, a Democrat, had long been pushing the legislature to reduce the state's prison population, particularly in his role as head of the Missouri Sentencing Advisory Commission, which sought to give judges avenues for punishment of nonviolent offenders other than sending them to prison.[26] Wolff, in fact, made the point that the state's corrections system included a perverse incentive to increase costs in a concurring Missouri Supreme Court opinion issued that year. That's because the state reimburses counties for detainees—including for pretrial detention—as long as they are found guilty of an offense and sentenced to state prison, as compared to county jail, which is generally much less expensive for taxpayers.

"The incentive, of course, is for local prosecutors to urge judges to send offenders to state prisons at a far greater cost than the cost of punishing those who otherwise could be punished through greater use of county jail facilities," Wolff wrote. "This shows that sometimes not paying for something ends up costing more."[27] Despite the leadership and support of a bipartisan group of lawmakers and judges, including key members of the majority Republican Party, there would be no prison closed that year.

"We did not do a very good job of moving the best ideas out of the room into law," Bartle remembers. "but it was a reminder to me that people can get excited and innovative when they are asked to take off their normal hat and join a team if even for a couple of hours."

In the decade to follow, before Parson proposed closing a prison, the corrections budget continued to climb. The jail and prison populations went up, not down.[28] Missouri was hardly alone in this phenomenon, as prison populations soared across the country. Among women, the rate of incarceration nationally was increasing twice as quickly as the rate for men between 1980 and 2017. During that time, Oklahoma had the highest rate of incarceration among women, at 157 per 100,000 of population.[29] The other states with the highest incarceration rate for women during that time were Arizona, Kentucky, South Dakota, Idaho, and Missouri. Altogether, the U.S. remains the country with the highest known rate of incarceration in the world. Like Bartle, lawmakers in various states and the federal government, post–Great Recession, realized that they couldn't keep allowing corrections budgets to increase unchecked year after year. A slight decrease in prison population began.

In 2011, the combined state and federal prison population in the U.S. dropped just below 1.6 million.[30] That figure does not include the population of city and county jails. In 2017, the combined prison population dropped below 1.5 million.[31] In 2018, the country's incarceration rate dropped to its lowest rate since 1996, with 431 incarcerated people per 100,000 total population.[32] When you take into account city and county jails, the U.S. incarceration rate in 2018 was 698 per 100,000 population.[33] Cracks were finally showing in the tough-on-crime narrative that had been the fiat mantra of American criminal justice policy for decades.

It was in this context that in 2019 Parson signed a bill to close a prison.[34] He was following a national trend. In New York,[35] California,[36] Arizona,[37] and Mississippi,[38] governors of both parties were planning to close at least one prison, in part because rising costs were simply unaffordable in cash-strapped state budgets.

In 2019, New York governor Andrew Cuomo, a Democrat, closed two prisons. "Not needing prisons is a good thing by the way," Cuomo told reporters in 2019. "Not locking up people in jail cells is a good thing. Alternatives to incarcerations is a good thing."[39] In 2020, he sought legislative authority to close more.[40]

Closing prisons attracts strange bedfellows: from the left, the American Civil Liberties Union, and from the right, Americans for Prosperity.

President Trump's first campaign ad going into the 2020 election ran on February 2, 2020, during the Super Bowl. "I'm free to start over. This is the greatest day of my life," says Alice Marie Johnson during the segment.[41] The sixty-three-year-old Memphis grandmother had been convicted of attempting to possess cocaine in 1996.[42] She had served twenty-one years of a life sentence she had received for a nonviolent drug conviction.

"My heart is just bursting with gratitude. I want to thank the president, Donald John Trump," Johnson said in the Super Bowl ad.[43]

Trump used the commutation to help establish his criminal justice reform bona fides, having already signed in late 2018 the FIRST STEP Act, which allows federal judges more leeway to avoid harsh mandatory sentencing guidelines in nonviolent drug cases, and also led to the release of about 3,000 federal detainees who were in a situation similar to Johnson's.[44] The bill passed the Senate 87–12, with every Democrat and a clear majority of Republicans voting for it. Among the key organizations making sure the legislation had support from Republicans were a Texas-based conservative campaign called Right on Crime, and Americans for Prosperity.

"Beyond the fiscal implications, criminal justice reform resonates with people of faith," read a letter sent to President Trump by Right on Crime and signed by a group of nationally known conservatives, such as antitax activist Grover Norquist and former congressman Jim DeMint. "As you know from your recent meeting with urban pastors, prison and justice reforms have taken on a deeper meaning for those who believe in second chances and redemption. The FIRST STEP Act supports these concepts by encouraging those who have made mistakes to use their time in prison to reform themselves. Ninety-five percent of all federal inmates will eventually return home. When they do, we want them to be better versions of themselves."[45]

The first thing I saw when I walked into the Americans for Prosperity meeting were the red Make America Great Again hats that had become synonymous with support for President Trump. The hats had become the new Confederate flag. Some saw them as a unifying sign connecting Republicans to their heritage, or their new leader. Others felt the ubiquitous red hats represented the rise of white supremacy in the Trump era, a clear sign of division.[46]

Count me among the others. Just seeing the hat creates a physiological reaction, an involuntary pang of disgust. But here I was, a guest in a sea of red MAGA hats. I swallowed my pride. As I poured myself a cup of coffee in a side room, the whispers about the topic of the day grew louder: Donald Trump vs. Nancy Pelosi.

Earlier that day, President Trump had canceled the Speaker of the House's planned secret trip to visit American troops in Afghanistan. The gambit was political payback for Pelosi's suggestion to the president that he delay the State of the Union speech amid the ongoing federal shutdown in which hundreds of thousands of federal workers were wondering when they'd receive their next paycheck as Congress and the president debated the budget and debt ceiling.[47]

To this St. Charles County crowd, Pelosi was a four-letter word to be uttered with disdain. I shook some hands and sat in the corner awaiting my introduction as the group's speaker that night.

Sitting in the front row with his wife, Eva, was a newly elected Republican state representative named Tony Lovasco. From O'Fallon originally, Lovasco had grown up in St. Charles County.[48] It's a Republican hotbed, the most populous suburban county in St. Louis, just west of the Missouri River from St. Louis County.[49]

More than any other place in Missouri, St. Charles County straddles the rural-urban divide that so often defines political disputes in the state. The county continues to be the fastest growing in the St. Louis region, with its gains—up to nearly 400,000 in population—coming at the expense of St. Louis City, down to just more than 300,000.[50]

St. Charles County had become the ending place for those traveling the White Flight Trail.[51]

The St. Louis region has a long history of racial segregation in housing, going back to 1916, when the city became the first in the country to pass an ordinance actually requiring such segregation, limiting housing purchases in neighborhoods that were 75 percent or more occupied by one race. The measure was deemed unconstitutional a year later, but that didn't stop decades of redlining and white flight, first from the city to newly formed municipalities with protective covenants in St. Louis County, and then from the county across the river into St. Charles County.[52]

A mix of rich soil fed by seasonal floods makes the bottomland soybean and corn farms in St. Charles some of the most productive by yield in the country.[53] Farther away from the river, however, former farmlands are being turned into suburban housing tracts, with some, such as the new urbanist development called New Town, trying to mimic life in the city.[54]

This is a county where gun ownership is high and taxes are low.[55] More than 60 percent of its voters cast a ballot for Trump in 2016.[56] When it comes to the debtors' prison issue that I was at the Americans For Prosperity group to talk about, however, St. Charles County leans more urban than rural. If you spend time in the county jail there, you might receive a board bill for your time behind bars, like nearly every other rural county in Missouri.[57] But unlike most, St. Charles County takes a person's ability to pay into consideration.

"Our general rule of thumb is if the person is indigent—which is about 80 percent of our defendants—we don't try to collect it," says St. Charles County prosecuting attorney Tim Lohmar, a Republican.[58]

That number of poor defendants—80 percent—is not unusual. Various studies have shown that is the percentage of people charged with crimes in the U.S. that qualify for a public defender, a fair definition of living in some stage of poverty.[59]

But few counties in Missouri take ability to pay into account when charging board bills or other court costs or fees.[60] That should offend the sensibilities of conservatives, Lovasco told me that night. He'd get a chance to test that theory.

In the upcoming legislative session, Lovasco would find himself on the House Special Committee on Criminal Justice chaired by Dogan. That committee would hear, and pass, DeGroot's bill that made it illegal to put people in jail who couldn't afford to pay for court fines and fees, including board bills.[61]

Here's the truth about Lovasco and his fellow MAGA-hat-wearing conservatives that night: They got it. They understood and cared about the injustice of their fellow Missourians being jailed again simply because they couldn't afford the bill they received for previous time spent in jail. They helped answer a question that had been bugging me ever since I started writing my series of columns on the new American debtors' prisons. Why was it that conservatives were joining liberals in advocating for criminal justice reform, particularly related to how the judicial system was being used to criminalize poverty? Early on, as I wrote about rural Missourians who were caught in this never-ending cycle of abuse, I'd receive letters that began with some version of this:

"I normally disagree with your columns, but . . ." They were invariably from readers on the right side of the political aisle.

Some folks saw a form of double jeopardy, people being punished twice for the same, minor crimes. Others recognized it as a backdoor tax. Some saw the tyranny of big government. Still others, like the Catholic priest who wrote me several times asking for the names of county commissioners in the various places I wrote about, saw it as a matter of faith that punishing people because they're poor wasn't a very godly thing to do.

Amid the most divided political landscape of my life, I had stumbled upon a unifying issue.

"Criminal justice reform is not a right and left issue, but a right and wrong issue," Cady said.[62]

Indeed, in 2019, Americans For Prosperity would join hands with the American Civil Liberties Union and Empower Missouri, a nonpartisan, but left-leaning, organization that lobbied the legislature on anti-poverty measures, to hold a series of public meetings pushing criminal justice reform issues. They worked together to put on panel discussions in four Missouri cities featuring Matthew Charles, the first person released from federal prison under the FIRST STEP Act.[63] Charles had served more than two decades in prison for a nonviolent drug offense, then was released for two years on parole, and sent back to federal prison because a court determined his release was premature.[64]

I met Marc Levin in September 2019 at John Jay College in New York. We were both panelists at a two-day symposium for journalists called Cash Register Justice.[65] The name synthesizes the problem that had become the focus of my work as a journalist and Levin's work as a conservative advocate and author.

Think back to Cory Booth's description of robbing Peter to pay Paul, of using his "Judge Kanoy" money for medicine for his kids. Booth takes care of the family's children while his wife works at a local hotel making not much more than minimum wage. They've made the decision a lot of folks in rural Missouri make: it's cheaper to have one parent not work than it is to pay for childcare. In Missouri, the average cost of childcare for one school-age child tops $7,000 a year.[66] The cost for an infant is more than $10,000. That's nearly 50 percent of a person's income if they made $8.60 an hour (Missouri's minimum wage in 2020) and worked forty hours a week, for one child, let alone four.

Booth had worked previously as a corrections officer, but in Missouri, corrections officers are the lowest paid in the country. So he stayed home and took care of the children while his wife worked. The per capita income in Caldwell County is just more than $24,000 a year.[67] After rent, gas, utility bills, car repairs, medical bills, and food, there isn't much left for the monthly payment to the courts. This is one reason why conservatives like Levin have become so active in the national push to reduce court fines and fees. These backdoor taxes make it harder for people living in impoverished conditions to make ends meet, to do anything other than live paycheck to paycheck.

When I met him, Levin was the vice president of criminal justice policy at the Texas Public Policy Foundation, a right-leaning think tank that founded the Right on Crime movement. He's a former staff attorney for the Texas Supreme Court.[68]

Levin was on the day's first panel, along with Lisa Foster, from the Fines and Fees Justice Center, and Samuel Brooke, the deputy legal director of the Southern Poverty Law Center.[69]

"Court costs and fees are the tail that wags the dog," Brooke said that day.[70] He works for an organization seen by most as representing the left side of the political spectrum. But on this issue, he and Levin are simpatico.

If the courts are used as a debt-collection service, and that drives law enforcement decisions, then it bastardizes the entire purpose of the judicial branch of government and puts public safety at risk, Levin says.

He speaks in a language understood by conservatives about the tyranny of government and the deprivation of liberty by courts that don't take into consideration the civil rights protections for the people who come before judges but can't afford to pay the costs heaped upon them.

If cops and courts are being used to raise money by collecting fines and fees, Levin says, "[t]hey actually solve fewer crimes."[71]

I sat in the audience during the first panel discussion before my appearance at Cash Register Justice later that morning, and as Levin talked I thought back to the red MAGA hats in the St. Charles County meeting where I spoke. Take any issue today, and it's difficult to get people to listen to an opposing viewpoint if the messenger is wearing the hat, or flying the flag, that represents a political opponent.

"I think it is important to both utilize coalitions across ideological lines, such as Free to Drive and the Texas Smart on Crime Coalition, but also continue to have both conservative and liberal groups each speak to their own constituencies, both within the public and among policymakers," Levin would tell me later. "Cognition research has demonstrated that people are most apt to respond favorably to trusted messengers, so advocates on both sides of the spectrum should continue working together while also appealing to their audiences with the strongest respective arguments."

Indeed, while it is refreshing that Americans for Prosperity and the ACLU would appear at a conference together singing from the same hymnal, in the end, for there to be progress on the issue, each "side," so to speak, will have to go back and preach to their home church to rally the faithful behind the cause. It's a little bit like how the late evangelist Billy Graham used to conduct his crusades.

Before Graham would arrive in towns where he would fill stadiums with tens of thousands for several nights in a row, he would send pastors and educators from his organization to those cities. There, they would meet with religious leaders, and train them to be near the stage during the altar call at the end of his preaching.[72]

When Graham asked thousands of folks to accept Jesus Christ as their savior, an act evangelical Christians refer to as salvation, he knew that they weren't all raised with his Southern Baptist roots. They were Catholics and Methodists, Presbyterians and Lutherans, people raised in different faith traditions who all speak of salvation and baptism in different terminology.[73]

In the summer of 1987, Graham came to Denver's Mile High Stadium to preach for ten days. Mile High Stadium was my cathedral, home of the Denver Broncos, my favorite NFL football team.[74] In my family, it is said we are born with blue-and-orange blood, but for a bit more than a week, this football cathedral was Graham's church. I was there on one particular night, mostly to take in the spectacle. I was born and raised Catholic, and one of my favorite Catholic priests, Father Ken Leone, had been one of the religious leaders who helped Graham's new converts understand his message in their religious native tongue. Graham's goal wasn't to recruit new Baptists but to spread the Gospel and send people whose faith had been rekindled back to their home churches, or in search of new ones.

It's the sort of unifying strategy that seems almost quaint three decades later during a political time in which people are defined by which cable television show they watch or the color of their political hat. But this is the time we live in, and so if progress is to be made in the realm of cutting the profit motive out of the criminal justice system, then the messengers must be trusted by those receiving the message on the left, the right, and everywhere in between.[75]

I'm embarrassed by a conscious decision I made while writing my debtors' prison series of columns in Missouri. That's one of the things I told the Cash Register Justice forum, on the panel where I spoke following Levin and Foster and Brooke.

My early subjects from rural Missouri—Victoria Branson, Brooke Bergen, Amy Murr, Cory Booth—all share a characteristic. They're white. Part of that is just circumstance. Rural Missouri is the very definition of whiteness. Caldwell County is 96 percent white;[76] Dent County is 95 percent;[77] St. Francois County is 93 percent.[78]

The majority of the defendants being abused by the judicial system as a source of profit in rural Missouri are white.[79] That's not the case in urban areas across the country—in Tulsa, in Milwaukee, in Columbia, South Carolina, and even in the rural South—where fines and fees and driver's license suspensions overwhelmingly affect communities of color in higher numbers.[80] It's not the case in New Mexico, Nevada, or Colorado and California, where many of the victims of fines-and-fees schemes are Hispanic.

But in Missouri, if I wanted to get the attention of the legislature, which is populated and run by a supermajority of white Republicans, then the characters of my column had to look like their voters. So even when I came across stories of Black Missourians abused by the same system, I sat on them for a while—focusing on the white faces early on.

There was Precious Jones, a Black woman from north St. Louis who got a speeding ticket in rural Lafayette County and ended up doing twenty days in jail and serving two years under the supervision of a private probation company. Jones asked to do her jail time in a local jail so she didn't have to get a ride across the state—her license had been suspended because of the ticket—but the judge said no.[81] The jail in the city of St. Louis does not charge pay-to-stay fees. If Jones spent her time in the St. Louis jail, Lafayette County would be unable to collect money for her time behind bars.

Then there was Clifton Harris, a forty-three-year-old Black man with mental illness issues who spent three months in the same Lafayette County Jail on a misdemeanor charge because he couldn't afford to make bail. He pleaded guilty to time served to get out of jail—a common practice in Missouri—and then was called before Associate Circuit Court Judge Kelly Rose month after month to collect his $2,000 board bill. Harris's mother, who lives on federal disability income and takes care of her son, was doing her best to pay the bill.[82] When Harris missed a hearing in 2016, Rose put him back in jail. Harris and Jones had compelling stories, but I pushed them aside, for a while, until there was widespread support building for upending Missouri's pay-to-stay jail scheme.

In reality, what was happening in rural Missouri was an extension of what had been happening in north St. Louis County, in Ferguson and surrounding municipalities, where the victims were primarily Black.

"The primary difference between the poor people who have been 'terrorized' in Edmundson or Jennings or Ferguson, compared with those in Salem and Hamilton and Farmington, is the color of their skin," I wrote in the *Post-Dispatch* in December 2019. "Black in the city. White in rural Missouri."[83]

In October 2016, at the height of the presidential race between Trump and Clinton, the NBC comedy show *Saturday Night Live* produced a skit that in some ways puts the racial politics of poverty in its proper context.

The skit starts out predictably. It's an episode of "Black Jeopardy!" with African American comedian Kenan Thompson portraying the host,

Darnell Hayes.[84] In this episode, there are two Black female contestants, Keeley (played by Sasheer Zamata) and Shanice (played by comedian Leslie Jones), and one white contestant, played by actor Tom Hanks. He's a MAGA-hat-wearing, Trump-loving, rural American named Doug.

As the show begins, it's easy to see where this is headed: it's time to make fun of Trump's "deplorables," the redneck, racist extremists who wave Confederate flags at his rallies and cheer when he demeans immigrants. But that's not what happens.

The first question Doug answers is in the category "They Out Here Saying." Given a clue of "They out here saying: The new iPhone wants your thumbprint 'for your protection,'" Doug nails the answer.

"What is: I don't think so, that's how they get you," he says.

A surprised Hayes, the host, exclaims: "Yes, yes, that's it!" Keeley and Shanice nod along.[85]

It turns out white and Black Americans share a distrust of government. Go figure.

In answer after answer, in a skit that typically highlights differences between whites and Blacks, Doug turns out to be more like his new friends Keeley and Shanice than anybody expected.

"I'll take 'Big Girls' for $200," Doug says.

The clue: "Skinny women can do this for you."

Doug is quick with his answer: "Not a damn thing."

"You're damn right," Hayes says, practically hyperventilating over his enthusiastic agreement with the white man in the MAGA hat.[86]

The episode takes a turn back to a more predictable tone when the final *Jeopardy!* category is announced: Lives That Matter.

"Well, it was good while it lasted," Hayes says. "When we come back, we'll play the national anthem and just see what happens."[87]

It was the sort of instant classic *Saturday Night Live* that cut right through the current events of the day with a smart and lasting take: despite the division of our times, for poor people at least, there is an underlying connection between Black and white, particularly when it comes to their distrust of a government that all too often tramples on their rights.

There is not much difference between being poor and Black and stuck in jail in Ferguson because of unpaid traffic tickets and being poor and white and in jail in Salem because of unpaid court costs and fines that emanated from the theft of an $8 tube of mascara. The consequences for both are deadly. This is not to say that white and Black Americans experience the criminal justice system equally. Rather, once anyone finds themselves locked in the cycle I've explored throughout this book, the tragedy remains uniformly unjust.

"For far too long, America's poor have been criminalized by intersecting systems that impact low-income individuals at all levels," wrote Peter Edelman, a Georgetown law professor, in April 2020, for a paper published by the *Duke Law Journal*.[88] Edelman is the author of two books on poverty in America.[89] "The punishing fines and fees that often result from a low-income individual's interaction with these systems have exacerbated the cycle of poverty."

If America wants to ever win the so-called War on Poverty, then the criminal justice system must be the front lines, with an ever-increasing focus by those in charge of it to protect the civil rights of the people too often abused by a system more focused on tax collection than keeping local communities safe. Every judge, every prosecutor, every public defender in the country must ask themselves before they make a decision in the sorts of misdemeanor and traffic cases they rush through every day on crowded dockets:

Can this person afford to pay the fines and fees the statutes call for in this case?

Will jailing this person make my community safer?

What must be done to make sure every defendant in this courtroom has their civil rights defended in the same way, regardless of if they are Black, white, or brown, or have money, or don't?

Fixing this system of injustice that abuses people living in poverty will take more than lawsuits and legislation, says Alec Karakatsanis. "It's about political power," he says, on both the left and the right, which, in some ways, have found bipartisan agreement that the criminal justice system is in need of serious reform. For serious change to occur,

Karakatsanis says, that newfound political power "must demand that the system stop extracting wealth from poor people."

The solutions that are making their way through both the courts and state capitols all have some form of bipartisan support:

- Get rid of cash bail.
- Stop using court fines and fees as a primary revenue source for local or state governments.
- Don't put people back in jail if they can't afford a bill for their previous stay in jail, and, better yet, don't charge poor people for their time behind bars.
- Stop suspending driver's licenses simply because somebody has fallen behind on court costs.
- Limit the amount of revenue cities and counties can collect from driving tickets or court fines and fees. Taking this concept a step further, Pennsylvania Treasurer Joe Torsella in early 2021 wrote the nation's credit-rating agencies and asked them to take into consideration a city's reliance on fines and fees for revenue when considering municipal bond ratings.

None of these ideas are radical, and each have been adopted or supported in some capacity by lawmakers in both Democratic-and Republican-leaning states. But to fully implement them, they must go national, and lawmakers are going to have to deal with the consequences of not relying on the revenue sources they have depended upon to the detriment of their constituents who live in a state of poverty.

America's judicial branch, and the legislative branch that funds it, must reach back to the constitution that created our system of government, and the system of English law upon which our courts are built, and get back to the basics, or, if necessary, redefine the system so that it protects those most unalienable of rights.

There can be no sale of justice in a free America. Until the country elevates that value, Lady Justice isn't blind, and her scales are completely out of balance.

11

·················

A TALE OF TWO LETTERS

Lashawn Casey helped me realize that for Americans to demand change in the criminal justice system, they would have to care about the people stuck in county jails.

I introduced Casey in Chapter Five, but I want to tell a bit more of her story, because it helps explain what the future could look like in a criminal justice system that doesn't prey on poor people just because it can. Casey wrote me two letters from jail, one as I started writing on the crisis and one after the Missouri Supreme Court made the law a little bit more just. The stark difference of how she described what was happening in one county jail tells an important story.

Rolla, Missouri
November 2018

Casey was on the run when I met her. She had an outstanding warrant for drug possession. It was early November 2018. We were meeting to talk about the use of the courts to keep people living in poverty.

Casey's eyes darted to and fro under the incognito protection of her pink hoodie. It was a brisk fall day, the sun's glare dulled by gray Midwest cloudiness. We met on a quiet street outside a pizza joint in

Rolla, the same college town just north of her home in Salem, Missouri, where I first met Brooke Bergen.

A few months earlier, Casey had written me a letter about conditions in the Dent County Jail. She was forty-three at the time, divorced, the mother of two grown children.

Casey had been in jail with Bergen, Leann Banderman, and Amy Murr. They were all single mothers who had become caught up in the region's epic drug culture. Casey was a veteran of the jail—she had done a stint in prison for drug possession also.

Casey had spent plenty of time in jail. She knew she belonged there at times. She owned her decisions. In another life, she would have been an entrepreneur or a CEO. She's smart and savvy. She's a good writer with a caring heart. And she's self-aware. She recognized something about her cellmates: they didn't belong there.

The truth is that most of the women who had been crowded into the cell with her were out of place. They were there because they couldn't afford bail, because one week turned into thirty days, and then came a $1,500 jail board bill that could never be paid down.

This is the criminal justice system in America, Casey told me in her letter, where people of little means have almost no chance to escape, even after paying for their sins.

"I am a life-long resident of Dent County and have been following your articles on judicial misconduct in this and other rural counties. This issue has affected my life on every level. Thank you for standing up for people who can't defend themselves," Casey wrote me. Then she described the specifics of the scheme that creates two versions of justice in rural counties all over America. If you have money, you walk out of the jailhouse doors on day one and await your day in court. If you don't, you're stuck behind bars on a bail you can't afford, and then are subject to the for-profit whims of a prison industrial complex seeking to profit off your misery.

"The best of luck battling giants, now and in the future," Casey wrote.[1]

After lunch, Casey took me to meet Janice Bote. Also on the run with a drug charge pending, she was living in an apartment on Rolla's north side, hiding out from the law while she figured out what to do. Both Casey and Bote planned to turn themselves in, but first, they were trying to get their affairs in order.

Bote is a drug addict. She grew up in St. Charles County, just across the Missouri River west of St. Louis. She turned to meth after a battle with thyroid cancer in 2014.

"It helped me cope."

She met Casey in the Dent County Jail, after being arrested for the first time in her life. A drug task force broke down the door at her boyfriend's house. There was meth in the house. She got charged with dealing, something Janice says she's never done.

But her real problems began after she made bail, a couple of weeks after she was arrested. She signed the same pretrial release agreement everybody signs in Dent County, which required her to submit to, and pay for, drug testing by the private probation company.[2]

Of course, she tested dirty. She is an addict, after all.

In Dent County, this became a matter of public record. Before Janice ever had her day in court, the private probation company was posting her failed drug tests on a public court website, for all to see.

Later, I asked St. Louis University law professor Brendan Roediger about this practice. He was indignant.

"There is no time prior to trial where it is appropriate for anyone to just file evidence with the court. The court is not a repository for good or bad information about the client," Roediger said.[3] He compared the uploading of drug test results without a hearing to a defense attorney discovering evidence beneficial to a client and just filing it with the court without a written motion or any proper legal foundation.

Roediger is himself a recovering drug addict. He knows firsthand how public consumption of one's drug history can have consequences.[4]

"I've been in recovery for 19 years and I've seen shame kill a lot of addicts, but I've never seen it keep someone clean."[5]

The Dent County Court stopped posting public drug test results after I wrote about it.

Bote chain-smoked in her small apartment kitchen while we talked. Casey choked back tears thinking about her frail friend ending up back in jail. When they go, they'll likely go together, they said. There's power in pairs.

Months after Casey introduced me to this pervasive American problem, she wrote me another letter.

It was early spring in 2019. The Missouri Supreme Court had issued its unanimous ruling in the Richey and Wright cases that judges could no longer threaten jail time for indigent defendants who couldn't afford to pay their jail bills. The Missouri Legislature was poised to pass a bill that would change the law to say that any court costs owed by indigent defendants could not be used to threaten jail time, that there could only be civil consequences for such a situation.

Things weren't going so well for Casey. While on the run, she had gotten some affairs in order, including trying to help get her daughter out of her own legal jam. She was back in the Dent County Jail, awaiting trial on charges that were likely to send her to prison.

But she wasn't upset when she wrote me.

"You wouldn't believe the changes that have taken place around here," Casey wrote. "What you probably haven't heard is how the atmosphere has changed. The jail is emptying out. People that do come in are able to bond out quickly. None of the girls here are being held for financial reasons. This place isn't the terrifying dungeon it used to feel like. The new judges are actually listening to people's needs instead of sending them straight to prison."[6]

The Dent County Jail was built in 1978 to house up to twenty-one prisoners.[7] In 2018, at one point, it was housing sixty-five people, more than three times its capacity. At the end of April 2019, around the time Casey wrote me, only seventeen people were in the jail.

The Missouri Supreme Court ruling was only part of the reason. The court had also instituted new bail rules designed to bring the use of bail in the state more in line with the constitution. The combination of the two events emptied county jails.[8] It wasn't just Dent County where this was happening. In May, after receiving Casey's letter, I wrote about a few judges in Caldwell, Andrew, and Scott counties who were still holding payment review hearings after the Missouri Supreme Court ruling and threatening defendants with jail time, or in some cases still holding them behind bars.[9] Judge David Andrew Dolan, who presided over the Mississippi and Scott County courts, wasn't happy about it.

"The judges of the 33rd Circuit were surveyed after your article of May 12, 2018," Judge Dolan wrote me. He signs his emails with his initials, DAD, and his tone fits the metaphor. "If you have knowledge of a specific case where jail board hearings are being held or warrants issued please let me know."[10]

So I let the judge know about Tonya Burgess. She was sitting in Scott County's jail that very day, for failing to appear to a payment review hearing on a $1,400 jail bill that stemmed from a three-year-old misdemeanor case.

Burgess was released from jail within twenty-four hours.

For most of the people who had been caught up in Missouri's debtors' prison scheme, the damage to their lives has been done, and carries over to this day. During much of the time I spent writing this book in 2020, many of the people I wrote about were back in county jail, or state prison: George Richey, Brook Bergen, Leann Banderman, and, of course, Lashawn Casey, who caught COVID-19 while in the Chillicothe Correctional Center. She recovered, and was released from prison in October 2020. She is living in St. Louis in an apartment run by a nonprofit called Criminal Justice Ministry. She is sober and working two jobs.

The emptying of Missouri's county jails, at least temporarily, tells a story about criminal justice reform that should help guide the national debate by focusing on how the courts are treating people living in poverty.

Let's go back to Scott County, where Burgess was released after I let the judge know she was still being jailed for failure to pay a jail board bill after the Missouri Supreme Court said it was illegal.

In 2017, Scott County, population 38,500, smack-dab in the middle of one of the poorest congressional districts in the country,[11] took in $143,000 in jail board bill revenue, more than all but 5 of Missouri's 114 counties.[12] Right next door, to the west, is Stoddard County, which is even smaller, with only 29,300 residents.[13] How poor is the Eighth Congressional District in southeast Missouri? It is the poorest in the state, with more than 18 percent of its adults and 24 percent of its children living below the federal poverty line.[14]

How much did Stoddard County raise in jail board revenue in 2017?

Zero. It is one of two rural counties in the state that doesn't charge such bills.[15]

"We have never, ever charged room and board for our inmates," said former Stoddard County presiding commissioner Greg Mathis. He's a funeral director for a living, with his funeral home located directly across the street from the county courthouse. "It's never been brought up."

Mathis knows what some of his rural Missouri colleagues are now figuring out. Putting people in jail just because they're struggling to make ends meet doesn't add up. There is a better way.

"Why would I want to overcrowd our jail with people who would be there just because they couldn't pay their jail bill?" he asked. "It's just a never-ending vicious cycle that targets poor people."

Epilogue

· · · · · · · · · · · · · · · · · · · ·

POVERTY IS RELATIVE

Norman, Oklahoma
August 2020

Kendy Killman gestured to the packed dinner table and asked a question. Well, it wasn't a table, but several mismatched tables pushed together so a gathering of about twenty family members—and me—could crowd into Killman's apartment in Norman for dinner in August of 2020.

Killman and most of her family live at the Vicksburg Village Apartments in Norman, east of downtown. The series of one- and two-story redbrick buildings are subsidized by the U.S. Department of Housing and Urban Development.[1] Killman lives there with her boyfriend, Steven, who does maintenance on the properties. Her mom lives there, and several of her children and grandchildren, spread out over several buildings. They gather on the picnic benches in common green space, or around the charcoal grill outside Killman's building.

She wanted me to meet her family, so here we were at dinner, swapping stories, talking about making it through life when the court system hangs additional debt on you as you decide whether or not to run the window air-conditioning unit on a ninety-degree, humid August day because the local electric cooperative charges extra during the peak usage time.

"How many of you are overdrawn in your checking accounts?" Killman asked.

Her mom's hand went up. So did Steven's and a couple of her children's. Meranda, the oldest, kept her hand down. She's got a good job working for the state government, though with about $100,000 in college debt that allowed her to reach closer to the middle class, she doesn't feel much different from those whose bank accounts often show a negative balance just a few days after payday.

Payday for Killman is when her federal disability check of $543 arrives, the check that she receives to take care of Bubba, who still lives with her. That's what she lives on. When she asked the question about being overdrawn, there was no shame to it. She doesn't lament her lot in life. Sure, she can point to a few moments in history when maybe a different decision might have led to a better result—don't date that guy, don't buy a car from your ex-husband, pay this bill, not that one—but that's the reality of living in poverty for many Americans.

There are no good choices.

We talked about what mealtime was like toward the end of the month when the money dried up. Some of her kids remember eating ramen noodles for days. Others remember peanut butter sandwiches, or Hamburger Helper, spreading the food out as long as the money would allow. As the conversation went on, I briefly thought about the "community rag." That's what some of my kids and I used to call the dish towel we would share during a family meal when I didn't have napkins or a roll of paper towels. It was usually on a Friday night, during the time when I was divorcing from my first wife, their mother. On those nights, usually after I got off work and drove to pick them up and bring them back to my apartment, I'd order a pizza and we'd eat late, passing around our community rag.

One of those meals is most memorable. I was living in Columbia, Missouri, and it was the middle of the summer. Two of my children were visiting after I had driven to Colorado to pick them up. That summer, I had a choice to make. I could get my car payments caught up, or I could save enough money to be able to feed and take care of my children for the summer. I wasn't poor, not like Killman, but poverty is relative. I lived paycheck to paycheck, with child support, rent, and utilities eating up most of what I made at the time working for a small daily newspaper in the middle of America.

As we ate lunch, and passed around the community rag, I heard the "beep, beep, beep" of a large vehicle backing up and I knew what was about to happen.[2] My car was being repossessed. I had pushed off the inevitable for several months, taking out payday loans to extend the time as long as I could. But as my children and I sat in my apartment, I realized that there would be no car for the rest of the summer.

We made do. We walked to the grocery store and the park. I rode my bike to work. Eventually, I saved up enough to buy a $700 beater that would work for a while. The woman who would become my second wife, mother of my two youngest children, and the love of my life, drove me to buy that car, down a country road in the woods. Marla knew I was not very good with money and had my financial struggles, but she married me anyway, and helped me get to better times.

I don't know if my kids remember the day their dad's car got repossessed, but I doubt it. Most of the people I've written about in this book, people who grew up poor, and then were made poorer by a criminal justice system seeking to extract money from them in unconstitutional ways, tell me that they never really thought of themselves as poor.

They just lived in the circumstances that were dealt them, and they made do.

Killman and I are about the same age. We have about the same number of children and grandchildren. We've both survived at times because of the support of the government, and the kindness of strangers, and we live in different financial circumstances today as a combination of the decisions we've made, but also those made by others around us, some of them completely out of our control.

That's one of the key messages I would hope readers of this book come away with. When I first started writing about people in jail or prison, I would regularly get emails from some readers who lacked any empathy for their plight.

They shouldn't have broken the law.

They got what's coming to them.

But over time, many of those same readers began to see through a person's initial mistake—shoplifting, taking drugs, losing one's temper, driving too fast—and see themselves, or the people they know, in my characters' stories. Most of us have somebody in our family who struggles with addiction. We've been pulled over for driving too fast. We received Women, Infants, and Children payments from the state when we had that first child when we were barely making ends meet at our first job.

But what happened next? How did your circumstance, and how the criminal justice system treated you, differ from the people in this book? That's the question I hope many of you ask. Are your civil rights worth more than those of Kendy Killman, Brooke Bergen, and Sasha Darby?

ACKNOWLEDGMENTS

There is no greater honor in journalism than having people at the most vulnerable moments of their lives trust you to tell their stories. That has been my journey for the past few years as I worked first on a series of columns for the *St. Louis Post-Dispatch* that exposed the criminalization of poverty in rural Missouri counties, and then pursued the national version of that story for this book.

Brooke Bergen, Kendy Killman, and Sasha Darby didn't have to share their painful journeys in the criminal justice system with me, but they did, and for that I will be forever grateful to them and all the other people abused by this system who agreed to tell me their stories so that others might see the injustice inherent in a judicial process that often serves as a backdoor tax collection system.

This is my first book, and that means I made more mistakes than I care to remember. Along the way, several people offered me crucial guidance and help. *Profit and Punishment* would not exist if not for them. First, my editors at the *Post-Dispatch*, Marcia Koenig and Gilbert Bailon, gave me the room and the support I needed to explore this story before any of us really knew how important it was. They let me traverse the state of Missouri, writing about people in areas where the newspaper has little circulation, because as the columns built upon each other, we became convinced it was important work, and they supported my efforts to pursue a book project.

As I thought about writing this book, and when the idea was in its formative stages, many advocates in the criminal justice reform world encouraged me, namely Blake Strode, Thomas Harvey, and Michael-John Voss, of ArchCity Defenders; Joanne Weiss and Lisa Foster of the Fines and Fees Justice Center; and Lauren-Brooke Eisen of the Brennan Center for Justice. Several friends, including retired Judge Michael Wolff, attorney Mark Pedroli, law professor Brendan Roediger, and publicist Richard Callow, also listened to my deliberations and pushed me over the edge to write the book. My research assistant, Hayley Landman, was an integral part of improving the book's accuracy and making sure readers had a clear-to-follow map of the research.

Author and historian Walter Johnson introduced me to my first agents, Sandra Dijkstra and Elise Capron, who guided me through several revisions of my book proposal and prepared me for the process of trying to get a book contract. While we parted ways, their wisdom made this book better. So did that of my agent, Jim Hornfischer, who believed in the project, saw its potential, and led me to St. Martin's Press.

There, editor Pronoy Sarkar was patient with me. He helped me probe the book's best narrative angles, taught me to breathe, and opened my eyes to new structures that made the complex topic much easier to understand. Pronoy made this book better because he cared about the people on its pages, and he helped me bring them to life in a way that, I hope, makes a difference as this nation tries to fix a broken criminal justice system.

The people who are doing this important work on the streets, the victims of the system, the attorneys fighting for justice in courtrooms, the advocates seeking more just laws, all of them inspired me, as the march for change took place across the country during the process of writing this book. My wish is that some of them feel renewed by the energy of this call to action.

NOTES

PROLOGUE: THE POVERTY PENALTY

1. Tony Messenger, "Judge Tries to Block Access to Debtors' Prison Hearings in Dent County," *St. Louis Post-Dispatch*, November 5, 2018, https://www .stltoday.com/news/local/columns/tony-messenger/messenger-judge -tries-to-block-access-to-debtors-prison-hearings-in-dent-county/article _ec6a9526-e652–5819–88b0-b5e8fd3b28dc.html.
2. Lauren-Brooke Eisen, *Charging Inmates Perpetuates Mass Incarceration* (New York: Brennan Center for Justice at NYU School of Law, 2015), 4, https:// www.brennancenter.org/sites/default/files/2019–08/Report_Charging _Inmates_Mass_Incarceration.pdf.
3. *Fueling an Epidemic* (U.S. Senate Homeland Security & Governmental Affairs Committee 2018), 10, 12, https://www.hsgac.senate.gov/imo /media/doc/REPORT-Fueling%20an%20Epidemic-A%20Flood%20 of%201.6%20Billion%20Doses%20of%20Opioids%20into%20Mis- souri%20and%20the%20Need%20for%20Stronger%20DEA%20Enforce- ment.pdf; Andrew Sheeley, "Dent County Among State's Hardest Hit by Opioids, According to McCaskill Report," *Salem News Online*, July 17, 2018, https://www.thesalemnewsonline.com/news/local_news/article _fa91ffc6–89d4–11e8-a8c3–1faaa1264e18.html.
4. "2010 Census: Center of Population," United States Census Bureau, ac- cessed October 7, 2020, https://www.census.gov/2010census/data/center-of -population.html#:~:text=The%20National%20Mean%20Center%20of,res- idents%20were%20of%20identical%20weight.
5. Alexandra Natapoff, *Punishment Without Crime* (New York: Basic Books, 2018), 2, 125.
6. Peter Edelman, *Not a Crime to Be Poor: The Criminalization of Poverty in America* (New York: The New Press, 2017), 18.

7. Tony Messenger, "St. Francois County Judge Sends Another Grandma to Prison Over Court Costs," *St. Louis Post-Dispatch*, August 22, 2017, https://www.stltoday.com/news/local/columns/tony-messenger/messenger -st-francois-county-judge-sends-another-grandma-to-prison/article _8e7408d5-afec-5e69-bc3a-50fa93706deb.html.

8. "2020 Poverty Guidelines," Office of the Assistant Secretary for Planning and Evaluation, U.S. Department of Health & Human Services, January 21, 2020, https://aspe.hhs.gov/2020-poverty-guidelines.

9. Lauren-Brooke Eisen, "Paying for Your Time: How Charging Inmates Fees Behind Bars May Violate the Excessive Fines Clause," Brennan Center for Justice at NYU School of Law, July 31, 2014, https://www.brennancenter .org/our-work/research-reports/paying-your-time-how-charging-inmates -fees-behind-bars-may-violate.

10. Edelman, *Not a Crime to Be Poor*, 18.

11. Messenger, "St. Francois County Judge Sends Another Grandma to Prison."

12. Unless otherwise noted, all interviews in this book were conducted by the author by phone, email, or in person between January 2019 and October 2020, including: Brooke Bergen, Kendy Killman, Sasha Darby, Lisa Foster, Joanna Weiss, Jill Webb, Matthew Mueller, Michael Barrett, Alec Karakatsanis, Michael-John Voss, Peter Edelman, Bruce DeGroot, Michael Wolff, Loretta Radford, Meagan Taylor, Nusrat Choudhury, Michael Milton, Anna Odegaard, John Lesch, Nancy Pelosi, Jim Roth, Brad Colbert, Lauri Traub, Lashawn Casey, Samuel Brooke, Keilee Fant, Ashley Gantt, Blake Strode, Frank Vatterott, Atteeyah Hollie. Some of the reporting for this book came from the author's work for the *St. Louis Post-Dispatch*. Any quotes or facts taken from that reporting are cited with the original published work.

13. "Team: Leadership," Fines & Fees Justice Center, updated 2018, https:// finesandfeesjusticecenter.org/team/.

14. Peter B. Edelman, "Criminalization of Poverty: Much More to Do," *Duke Law Journal Online* 69 (April 2020): 114, https://dlj.law.duke.edu/2020/04 /criminalizationofpoverty/.

15. Michelle Alexander, *The New Jim Crow: Mass Incarceration in the Age of Color-blindness* (New York: The New Press, 2012), 60.

16. John F. Pfaff, *Locked In: The True Causes of Mass Incarceration and How to Achieve Real Reform* (New York: Basic Books, 2017), 94.

17. "Trends in Rates of Homicide—United States, 1985–1994," *Morbidity and Mortality Weekly Report*, Centers for Disease Control and Prevention, last reviewed May 2, 2001, https://www.cdc.gov/mmwr/preview/mmwrhtml /00042178.htm#00000888.gif.

18. Sheryl Gay Stolberg and Astead W. Herndon, "'Lock the S.O.B.s Up': Joe Biden and the Era of Mass Incarceration," *New York Times*, June 25, 2019, https://www.nytimes.com/2019/06/25/us/joe-biden-crime-laws.html.

19. Alexander, *The New Jim Crow*, 56.

20. Pub. L. 103–322, "Violent Crime Control and Law Enforcement Act of 1994," 42 U.S.C. § 136 (1994).

21. Alexander, *The New Jim Crow*, 57.

22. Alma Carten, "The Racist Roots of Welfare Reform," *New Republic*, August 22, 2016, https://newrepublic.com/article/136200/racist-roots-welfare-reform.

23. Pub. L. 104–193, "Personal Responsibility and Work Opportunity Reconciliation Act," 110 Stat. 2105; 42 U.S.C. § 862(a); Alexander, *The New Jim Crow*, 157–58.

24. David K. Shipler, *The Working Poor* (New York: Vintage Books, 2005), 41–42.

25. Tony Messenger, "Pelosi Suggests a 'Revisit' of '90s Crime Policies; Lamar Johnson Case Offers That Chance," *St. Louis Post-Dispatch*, August 21, 2019, https://www.stltoday.com/news/local/columns/tony-messenger/messenger -pelosi-suggests-a-revisit-of-90s-crime-policies-lamar-johnson-case-offers -that-chance/article_47217076-b904–592d-9c8a-7eabba8e350e.html.

26. Barb Rosewicz, Justin Theal, and Alexandre Fall, "Decade After Recession, Tax Revenue Higher in 45 States," Pew Charitable Trusts, January 9, 2020, https://www.pewtrusts.org/en/research-and-analysis/articles/2020/01/09 /decade-after-recession-tax-revenue-higher-in-45-states.

27. "Fiscal 50: State Trends and Analysis," Pew Charitable Trusts, Pew Center for the States, last updated September 4, 2020, https://www.pewtrusts.org /en/research-and-analysis/data-visualizations/2014/fiscal-50#ind0.

28. Tracy Gordon, "State and Local Budgets and the Great Recession," *Brookings*, December 31, 2012, https://www.brookings.edu/articles/state-and -local-budgets-and-the-great-recession/; Lisa Lambert, "States Seek to Escape Rising Prison Costs," *Reuters*, May 20, 2011, https://jp.reuters.com /article/instant-article/idUSTRE74J3S920110520.

29. "About the Taxpayer Protection Pledge," Americans for Tax Reform, accessed October 10, 2020, https://www.atr.org/about-the-pledge.

30. Bob Dreyfuss, "Grover Norquist: 'Field Marshal' of the Bush Plan," *Nation*, April 26, 2001, https://www.thenation.com/article/archive/grover-norquist -field-marshal-bush-plan/.

31. Paul Waldman, "Nearly All the GOP Candidates Bow Down to Grover Norquist," *Washington Post*, August 13, 2015, https://www.washingtonpost .com/blogs/plum-line/wp/2015/08/13/nearly-all-the-gop-candidates-bow -down-to-grover-norquist/.

32. Corey Jones, "How Much Does Oklahoma Rely on Court Collections to Fund Government? 'We Reach a Point Where We Begin to Criminalize Poverty,'" *Tulsa World*, May 7, 2019, https://tulsaworld.com/news/local /crime-and-courts/how-much-does-oklahoma-rely-on-court-collections -to-fund-government-we-reach-a-point/article_81cb716e-791d-5053 -a6d0–6e22d9a2229a.html.

33. Karin D. Martin, Sandra Susan Smith, and Wendy Still, "Shackled to Debt: Criminal Justice Financial Obligations and the Barriers to Re-Entry They

Create," *New Thinking in Community Corrections*, no. 4 (January 2017): 5, https://www.ncjrs.gov/pdffiles1/nij/249976.pdf.

34. Joseph Cranney, "These SC Judges Can Have Less Training Than Barbers but Still Decide Thousands of Cases Each Year," *Post and Courier*, September 14, 2020, https://www.postandcourier.com/news/these-sc-judges-can-have -less-training-than-barbers-but-still-decide-thousands-of-cases/article _deeac12e-eb6f-11e9–927b-5735a3edbaf1.html.

35. Natapoff, *Punishment Without Crime*, 154; Tony Messenger, "Latest Debtors' Prison Lawsuit Straddles Missouri's Urban-Rural Divide," *St. Louis Post-Dispatch*, December 15, 2018, https://www.stltoday.com/news/local /columns/tony-messenger/messenger-latest-debtors-prison-lawsuit -straddles-missouris-urban-rural-divide/article_c0ea89b0-a271–59ce-95a4 -aaae96e0d535.html.

36. Eisen, *Charging Inmates Perpetuates Mass Incarceration*, 3.

37. Edelman, *Not a Crime to Be Poor*, 30.

38. Eric Schmitt, "'Taxation by Citation' Undermines Trust Between Cops and Citizens," *Wall Street Journal*, August 7, 2015, https://www.wsj.com /articles/taxation-by-citation-undermines-trust-between-cops-and-citizens -1438987412.

39. Tony Messenger, "New Attorney General Joins the Fight Against Debtors Prisons in Missouri," *St. Louis Post-Dispatch*, January 8, 2019, https:// www.stltoday.com/news/local/columns/tony-messenger/messenger-new -attorney-general-joins-the-fight-against-debtors-prisons-in-missouri /article_7f77d9ce-e7e2–5ff5-b905-e034a6c1ceb8.html.

40. Oral Argument at 1:20, *State v. Richey*, 569 S.W.3d 420, 421 (Mo. banc 2019).

41. Tony Messenger, "Poor Defendants in Dent, Caldwell Counties Join Not-So-Exclusive $10,000 Club," *St. Louis Post-Dispatch*, October 16, 2018, https://www.stltoday.com/news/local/columns/tony-messenger/messenger -poor-defendants-in-dent-caldwell-counties-join-not-so/article_aef8e1bf -96c6–56a5–9c82–10feff656721.html; Tony Messenger, "Jailed for Being Poor Is a Missouri Epidemic," *St. Louis Post-Dispatch*, October 9, 2018, https://www.stltoday.com/news/local/columns/tony-messenger/messenger -jailed-for-being-poor-is-a-missouri-epidemic/article_be783c96 -e713–59c9–9308–2f8ac5072a0c.html.

42. Tony Messenger, "Judge Tries to Block Access to Debtors' Prison Hearings in Dent County," *St. Louis Post-Dispatch*, November 5, 2018, https:// www.stltoday.com/news/local/columns/tony-messenger/messenger-judge -tries-to-block-access-to-debtors-prison-hearings/article_ec6a9526 -e652–5819–88b0-b5e8fd3b28dc.html.

43. Court Operating Rule 16.03(b), Your Missouri Courts, updated July 1, 2018, https://www.courts.mo.gov/courts/ClerkHandbooksP2RulesOnly.nsf/e2aa 3309ef5c449186256be20060c329/8d8476459573196786256c240070a979.

CHAPTER 1: THE ARREST

1. Douglas Martin, "The Town That Oil Built," *New York Times*, February 22, 1981, https://www.nytimes.com/1981/02/22/business/the-town-that-oil-built.html.
2. "Tammy Wynette: The 'Tragic Country Queen,'" *NPR*, March 14, 2010, https://www.npr.org/templates/story/story.php?storyId=124540180.
3. "Dewey City, Oklahoma," U.S. Census Bureau, accessed October 9, 2020, https://data.census.gov/cedsci/table?q=Dewey%20city,%20Oklahoma&tid=ACSDP5Y2018.DP05.
4. "Poverty, Housing Insecurity and Student Transiency in Rural Areas," Penn State College of Education, Center on Rural Education and Communities, accessed October 9, 2020, https://ed.psu.edu//crec/research/poverty.
5. David K. Shipler, *The Working Poor: Invisible in America* (New York: Vintage Books, 2004), 11.
6. Kevin Latham, "Cleveland County Courthouse," Exploring Oklahoma History, accessed October 8, 2020, http://blogoklahoma.us/place.aspx?id=732.
7. Alexandra Natapoff, *Punishment Without Crime* (New York: Basic Books, 2018), 2.
8. Natapoff, *Punishment Without Crime*, 3–4.
9. U.S. Const. amend. VI.
10. *Gideon v. Wainwright*, 372 U.S. 335, 339–40 (1963).
11. Bryan Furst, *A Fair Fight: Achieving Indigent Defense Resource Parity* (Brennan Center for Justice, September 9, 2019), 5, https://www.brennancenter.org/sites/default/files/2019–09/Report_A%20Fair%20Fight.pdf; Department of Justice, Bureau of Justice Statistics, *Special Report: State Public Defender Programs, 2007*, September 2010, 3, https://www.bjs.gov/content/pub/pdf/spdp07.pdf.
12. Ryan Gentzler, *The Cost Trap: How Excessive Fees Lock Oklahomans Into the Criminal Justice System without Boosting State Revenue* (Tulsa: Oklahoma Policy Institute, February 2017), 5, https://okpolicy.org/wp-content/uploads/The-Cost-Trap-How-Excessive-Fees-Lock-Oklahomans-Into-the-Criminal-Justice-System-without-Boosting-State-Revenue-updated.pdf?x35308.
13. Ryan Gentzler, "The Indigent Defense System Needs $1.5 million to Avoid Another Constitutional Crisis," Oklahoma Policy Institute, April 19, 2017, https://okpolicy.org/indigent-defense-system-needs-1–5-million-avoid-another-constitutional-crisis/; "Oklahoma Indigent Defense System" (presentation, 2018), accessed October 9, 2020, https://oksenate.gov/sites/default/files/agencies_documents/OIDS_FY19BPR_Presentation.pdf.
14. Bryan Furst, A Fair Fight: Achieving Indigent Defense Resource Parity (Brennan Center for Justice, September 9, 2019), 13, https://www.brennancenter.org/sites/default/files/2019–09/Report_A%20Fair%20Fight.pdf.
15. Furst, *A Fair Fight*, 6–7.
16. Tony Messenger, "New Report Highlights Failure of Missouri, Other States, to Fund Public Defenders," *St. Louis Post-Dispatch*, September 9, 2019, https://www.stltoday.com/news/local/columns/tony-messenger/messenger

-new-report-highlights-failure-of-missouri-other-states-to-fund-public
-defenders/article_ea9fa7ac-9fdf-5f8c-8697–65d942e0a0f1.html.

17. Messenger, "New Report Highlights Failure of Missouri."

18. Margaret Stafford, "Missouri Sued over Low Funding for Public Defender System," *Springfield News-Leader*, March 9, 2017, https://www.news-leader .com/story/news/local/missouri/2017/03/09/missouri-sued-low-funding -public-defender-system/98963436/.

19. Stafford, "Missouri Sued over Low Funding for Public Defender System."

20. Matt Ford, "A Governor Ordered to Serve as a Public Defender," *Atlantic*, August 4, 2016, https://www.theatlantic.com/politics/archive/2016/08 /when-the-governor-is-your-lawyer/494453/; Alex Johnson, "Missouri Governor, Who Vetoed Relief for Public Defenders, Appointed as Public Defender," *NBC News*, August 4, 2016, https://www.nbcnews.com/news/us -news/missouri-governor-who-vetoed-relief-public-defenders-appointed -public-defender-n623326; Elise Schmelzer, "Missouri Public Defender, Fed Up with Meager Funding, Appoints Governor to Defend Assault Suspect," *Washington Post*, August 4, 2016, https://www.washingtonpost .com/news/morning-mix/wp/2016/08/04/mo-public-defender-blames -governor-for-huge-caseload-problem-appoints-him-to-defend-assault -suspect/; Katie Reilly, "Missouri's Governor Cut Funding to the State's Public Defenders. So They Assigned Him a Case," *Time*, August 4, 2016, https://time.com/4439083/missouri-public-defender-governor-jay-nixon/.

21. "The Cost of Child Care in South Carolina," Economic Policy Institute, accessed October 27, 2020, https://www.epi.org/child-care-costs-in-the -united-states/#/SC.

22. Joseph Cranney, "These SC Judges Can Have Less Training Than Barbers but Still Decide Thousands of Cases Each Year," *Post and Courier*, September 14, 2020, https://www.postandcourier.com/news/these-sc-judges-can-have -less-training-than-barbers-but-still-decide-thousands-of-cases/article _deeac12e-eb6f-11e9–927b-5735a3edbaf1.html.

23. Karin D. Martin, "Monetary Myopia: An Examination of the Institutional Response to Revenue from Monetary Sanctions for Misdemeanors," *Criminal Justice Policy Review* 29, Nos. 6–7 (May 10, 2018): 630–662.

24. Anne Wolfe and Michelle Liu, "Think Debtors Prisons Are a Thing of the Past? Not in Mississippi," The Marshal Project, January 9, 2020, https://www .themarshallproject.org/2020/01/09/think-debtors-prisons-are-a-thing-of -the-past-not-in-mississippi; Cranney, "These SC Judges Can Have Less Training Than Barbers."

25. "Salem, Missouri Population 2020," World Population Review; Jessica Semega, Melissa Kollar, Emily A. Shrider, and John Creamer, "Income and Poverty in the United States: 2019," U.S. Census Bureau, September 15, 2020, https:// www.census.gov/library/publications/2020/demo/p60–270.html#:~:text =The%20official%20poverty%20rate%20in,and%20Table%20B%2D5).

26. "Poverty Guidelines," U.S. Department of Health & Human Services, Office of the Assistant Secretary for Planning and Evaluation, January 8, 2020, https://aspe.hhs.gov/poverty-guidelines.
27. Andrew Sheeley, "Struggling with Poverty: In Dent County and the Ozarks, Another World Exists," *Salem News*, February 10, 2015, https://www.thesalemnewsonline.com/news/article_f023a66e-b130-11e4-89a6-e730be7ec6de.html.
28. "Dent County," Meramec Regional Planning Commission, accessed November 3, 2020, https://www.meramecregion.org/counties/dent-county/.
29. Leah Thorsen, "Missouri Is No Longer the Meth Capital of the U.S.," *St. Louis Post-Dispatch*, March 31, 2014, https://www.stltoday.com/news/local/crime-and-courts/missouri-is-no-longer-the-meth-capital-of-the-u-s/article_358b8c90-29ba-5c8f-acba-2bdaf5d6523f.html.
30. Camille Phillips, "Prescription Painkiller Abuse Cases on the Rise in Missouri Hospitals," St. Louis Public Radio, October 12, 2015, https://news.stlpublicradio.org/health-science-environment/2015-10-12/prescription-painkiller-abuse-cases-on-the-rise-in-missouri-hospitals.
31. Stephan J. Goetz and Hema Swaminathan, *Wal-Mart and County-Wide Poverty*, *Social Science Quarterly* 87, no. 2 (June 2006): 220, https://aese.psu.edu/nercrd/economic-development/for-researchers/poverty-issues/big-boxes/wal-mart-and-poverty/article-wal-mart-and-county-wide-poverty.
32. Tony Messenger, "Poor Defendants in Dent, Caldwell Counties Join Not-So-Exclusive $10,000 Club," *St. Louis Post-Dispatch*, October 16, 2018, https://www.stltoday.com/news/local/columns/tony-messenger/messenger-poor-defendants-in-dent-caldwell-counties-join-not-so/article_aef8e1bf-96c6-56a5-9c82-10feff656721.html.
33. "Henry T. Kirkland Apartments," Panama City Housing Authority, accessed November 3, 2020, https://panamacityhousing.org/henry-t-kirkland-apartments/.
34. Carol Marbin Miller and Marc Caputo, "New Claims of Abuse at Boys Camp, October 14, 2006," *Miami Herald*, October 12, 2007, https://www.miamiherald.com/latest-news/article1928434.html.
35. Colson Whitehead, *The Nickel Boys* (New York: Doubleday, 2019).
36. "Department of Justice Releases Investigative Findings on the Arthur G. Dozier School for Boys and the Jackson Juvenile Offender Center in Florida," Department of Justice (Press Release), December 2, 2011, https://www.justice.gov/opa/pr/department-justice-releases-investigative-findings-arthur-g-dozier-school-boys-and-jackson.
37. *Fueling an Epidemic: Report Three: A Flood of 1.6 Billion Doses of Opioids into Missouri and the Need for Stronger DEA Enforcement* (Washington, DC: U.S. Senate Homeland Security & Governmental Affairs Committee, Ranking Member's Office, July 2018), 1, https://www.hsgac.senate.gov/imo/media/doc/REPORT-Fueling%20an%20Epidemic-A%20Flood%20of%201

.6%20Billion%20Doses%20of%20Opioids%20into%20Missouri%20
and%20the%20Need%20for%20Stronger%20DEA%20Enforcement.pdf.

38. Andrew Sheeley, "Dent County Listed Among Regional Leaders for Opioids," *Salem News*, August 7, 2019, https://www.thesalemnewsonline.com
/article_267f8506-b2db-11e9–8997–8fb43e0700b5.html.

39. Phillips, "Prescription Painkiller Abuse Cases on the Rise in Missouri
Hospitals."

40. "Confined and Costly: How Supervision Violations Are Filling Prisons and
Burdening Budgets," Justice Center, Council of State Governments, June 18,
2019, https://csgjusticecenter.org/publications/confined-costly/.

41. Tony Messenger, "Judge Tries to Block Access to Debtors' Prison Hearings in Dent County," *St. Louis Post-Dispatch*, November 5, 2018, https://
www.stltoday.com/news/local/columns/tony-messenger/messenger-judge
-tries-to-block-access-to-debtors-prison-hearings/article_ec6a9526
-e652–5819–88b0-b5e8fd3b28dc.html.

42. Peter Edelman, *Not a Crime to Be Poor* (New York: The New Press, 2017), 30.

43. Messenger, "Judge Tries to Block Access."

CHAPTER 2: TAXATION BY CITATION

1. Micah Schwartzbach, "What Does Pleading 'No Contest' Mean?" Nolo,
accessed October 9, 2020, https://www.nolo.com/legal-encyclopedia/what
-pleading-guilty-contest.html.

2. Rodney J. Uphoff, "The Criminal Defense Lawyer as Effective Negotiator:
A Systemic Approach," *Clinical Law Review* 2 (Fall 1995): 73, 89n63 ("In
Oklahoma, for example, prosecutors in Cleveland County routinely offer to
first offenders to recommend a deferred sentence in exchange for a plea . . .").

3. For a generic breakdown of costs, see Ryan Gentzler, *The Cost Trap: How Ex-
cessive Fees Lock Oklahomans Into the Criminal Justice System without Boosting
State Revenue* (Tulsa: Oklahoma Policy Institute, February 2017), 5, https://
okpolicy.org/wp-content/uploads/The-Cost-Trap-How-Excessive-Fees
-Lock-Oklahomans-Into-the-Criminal-Justice-System-without-Boosting
-State-Revenue-updated.pdf?x35308.

4. Gentzler, *The Cost Trap*, 7; Tianna Mays and Phylicia H. Hill, "Point of
View: Oklahoma Should Address the Trap of Fees, Fines," *Oklahoman*, May
31, 2019, https://oklahoman.com/article/5632676/point-of-view-oklahoma
-should-address-the-trap-of-fees-fines.

5. Gentzler, *The Cost Trap*, 5.

6. "New ABA Study Captures Impact of Fines, Fees on the Poor," American Bar Association, June 29, 2020, https://www.americanbar.org/news
/abanews/aba-news-archives/2020/06/new-aba-report-captures/.

7. Tony Messenger, "In North St. Louis County, the Courts and Poverty Intertwine," *St. Louis Post-Dispatch*, May 29, 2017, https://www

.stltoday.com/news/local/columns/tony-messenger/messenger-in-north
-st-louis-county-the-courts-and-poverty/article_f7d7ac14-3cc6-5f42-
b070-6609a459c243.html; Radley Balko, "How Municipalities in St. Louis
County, Mo., Profit from Poverty," *Washington Post*, September 3, 2014,
https://www.washingtonpost.com/news/the-watch/wp/2014/09/03/how
-st-louis-county-missouri-profits-from-poverty/.

8. Walter Johnson, *The Broken Heart of America: St. Louis and the Violent History
of the United States* (New York: Basic Books, 2020), 160, 340.

9. Radley Balko, "How Municipalities in St. Louis County, Mo., Profit from
Poverty"; Ken Leiser, "St. Louis County Cities Tag Speeders with Heavy
Fines on I-70," *St. Louis Post-Dispatch*, January 17, 2011, https://www.stltoday
.com/news/local/metro/st-louis-county-cities-tag-speeders-with-heavy
-fines-on-i-70/article_352c3f26–2208–11e0-abb3–00127992bc8b.html.

10. Thomas Harvey, John McAnnar, Michael-John Voss, Megan Conn, Sean
Janda, and Sophia Keskey, *Municipal Courts White Paper* (St. Louis, MO:
Arch City Defenders, 2014), 9, https://www.courts.mo.gov/file.jsp?id
=98433.

11. *Targeted Fines and Fees Against Communities of Color: Civil Rights & Consti-
tutional Implications* (Washington, DC: U.S. Commission on Civil Rights,
September 2017), 12, n51 https://www.usccr.gov/pubs/2017/Statutory
_Enforcement_Report2017.pdf.

12. Harvey *et al.*, *Municipal Courts White Paper*, 31.

13. *Targeted Fines and Fees Against Communities of Color*, 12, n. 51.

14. Jeremy Kohler, Jennifer S. Mann, and Walker Moskop, "For People Living
Under Threat of Arrest Around St. Louis, a Constant Stress," *St. Louis Post-
Dispatch*, September 21, 2014, https://www.stltoday.com/news/local/crime
-and-courts/for-people-living-under-threat-of-arrest-around-st-louis-a
-constant-stress/article_5135fe78–02f4–5ff2–8283–3b7c0b178afc.html.

15. Kohler *et al.*, "For People Living Under Threat of Arrest."

16. Kohler *et al.*, "For People Living Under Threat of Arrest."

17. Tony Messenger, "Latest Debtors' Prison Lawsuit Straddles Missouri's
Urban-Rural Divide," *St. Louis Post-Dispatch*, December 15, 2018, https://
www.stltoday.com/news/local/columns/tony-messenger/messenger-latest
-debtors-prison-lawsuit-straddles-missouris-urban-rural-divide/article
_c0ea89b0-a271–59ce-95a4-aaae96e0d535.html.

18. Harvey *et al.*, *Municipal Courts White Paper*, 1–2.

19. Class Action Complaint of Keilie Fant *et al.* at ¶ 1, *Fant v. Ferguson*, No.
4:15-cv-00253 (ED. Mo. February 8, 2015).

20. Class Action Complaint of Keilie Fant *et al.* at ¶ 1.

21. Robert Patrick, "Judge Approves $4.7 Million Settlement to Those Jailed
for Unpaid Fines in Jennings," December 14, 2016, *St. Louis Post-Dispatch*.

22. Campbell Robertson, "Missouri City to Pay $4.7 Million to Settle Suit
Over Jailing Practices," *New York Times*, July 15, 2016, https://www.nytimes

.com/2016/07/16/us/missouri-city-to-pay-4–7-million-to-settle-suit-over
-jailing-practices.html.

23. Mike Maciag, "Addicted to Fines: A Special Report," *Governing*, August 21,
2019, https://www.governing.com/topics/finance/fine-fee-revenues-special
-report.html.

24. Carrie Teegardin, "Why Georgia Traffic Tickets Have So Many Extra
Fees," *Atlanta Journal-Constitution*, May 2, 2017, https://www.ajc.com
/blog/investigations/why-georgia-traffic-tickets-have-many-extra-fees
/a3932GuCyWy8IC6NMNz8OO/.

25. "Georgia State Conference of the NAACP et al. v. City of LaGrange,
Georgia," Fines & Fees Justice Center, February 29, 2020, https://
finesandfeesjusticecenter.org/articles/georgia-state-conference-of-the
-naacp-et-al-v-city-of-lagrange-georgia/.

26. "QuickFacts: LaGrange City, Georgia," U.S. Census Bureau, accessed October 31, 2020, https://www.census.gov/quickfacts/lagrangecitygeorgia.

27. Hannah Riley, "Eleventh Circuit Reverses Dismissal of Lawsuit Chal-
lenging Policies Unlawfully Restricting Access to Basic Utility Services,"
Southern Center for Human Rights, October 14, 2019, https://www.schr
.org/eleventh-circuit-reverses-dismissal-of-lawsuit-challenging-policies
-unlawfully-restricting-access-to-basic-utility-services/; Complaint of
Georgia State Conference of the *NAACP v. City of LaGrange*, No. 18–10053
(N.D. Ga. May 18, 2017).

28. *NAACP v. LaGrange* at ¶ 33.

29. *NAACP v. LaGrange*, 940 F.3d at 634.

30. Hunter Riggall, "LaGrange Settles Utilities Lawsuit Alleging Discrimination," *LaGrange Daily News*, November 2, 2020, https://www.lagrangenews
.com/2020/11/02/lagrange-settles-utilities-lawsuit-alleging-discrimination/.

31. Maciag, "Addicted to Fines."

32. Donald R. Ford, *Village of Fenton, Louisiana, Annual Financial Report: Year Ended
June 30, 2018* (Zachary, LA, 2018), 54, http://app.lla.state.la.us/PublicReports
.nsf/0/F03C7A56772A8E37862584D3007A3434/$FILE/0001EC7C.pdf.

33. Samuel Brooke, "The Hidden Costs of U.S. Justice" (panel presentation, "Cash
Register Justice," John Jay College, New York, NY, September 26, 2019).

34. Maciag, "Addicted to Fines."

35. Tony Messenger, "This Is Not St. Louis," *St. Louis Post-Dispatch*, August
14, 2014, https://www.stltoday.com/opinion/editorial/video-editorial-this
-is-not-st-louis/html_4002ac18–9250–58dd-b61e-88229ba108c0.html.

36. Tony Messenger, "Justice in Ferguson Is About Long-Term Change," *St.
Louis Post-Dispatch*, November 12, 2014, https://www.stltoday.com/opinion
/columnists/messenger-justice-in-ferguson-is-about-long-term-change
/article_1b33925f-a3ef-5428–9b83–98a324415057.html.

37. Deaconess Foundation, "Rev. Dr. Starsky Wilson," accessed October 16,
2020, https://deaconess.org/rev-dr-starsky-wilson/; Rachel Rice, "Deaconess Foundation CEO Wilson to Leave for National Role," *St. Louis*

Post-Dispatch, September 2, 2020, https://www.stltoday.com/news/local/metro/deaconess-foundation-ceo-wilson-to-leave-for-national-role/article_fb211f3c-cd39-5d37-b19c-870e219a3aa6.html.

38. *Forward Through Ferguson: A Path Toward Racial Equity* (Ferguson Commission, October 14, 2015), 32, https://3680or2khmk3bzkp33juiea1-wpengine.netdna-ssl.com/wp-content/uploads/2015/09/101415_FergusonCommissionReport.pdf.

39. *Forward Through Ferguson*, 32, 35.

40. Mo. S.B. 5, 0455S.18T (signed July 9, 2015), https://www.senate.mo.gov/15info/BTS_Web/Bill.aspx?SessionType=R&BillID=160.

41. Tony Messenger, "Old Jay Nixon Stirs to Life over Autism," *St. Louis Post-Dispatch*, July 9, 2009, https://www.stltoday.com/news/old-jay-nixon-stirs-to-life-over-autism/article_c88f8d2c-fdca-5d00-b71d-6564c3b36dcc.html.

42. Rachel Herndon Dunn, "Missouri Legislators Continue Autism Successes with Bill Signature," *Missouri Times*, June 29, 2015, https://themissouritimes.com/missouri-legislators-continue-autism-successes-with-bill-signature/.

43. Messenger, "Old Jay Nixon Stirs to Life over Autism."

44. Tony Messenger, "New Life for Autism Bill Bipartisan Push in Missouri—GOP Lawmakers Join Gov. Nixon in Effort to Make Sure Issue Takes Center Stage Next Session; Insurers Are Opposed," *St. Louis Post-Dispatch*, August 13, 2009, https://www.stltoday.com/news/new-life-for-autism-bill-bipartisan-push-in-missouri-gop-lawmakers-join-gov-nixon-in/article_b3bc7978-da67-5403-aedd-16aab23b4c07.html.

45. "Missouri Sen. Eric Schmitt (R)," TrackBill, accessed October 31, 2020, https://trackbill.com/legislator/missouri-senator-eric-schmitt/29-2791/#/details=true.

46. "Missouri Attorney General Eric Schmitt," Missouri Attorney General, accessed October 31, 2020, https://ago.mo.gov/about-us/about-ag-schmitt.

47. Tony Messenger, "Cities Look Foolish Fighting Against Higher Police Standards," *St. Louis Post-Dispatch*, December 20, 2015, https://www.stltoday.com/news/local/columns/tony-messenger/messenger-cities-look-foolish-fighting-against-higher-police-standards/article_6b6225b1-928a-5f97-84fc-1585624826fc.html.

48. Eric Schmitt, "Five Years After Ferguson, Reforms Are Yielding Positive Results," *St. Louis Post-Dispatch*, August 13, 2019, https://www.stltoday.com/opinion/columnists/article_5d6b02b5-061a-57ad-846f-88de8bcd3d90.html.

49. Messenger, "Cities Look Foolish Fighting Against Higher Police Standards."

50. Todd Frankel, "Speed Trap Law Is Full of Loopholes," *St. Louis Post-Dispatch*, May 17, 2009, https://www.stltoday.com/news/speed-trap-law-is-full-of-loopholes-macks-creek-the-town-that-inspired-measure-has/article_cdc4e8c1-4243-5d2b-96c3-487bda8bb60b.html.

51. John Tomerlin and Dru Whitledge, *The Safe Motorist's Guide to Speedtraps: State by State Listings to Keep Drivers Alert* (Chicago: Bonus Books, 1991).

52. Frankel, "Speed Trap Law Is Full of Loopholes."

53. John Rogers, "Missouri Town Was Driven by Speeding Tickets," *Washington Post*, July 19, 1998, https://www.washingtonpost.com/archive/politics /1998/07/19/missouri-town-was-driven-by-speeding-tickets/86c37ff6 -a437–4fb2–9d3e-46b19287cbfe/.

54. Rick Montgomery, "Small Towns: Villains or Victims of Missouri's Speed Trap Law?" *Kansas City Star*, updated May 16, 2014, https://www.kansascity .com/news/local/article312777.html.

55. Frankel, "Speed Trap Law Is Full of Loopholes."

56. Eddie O'Neill and Paul Hackbarth, "Local Towns Oppose Reducing Cap on Traffic Fines," *Rolla Daily News*, February 11, 2015, https://www .therolladailynews.com/article/20150211/NEWS/150219614.

57. "Edgar Springs, MO," Data USA, accessed October 31, 2020, https:// datausa.io/profile/geo/edgar-springs-mo.

58. Tony Messenger, "Speed Trap Highlights Policing-for-Profit Dilemma," *St. Louis Post-Dispatch*, September 7, 2016, https://www.stltoday.com/news /local/columns/tony-messenger/messenger-speed-trap-highlights-policing -for-profit-dilemma/article_6acba9a1-a618–5fa0-af5e-b9256966b841.html.

59. "Visit the Birthplace," The Pepsi Store, accessed October 31, 2020, https:// www.pepsistore.com/visit.asp.

60. Messenger, "Speed Trap Highlights Policing-for-Profit Dilemma."

61. Heather Hunt and Gene Nichol, *Court Fines and Fees: Criminalizing Poverty in North Carolina* (*North Carolina Poverty Research Fund*, Winter 2017), 4, http://www.ncpolicywatch.com/wp-content/uploads/2018/01/Court-Fines -and-Fees-Criminalizing-Poverty-in-NC.pdf.

62. Matthew Menendez, Michael F. Crowley, Lauren-Brooke Eisen, and Noah Atchison, *The Steep Costs of Criminal Justice Fines and Fees* (New York: Brennan Center for Justice at New York University School of Law, 2019), 5, https://www.brennancenter.org/sites/default/files/2020–07/2019_10 _Fees%26Fines_Final.pdf.

63. Mario Salas and Angela Ciolfi, *Driven by Dollars: A State-by-State Analysis of Driver's License Suspension Laws for Failure to Pay Court Debt* (Legal Aid Justice Center, Fall 2017), 1, https://www.documentcloud.org/documents /4061495-Driven-by-Dollars.html#document/p5/a377981.

64. Alex Bender, Stephen Bingham, Mari Castaldi, Elisa Della Piana, Meredith Desautels, Michael Herald, Endria Richardson, Jesse Stout, and Theresa Zhen, *Not Just a Ferguson Problem: How Traffic Courts Drive Inequality in California* (Berkeley: East Bay Community Law Center, Lawyers' Committee for Civil Rights, Western Center on Law & Poverty, A New Way of Life Reentry Project, and Legal Services for Prisoners with Children, 2015), 9, https://lccrsf.org/wp-content/uploads/Not-Just-a-Ferguson-Problem-How -Traffic-Courts-Drive-Inequality-in-California-4.20.15.pdf.

65. "Over 60 NY Groups Call on Gov. Cuomo to Sign Driver's License Suspension Reform Act," Fines & Fees Justice Center (Press Release), October 14, 2020, https://finesandfeesjusticecenter.org/2020/10/14/press

-release-dozens-of-ny-groups-call-on-gov-cuomo-to-sign-drivers-license
-suspension-reform-act/.

66. Carson Whitelemons, Ashley Thomas, and Sarah Couture, *Driving on Empty: Florida's Counterproductive and Costly Driver's License Suspension Practices* (Fines & Fees Justice Center, October 2019), 16, https://finesandfeesjusticecenter.org/content/uploads/2019/11/florida-fines-fees -drivers-license-suspension-driving-on-empty.pdf.

67. "About Us," Action Together Rochester, accessed October 31, 2020, http://actiontogether-rochester.org/.

68. Editorial Board, "There's No Reason to Let a Traffic Ticket Turn into a Financial Crisis," *Star Tribune*, May 1, 2018, https://www.startribune.com/there -s-no-reason-to-let-a-traffic-ticket-turn-into-a-financial-crisis/481431081/.

69. Kurt Erickson, "Missouri Governor Signs Law Targeting Municipal Courts," *St. Louis Post-Dispatch*, June 17, 2016, https://www.stltoday.com /news/local/govt-and-politics/missouri-governor-signs-law-targeting -municipal-courts/article_39b4461e-aa27–57b8-a614–33bc583c0a97.html.

70. Editorial Board, "Stunned by Our Fragmentation, Police Think-Tank Offers Some Ideas," *St. Louis Post-Dispatch*, May 3, 2015, https://www.stltoday.com /opinion/editorial/editorial-stunned-by-our-fragmentation-police-think-tank -offers-some-ideas/article_1bd7575d-5866–52f8-aca6-d22019a66fae.html.

71. *St. Louis City-County Governance Task Force Report to the Community* (St. Louis: Better Together, January 2019), 23, https://drive.google.com/file/d /1bOFQ3HTYUzQwEjJsl2y-3bqB8VyeY8j-/view.

72. Editorial Board, "Stunned by Our Fragmentation, Police Think-Tank Offers Some Ideas."

73. *Overcoming the Challenges and Creating a Regional Approach to Policing in St. Louis City and County* (Police Executive Research Forum, April 30, 2015), 2, https://www.policeforum.org/assets/stlouis.pdf.

74. Victoria Young, "Legislature Sends Municipal Court Reforms to Gov. Nixon," *St. Louis Post-Dispatch*, May 8, 2015, https://www.stltoday.com /news/local/govt-and-politics/legislature-sends-municipal-court-reforms -to-gov-nixon/article_9c0c71cb-e6e6–5c65–99bf-48470645a456.html.

75. Jeremy Kohler, "Court-Reform Law Survives Missouri Supreme Court, But No Longer Targets St. Louis County," *St. Louis Post-Dispatch*, May 16, 2017, https://www.stltoday.com/news/local/crime-and-courts/court-reform-law -survives-missouri-supreme-court-but-no-longer/article_81466cd3–3ec6– 5c12–8652–2fec5981e9a4.html.

76. Maciag, "Addicted to Fines."

77. ArchCity Defenders, "ArchCity Defenders Files Subsequent Debtors' Prison Lawsuit Against Edmundson," press release, December 12, 2018, https://www.archcitydefenders.org/archcity-defenders-files-subsequent -debtors-prison-lawsuit-against-edmundson-2/.

78. Tony Messenger, "Latest Debtors' Prison Lawsuit Straddles Missouri's Urban-Rural Divide," *St. Louis Post-Dispatch*, December 15, 2018, https://

www.stltoday.com/news/local/columns/tony-messenger/messenger-latest
-debtors-prison-lawsuit-straddles-missouris-urban-rural-divide/article
_c0ea89b0-a271–59ce-95a4-aaae96e0d535.html.

CHAPTER 3: NO SALE OF JUSTICE

1. Magna Carta, 1297, *Statutes of the Realm*, 25 Edw. 1, cl. 40.
2. Mo. H.B. 81 § 57.960 (1983); Mo. Rev. Stat. § 57.955.
3. Missouri Sheriff's Retirement System, "About Us," accessed October 12, 2020, http://sherretmo.com/about-us.
4. Tony Messenger, "Dispute over $3 Fee Pits Sheriffs vs. Judges," *St. Louis Post-Dispatch*, March 26, 2017, https://www.stltoday.com/news/local /columns/tony-messenger/messenger-dispute-over-fee-pits-sheriffs-vs -judges/article_9b11189b-4758–5065–8264-addd8b47de7f.html.
5. Alexandra Natapoff, *Punishment Without Crime* (New York: Basic Books, 2018), 2.
6. Messenger, "Dispute over $3 Fee."
7. Messenger, "Dispute over $3 Fee."
8. Mo. S.B. 601 (1984); Mo. Rev. Stat. Cum. Supp. § 56.790.2 (1984); *Harrison v. Monroe County,* 716 S.W.2d 263, 265 (Mo. Banc 1986).
9. *Harrison v. Monroe County,* 716 S.W.2d at 267.
10. *Harrison v. Monroe County,* 716 S.W.2d at 267.
11. Tony Messenger, "A Senator's Budget Threat Precedes Flip of Missouri's Top Court," *St. Louis Post-Dispatch*, March 27, 2017, https://www .stltoday.com/news/local/columns/tony-messenger/messenger-a-senator -s-budget-threat-precedes-flip-of-missouri/article_f5a2f577–617f-5e2b -a7c6–5b7ef2aefb17.html.
12. Messenger, "A Senator's Budget Threat"; Missouri Courts, "Office of State Courts Administrator," accessed October 13, 2020, https://www.courts.mo .gov/page.jsp?id=233.
13. Carl Reynolds and Jeff Hall, *Courts Are Not Revenue Centers* (Conference of State Court Administrators, 2011), https://cosca.ncsc.org/__data/assets/pdf _file/0019/23446/courtsarenotrevenuecenters-final.pdf.
14. Messenger, "A Senator's Budget Threat."
15. Messenger, "A Senator's Budget Threat." For an overview of the clerk of the Missouri Supreme Court's role, see "Clerk of the Supreme Court," Missouri Courts, https://www.courts.mo.gov/page.jsp?id=214.
16. "Order dated August 16, 2013, re: Schedules for Collection and Hierarchy for Disbursement of Court Costs, Fees, Miscellaneous Charges and Surcharges," Supreme Court of Missouri, *en banc*, August 16, 2013, https://www .courts.mo.gov/page.jsp?id=92265.
17. Tony Messenger, "Under Fire During Ferguson, Judge Waged Battle Behind the Scenes," *St. Louis Post-Dispatch*, March 28, 2017, https://www

.stltoday.com/news/local/columns/tony-messenger/messenger-under
-fire-during-ferguson-judge-waged-battle-behind-the/article_e0d017c7
-c653–53c4–85bc-1383439d9695.html.

18. Tony Messenger, "Sheriffs' Retirement Fund Had Its Day in Court; It
Didn't Show Up," *St. Louis Post-Dispatch*, March 27, 2017, https://www
.stltoday.com/news/local/columns/tony-messenger/messenger-sheriffs
-retirement-fund-had-its-day-in-court-it/article_a1214592-e36b-59f8
-bc15–27b5bd1b080f.html.

19. Messenger, "Dispute over $3 Fee."

20. Messenger, "Under Fire During Ferguson."

21. Lauren-Brooke Eisen, *Charging Inmates Perpetuates Mass Incarceration* (New
York: Brennan Center for Justice at NYU School of Law, 2015), 5, https://
www.brennancenter.org/sites/default/files/2019–08/Report_Charging
_Inmates_Mass_Incarceration.pdf.

22. Messenger, "A Senator's Budget Threat Precedes Flip of Missouri's Top Court."

23. Gene Perry, "SQ 640 Has Made Oklahoma Ungovernable," Oklahoma Policy Institute, last modified May 2, 2019, https://okpolicy.org/sq-640-made
-oklahoma-ungovernable/; Okla. S.Q. 640, Pet. 348 (May 25, 1990), available at https://www.sos.ok.gov/documents/questions/640.pdf.

24. Myesha Braden *et al.*, *Enforcing Poverty: Oklahoma's Reliance on Fines & Fees
Fuels the State's Incarceration Crisis* (Lawyer's Committee for Civil Rights
Under Law, 2020), 5, https://indd.adobe.com/view/6a8c0376-dba2–4aa2
-b64d-f537c63d65b5.

25. Corey Jones, "How Much Does Oklahoma Rely on Court Collections to
Fund Government? 'We Reach a Point Where We Begin to Criminalize
Poverty,'" *Tulsa World*, May 7, 2019, https://tulsaworld.com/news/local
/crime-and-courts/how-much-does-oklahoma-rely-on-court-collections
-to-fund-government-we-reach-a-point/article_81cb716e-791d-5053
-a6d0–6e22d9a2229a.html.

26. Clifton Adcock, "Offender's Story: Untying the Bonds of Court Debt,"
Oklahoma Watch, February 26, 2015, https://oklahomawatch.org/2015/02
/26/courts-push-collection-of-fines-and-fees/.

27. Colo. Const. art X § 20, The Taxpayer's Bill of Rights.

28. Missouri Const. Article X §§ 16–21; Thomas A. Schweich, Missouri State
Auditor, Review of Article X, Sections 16 Through 24, Constitution of
Missouri (No. 2012–25), i, https://app.auditor.mo.gov/repository/press
/2012–25.pdf.

29. Tony Messenger, "Missouri's Long Race to the Bottom Is Over. It's a Du-
bious Victory," *St. Louis Post-Dispatch*, May 29, 2020, https://www.stltoday
.com/news/local/columns/tony-messenger/messenger-missouri-s-long
-race-to-the-bottom-is-over-it-s-a-dubious-victory/article_93085fb4
-e3e6–51be-98fa-8c16f5c18f91.html.

30. Federal Reserve Board, Consumer and Community Research Section of
the Division of Consumer and Community Affairs, *Report on the Economic*

Well-Being of U.S. Households in 2019, Featuring Supplemental Data From April 2020 (May 2020), 9, https://www.federalreserve.gov/publications/files /2019-report-economic-well-being-us-households-202005.pdf.

31. Debra Cassens Weiss, "6% of Adults Have Debt From Court Costs or Legal Fees, Federal Reserve Report Says," *ABA Journal*, May 15, 2020, https:// www.abajournal.com/news/article/6-of-adults-have-debt-from-court-costs -or-legal-fees-federal-reserve-report-says.

32. Ryan Gentzler, *The Cost Trap: How Excessive Fees Lock Oklahomans Into the Criminal Justice System without Boosting State Revenue* (Tulsa: Oklahoma Policy Institute, February 2017), 4, https://okpolicy.org/wp-content /uploads/The-Cost-Trap-How-Excessive-Fees-Lock-Oklahomans-Into -the-Criminal-Justice-System-without-Boosting-State-Revenue-updated .pdf?x35308.

CHAPTER 4: FAILURE TO PAY

1. Class Action Second Amended Complaint at ¶ 3, *Brown v. Lexington County*, No. 3:17-cv-01426-MBS-SVH (D.S.C. October 19, 2017), available at https://www.aclu.org/legal-document/brown-v-lexington-county-et -al-class-action-second-amended-complaint.

2. John Raphling, "Plead Guilty, Go Home. Plead Not Guilty, Stay in Jail," *Los Angeles Times*, May 17, 2017, https://www.latimes.com/opinion/op-ed/la-oe -raphling-bail-20170517-story.html.

3. Corey Jones, "Day 1: How One Woman's Story Depicts Oklahoma's Struggle with Fines, Fees and Costs in the Justice System," *Tulsa World*, December 2, 2019, https://tulsaworld.com/news/local/crime-and-courts/day -1-how-one-womans-story-depicts-oklahoma-s-struggle-with-fines-fees -and-costs/article_935c0fb6–25ee-5599–952d-99551641c9d9.html.

4. Tony Messenger, "Jailed for Being Poor is a Missouri Epidemic: A Series of Columns from Tony Messenger," *St. Louis Post-Dispatch*, April 22, 2019, https://www.stltoday.com/news/local/columns/tony-messenger/jailed -for-being-poor-is-missouri-epidemic-a-series-of-columns-from-tony -messenger/collection_40e7d3ad-6b26–5dcb-8c10-d97b0eabc75e.html#1.

5. Tony Messenger, "St. Francois County Judge Sends Another Grandma to Prison Over Court Costs," *St. Louis Post-Dispatch*, August 22, 2017, https://www.stltoday.com/news/local/columns/tony-messenger/messenger -st-francois-county-judge-sends-another-grandma-to-prison/article _8e7408d5-afec-5e69-bc3a-50fa93706deb.html.

6. Tony Messenger, "Release from Debtor's Prison Raises Holiday Spirits of Missouri Woman," *St. Louis Post-Dispatch*, January 4, 2018, https://www .stltoday.com/news/local/columns/tony-messenger/messenger-release -from-debtors-prison-raises-holiday-spirits-of-missouri-woman/article _10bb2f09–7f24–55ff-a48f-49a357c09bd8.html.

7. Tony Messenger, "In St. Francois County, Judge and Prosecutor Treat Jail Like an ATM," *St. Louis Post-Dispatch*, September 28, 2018, https://www.stltoday.com/news/local/columns/tony-messenger/messenger-in-st-francois-county-judge-and-prosecutor-treat-jail/article_ddbd50f7-b3e9-547e-9675-2bb1539a45e3.html.

8. *State Ex Rel. Parrott v. Martinez,* 496 S.W.3d at 572 (2016).

9. Tony Messenger, "Missouri Supreme Court Draws a Line in the Sand on Rising Court Costs," *St. Louis Post-Dispatch*, April 12, 2017, https://www.stltoday.com/news/local/columns/tony-messenger/messenger-missouri-supreme-court-draws-a-line-in-the-sand/article_ab3d630f-908a-57a5-80c6-713bb45e6cfd.html

10. Vanita Gupta and Lisa Foster, "Dear Colleague Letter Regarding Law Enforcement Fees and Fines," Fines and Fees Justice Center, March 14, 2016, 2, https://finesandfeesjusticecenter.org/content/uploads/2018/11/Dear-Colleague-letter.pdf.

11. Matt Zapotosky, "Sessions Rescinds Justice Dept. Letter Asking Courts to Be Wary of Stiff Fines and Fees for Poor Defendants," *Washington Post*, December 21, 2017, https://www.washingtonpost.com/world/national-security/sessions-rescinds-justice-dept-letter-asking-courts-to-be-wary-of-stiff-fines-and-fees-for-poor-defendants/2017/12/21/46e37316-e690-11e7-ab50-621fe0588340_story.html.

12. Leroy Sigman, "Old Miners Recall the Brighter Days of Mining," *Daily Journal*, September 19, 2004, https://dailyjournalonline.com/news/local/old-miners-recall-the-brighter-days-of-mining/article_d3d23877-82a3-593e-aaba-23a6199f0bf5.html.

13. "Chrysler Plants Closing Causes $15 Billion Impact," *St. Louis Post-Dispatch*, September 16, 2011, https://www.stltoday.com/suburban-journals/metro/news/chrysler-plants-closing-causes-15-billion-impact/article_1519d934-b6f8-5617-8ce1-0826b80c4a23.html.

14. Tony Messenger, "In St. Francois County, Judge and Prosecutor Treat Jail Like an ATM."

15. Messenger, "In St. Francois County, Judge and Prosecutor Treat Jail Like an ATM."

16. Tony Messenger, "Judge Tries to Block Access to Debtors' Prison Hearings in Dent County," *St. Louis Post-Dispatch*, November 5, 2018, https://www.stltoday.com/news/local/columns/tony-messenger/messenger-judge-tries-to-block-access-to-debtors-prison-hearings/article_ec6a9526-e652-5819-88b0-b5e8fd3b28dc.html.

17. Komala Ramachandra and Sara Darehshori, *"Set Up to Fail": The Impact of Offender-Funded Private Probation on the Poor* (Human Rights Watch, 2018), 16, https://www.hrw.org/report/2018/02/21/set-fail/impact-offender-funded-private-probation-poor#.

18. Tony Messenger, "Lawmaker Targets Probation-for-Profit Companies in Missouri," *St. Louis Post-Dispatch*, November 19, 2018, https://www

.stltoday.com/news/local/columns/tony-messenger/messenger-lawmaker-targets-probation-for-profit-companies-in-missouri/article_57d95f5a-e745–5181–8280–74a1168e0608.html.

19. Ramachandra and Darehshori, *"Set Up to Fail."*

20. *Bearden v. Georgia,* 461 U.S. 660, 661–62 (1983).

21. Renee Montagne, "Unpaid Court Fees Land the Poor in 21st Century Debtors' Prisons," *NPR,* May 20, 2014, https://www.npr.org/transcripts/314138887.

22. Tony Messenger, "From Hamilton to Homeless; Another Debtors' Prison Tale from Rural Missouri," *St. Louis Post-Dispatch,* November 6, 2018, https://www.stltoday.com/news/local/columns/tony-messenger/messenger-from-hamilton-to-homeless-another-debtors-prison-tale-from-rural-missouri/article_0e68701e-dc14–58d8-a50f-9936ac4cd0bd.html.

23. Matthew Shaer, "How Cities Make Money by Fining the Poor," *New York Times,* January 8, 2019, https://www.nytimes.com/2019/01/08/magazine/cities-fine-poor-jail.html.

24. Shaer, "How Cities Make Money by Fining the Poor."

25. Anne Wolfe and Michelle Liu, "Think Debtors Prisons Are a Thing of the Past? Not in Mississippi," The Marshal Project, January 9, 2020, https://www.themarshallproject.org/2020/01/09/think-debtors-prisons-are-a-thing-of-the-past-not-in-mississippi.

26. Tony Messenger, "A Tale of Two Counties on Opposite Ends of Missouri's Debtors' Prison Cycle," *St. Louis Post-Dispatch,* November 30, 2018, https://www.stltoday.com/news/local/columns/tony-messenger/messenger-a-tale-of-two-counties-on-opposite-ends-of-missouris-debtors-prison-cycle/article_a182e3eb-a974–5f99–9ff0–72fb7de6e031.html.

27. Tony Messenger, "Missouri Teen Stole a Lawnmower in High School—11 Years Later He's Still Going to Court," *St. Louis Post-Dispatch,* November 16, 2018, https://www.stltoday.com/news/local/columns/tony-messenger/messenger-missouri-teen-stole-a-lawnmower-in-high-school-11-years-later-hes-still-going/article_d8dcbe9d-542b-561b-bb36–04f56c2e223f.html.

28. Messenger, "Missouri Teen Stole a Lawnmower in High School."

29. Tony Messenger, "She Was Late to a Hearing, So a Dent County Judge Tossed Her in Jail. Then She Got the Bill," *St. Louis Post-Dispatch,* November 16, 2018, https://www.stltoday.com/news/local/columns/tony-messenger/messenger-she-was-late-to-a-hearing-so-a-dent-county-judge-tossed-her-in/article_03e2a934-c094–5cb4-bf18–15bce4b825d4.html.

30. Messenger, "She Was Late to a Hearing."

31. Amanda Blackman, "The History of One of Colorado's Most Famous Venues," *Sentry,* February 21, 2018, http://cu-sentry.com/2018/02/21/history-one-colorados-famous-venues/; "300MPH Drag Racing Action on Thunder Mountain," Bandimere Speedway, accessed October 31, 2020, https://bandimere.com/.

32. "Morrison, Colorado Speed Traps," Speedtrap.org, accessed October 31, 2020, https://www.speedtrap.org/colorado/morrison/.

33. Mike Maciag, "Addicted to Fines," *Governing*, September 2019, https://www.governing.com/topics/finance/gov-addicted-to-fines.html.

34. Brief of the American Civil Liberties Union, the R Street Institute, the Fines and Fees Justice Center, and the Southern Poverty Law Center as Amici Curiae in Support of Petitioners at 18, *Timbs v. Indiana,* No. 17–1091, available at https://www.aclu.org/sites/default/files/field_document/timbs_amicus_brief_final.pdf.

35. Brief of the American Civil Liberties Union et al. as Amici Curiae at 18.

CHAPTER 5: PAY-TO-STAY

1. Tony Messenger, "Poor Defendants in Dent, Caldwell Counties Join Not-So-Exclusive $10,000 Club," *St. Louis Post-Dispatch*, October 16, 2018, https://www.stltoday.com/news/local/columns/tony-messenger/messenger-poor-defendants-in-dent-caldwell-counties-join-not-so/article_aef8e1bf-96c6–56a5–9c82–10feff656721.html.

2. Tony Messenger, "Jailed for Being Poor Is a Missouri Epidemic," *St. Louis Post-Dispatch*, October 9, 2018, https://www.stltoday.com/news/local/columns/tony-messenger/messenger-jailed-for-being-poor-is-a-missouri-epidemic/article_be783c96-e713–59c9–9308–2f8ac5072a0c.html.

3. Tony Messenger, "St. Charles County Points the Way As Lawmakers Seek to End Debtors Prisons in Missouri," *St. Louis Post-Dispatch*, December 9, 2018, https://www.stltoday.com/news/local/columns/tony-messenger/messenger-st-charles-county-points-the-way-as-lawmakers-seek/article_337547b9-cca9–5f53–91ec-bd1fe9ae6965.html; Titus Wu and Jennifer Mosbrucker, "In Rural Missouri, Going to Jail Isn't Free. You Pay for It," *Columbia-Missourian*, December 19, 2018, https://www.columbiamissourian.com/news/state_news/in-rural-missouri-going-to-jail-isnt-free-you-pay-for-it/article_613b219a-f4d7–11e8-bf90–33125904976d.html.

4. Wu and Mosbrucker, "In Rural Missouri, Going to Jail Isn't Free."

5. Lauren-Brooke Eisen, *Charging Inmates Perpetuates Mass Incarceration* (New York: Brennan Center for Justice at NYU School of Law, 2015), 2, https://www.brennancenter.org/sites/default/files/2019–08/Report_Charging_Inmates_Mass_Incarceration.pdf.

6. Eisen, *Charging Inmates Perpetuates Mass Incarceration,* 2.

7. "Bradford W. Colbert '85," Mitchell Hamline School of Law, accessed November 3, 2020, https://mitchellhamline.edu/biographies/person/bradford-colbert/.

8. *Jones v. Borchardt,* 775 N.W.2d 646 (Minn. 2009); "Minnesota Supreme Court Limits Fees for Jail Inmates," *Twin Cities Pioneer Press*, December 3, 2009, updated November 13, 2015, https://www.twincities.com/2009/12/03/minnesota-supreme-court-limits-fees-for-jail-inmates/.

9. Brief of Appellant at 13, *Jones v. Borchardt,* No. A08–0556 (Minn. 2009), available at https://mn.gov/law-library-stat/briefs/pdfs/a080556sca.pdf.

10. *Jones v. Borchardt*, 775 N.W.2d at 648; "Minnesota Supreme Court Limits Fees for Jail Inmates."
11. Minn. Stat. Ann. 641.12 (2019), available at https://www.revisor.mn.gov/statutes/cite/641.12.
12. "Fees," Olmsted County, Minnesota, accessed November 3, 2020, https://www.co.olmsted.mn.us/sheriff/divisions/ADC/WorkRelease/fees/Pages/default.aspx.
13. *Christianson v. Markquart*, 2018 WL 461134 (D. Minn. 2018), Civil No. 16–1034, 1, available at https://casetext.com/case/christianson-v-markquart.
14. *Christianson v. Markquart*, 2018 WL 461134, at 1.
15. *Christianson v. Markquart*, 2018 WL 461134, at 2.
16. Messenger, "Poor Defendants Join $10,000 Club."
17. Tony Messenger, "Private Probation Company Tries to Shame Dent County Woman Back to Jail," *St. Louis Post-Dispatch*, November 8, 2018, https://www.stltoday.com/news/local/columns/tony-messenger/messenger-private-probation-company-tries-to-shame-dent-county-woman-back-to-jail/article_6c5e866e-44ef-5567-8740-d6a2c992bed2.html.
18. Tony Messenger, "Lawmaker Targets Probation-for-Profit Companies in Missouri," *St. Louis Post-Dispatch*, November 19, 2018, https://www.stltoday.com/news/local/columns/tony-messenger/messenger-lawmaker-targets-probation-for-profit-companies-in-missouri/article_57d95f5a-e745-5181-8280-74a1168e0608.html.
19. Eli Hager, "Debtors' Prisons, Then and Now: FAQ," Marshall Project, February 24, 2015, https://www.themarshallproject.org/2015/02/24/debtors-prisons-then-and-now-faq.
20. Richard B. Gunderman, "Advocating for Children: Charles Dickens," *Pediatric Radiology* 50 (2020): 467–469, https://link.springer.com/article/10.1007/s00247-019-04608-w.
21. Hager, "Debtors' Prisons, Then and Now."
22. Mo. Const. art. I, § 11.
23. "Tour of the Dent County Jail-Feb. 23, 2017," SalemMoNews, video, 2:16, February 27, 2017, https://www.youtube.com/watch?v=524RCL-vAJc.
24. Tony Messenger, "She Was Late to a Hearing, So a Dent County Judge Tossed Her in Jail. Then She Got the Bill," *St. Louis Post-Dispatch*, November 16, 2018, https://www.stltoday.com/news/local/columns/tony-messenger/messenger-she-was-late-to-a-hearing-so-a-dent-county-judge-tossed-her-in/article_03e2a934-c094-5cb4-bf18-15bce4b825d4.html.
25. *Barnes v. Brown County*, 2013 WL 1314015 (E.D. Wis. 2012), No. 11-CV-00968, at 1.
26. *Barnes v. Brown County*, 2013 WL 1314015, at 6.
27. Izabela Zaluska, "Pay-to-Stay Fees Put Some Wisconsin Inmates in Sizable Debt," Associated Press, September 15, 2019, https://apnews.com/article/bb127e19eb454354ab1776d360fa4971.

28. "Is Charging Inmates to Stay in Prison Smart Policy?" Brennan Center for Justice, September 9, 2019, https://www.brennancenter.org/our-work/research-reports/charging-inmates-stay-prison-smart-policy.

29. Lauren-Brooke Eisen, "Paying for Your Time: How Charging Inmates Fees Behind Bars May Violate the Excessive Fines Clause," Brennan Center for Justice at NYU School of Law, July 31, 2014, https://www.brennancenter.org/our-work/research-reports/paying-your-time-how-charging-inmates-fees-behind-bars-may-violate.

30. "Is Charging Inmates to Stay in Prison Smart Policy?"

31. Eisen, "Paying for Your Time."

32. Holly Ramer, "N.H. to End 'Pay to Stay' for Prison Inmates," *Concord Monitor*, July 16, 2019, https://www.concordmonitor.com/New-Hampshire-to-end—pay-to-stay—for-inmates-27041265.

33. "Is Charging Inmates to Stay in Prison Smart Policy?"

34. Matthew Menendez, Michael F. Crowley, Lauren-Brooke Eisen, and Noah Atchison, *The Steep Costs of Criminal Justice Fines and Fees* (New York: Brennan Center for Justice at New York University School of Law, 2019), 5, https://www.brennancenter.org/sites/default/files/2020–07/2019_10_Fees%26Fines_Final.pdf.

35. Menendez *et al.*, *The Steep Costs of Criminal Justice Fines and Fees*, 5.

36. Tony Messenger, "St. Louis Woman Had a Bad Break Up in 2006. Camden County Still Keeps Putting Her in Jail Because of It," *St. Louis Post-Dispatch*, December 4, 2018, https://www.stltoday.com/news/local/columns/tony-messenger/messenger-st-louis-woman-had-a-bad-break-up-in-2006-camden-county-still-keeps/article_ef846be4–0bb9–5231-b8c9-ee9b9c1afa1b.html.

37. Messenger, "St. Louis Woman Had a Bad Break Up."

38. "06CM-CR014191—St v Nora Alicyn Rapp (CB) (E-Case)," Your Missouri Courts, Case.Net, accessed November 3, 2020, https://www.courts.mo.gov/casenet/cases/searchDockets.do.

39. Tony Messenger, "A Tale of Two Counties on Opposite Ends of Missouri's Debtors' Prison Cycle," *St. Louis Post-Dispatch*, November 30, 2018, https://www.stltoday.com/news/local/columns/tony-messenger/messenger-a-tale-of-two-counties-on-opposite-ends-of-missouris-debtors-prison-cycle/article_a182e3eb-a974–5f99–9ff0–72fb7de6e031.html.

40. "06CM-CR014191—St v Nora Alicyn Rapp (CB) (E-Case)."

41. "06CM-CR014191—St v Nora Alicyn Rapp (CB) (E-Case)."

CHAPTER 6: THE KEY TO THE JAILHOUSE DOOR

1. Tony Messenger, "Missouri Paid Bill for Woman's Jail Stay, But Judge Tries to Collect Again," *St. Louis Post-Dispatch*, January 22, 2019, https://www.stltoday.com/news/local/columns/tony-messenger/messenger-missouri

-paid-bill-for-womans-jail-stay-but-judge-tries-to-collect-again/article
_1fedcb20–49c4–5937–9337-dceed372b1d1.html.

2. "QuickFacts: Mississippi County, Missouri," U.S. Census Bureau, accessed November 3, 2020, https://www.census.gov/quickfacts/mississippicountymissouri.

3. "Missouri's Bootheel Region Is Fertile Ground," Missouri Department of Agriculture, *Farm Flavor*, February 5, 2013, https://www.farmflavor.com/missouri/missouri-crops-livestock/missouris-bootheel-region-is-fertile-ground/.

4. *State v. Tidwell*, 577 S.W.3d 816, 817 (Mo. Ct. App. 2019).

5. "David A. Dolan," Ballotpedia, accessed November 3, 2020, https://ballotpedia.org/David_A._Dolan.

6. Messenger, "Judge Tries to Collect Again."

7. "QuickFacts: Mississippi County, Missouri."

8. "QuickFacts: Pemiscot County, Missouri," U.S. Census Bureau, accessed November 3, 2020, https://www.census.gov/quickfacts/fact/table/pemiscotcountymissouri/PST045219.

9. Jacob Barker, "Noranda Aluminum Closure Marks the End of an Era in the Missouri Bootheel," *St. Louis Post-Dispatch*, February 21, 2016, https://www.stltoday.com/business/local/noranda-aluminum-closure-marks-the-end-of-an-era-in-the-missouri-bootheel/article_335027a8–2a8b-591f-9f9c-aaabbffab0a0.html.

10. "What Climate Change Means for Missouri," U.S. EPA, August 2016, https://19january2017snapshot.epa.gov/sites/production/files/2016–09/documents/climate-change-mo.pdf.

11. Emily Stahly, "The Child Poverty Rate in Mississippi County Is How High?" *Show-Me Institute* (blog), February 5, 2019, https://showmeinstitute.org/blog/business-climate/the-child-poverty-rate-in-mississippi-county-is-how-high.

12. Matt Ford, "A 'Constitutional Crisis' in Missouri," *Atlantic*, March 14, 2017, https://www.theatlantic.com/politics/archive/2017/03/missouri-public-defender-crisis/519444/.

13. Bryan Furst, *A Fair Fight: Achieving Indigent Defense Resource Parity* (Brennan Center for Justice, September 9, 2019), 13, https://www.brennancenter.org/sites/default/files/2019–09/Report_A%20Fair%20Fight.pdf.

14. Jordan Smith, "Missouri's Underfunded Public Defender Office Forces the Poor to Languish in Jail," *Intercept*, March 13, 2017, https://theintercept.com/2017/03/13/missouris-underfunded-public-defender-office-forces-the-poor-to-languish-in-jail/.

15. Furst, *A Fair Fight*, 14 n. 1; n. Complaint for Injunctive Relief at 3, Church v. Missouri, No.17-CV-04057-NKL (W.D. Mo. 2017), https://www.brennancenter.org/sites/default/files/2019–09/Report_A%20Fair%20Fight.pdf.

16. Tony Messenger, "New Report Highlights Failure of Missouri, Other States, to Fund Public Defenders," *St. Louis Post-Dispatch*, September 9, 2019, https://www.stltoday.com/news/local/columns/tony-messenger/messenger

-new-report-highlights-failure-of-missouri-other-states-to-fund-public
-defenders/article_ea9fa7ac-9fdf-5f8c-8697–65d942e0a0f1.html.

17. "Hannibal Attractions," Hannibal, Missouri, accessed October 30, 2020, https://www.visithannibal.com/attractions/.

18. "Office of Chief Disciplinary Counsel," Missouri Courts, accessed October 30, 2020, https://www.courts.mo.gov/page.jsp?id=217.

19. "For the Public: Disciplinary Hearings," Office of Chief Disciplinary Counsel, Missouri, accessed October 30, 2020, https://www.mochiefcounsel.org/ocdc.htm?id=24&cat=2.

20. Jesse Bogan, "Missouri's Sexually Violent Predator Treatment Program Eludes Federal Scrutiny," *St. Louis Post-Dispatch*, September 4, 2017, https://www.stltoday.com/news/local/crime-and-courts/missouris-sexually-violent-predator-treatment-program-eludes-federal-scrutiny/article_489da15a-40d9–5986-a2bb-5937f6d561c0.html.

21. Tony Messenger, "When Does a Prosecutor's Responsibility to Seek Justice End? A Tale of Two Cases," *St. Louis Post-Dispatch*, December 13, 2019, https://www.stltoday.com/news/local/columns/tony-messenger/messenger-when-does-a-prosecutor-s-responsibility-to-seek-justice-end-a-tale-of-two/article_18377c14–74d3–5036-a042–480ea82c74a3.html.

22. Tony Messenger, "Two Days After Debtors Prison Ruling, Missouri Judge Tries to Collect Pay-to-Stay Bills," *St. Louis Post-Dispatch*, March 22, 2019, https://www.stltoday.com/news/local/columns/tony-messenger/messenger-two-days-after-debtors-prison-ruling-missouri-judge-tries-to-collect-pay-to-stay/article_4e735ee5–1744–5ef4-a7b1-c3c73b2adeb8.html.

23. Tony Messenger, "In Missouri, the Road to Debtors' Prison Starts with Cash Bail," *St. Louis Post-Dispatch*, February 1, 2019, https://www.stltoday.com/news/local/columns/tony-messenger/messenger-in-missouri-the-road-to-debtors-prison-starts-with-cash-bail/article_cbb7e39f-b65f-53d3–9b89-e03e32ad87e9.html.

24. "Certified Ray County Jail Board Bill and Medical Expense as Court Cost," *Missouri v. Licata*, No. 13Ry-CR00111–01 (May 19, 2017), in possession of author.

25. Messenger, "In Missouri, the Road to Debtors' Prison Starts with Cash Bail."

26. Taryn A. Merkl, "New York's Latest Bail Law Changes Explained," Brennan Center for Justice, April 16, 2020, https://www.brennancenter.org/our-work/analysis-opinion/new-yorks-latest-bail-law-changes-explained.

27. Merkl, "New York's Latest Bail Law Changes Explained."

28. Merkl, "New York's Latest Bail Law Changes Explained."

29. Danny Wicentowski, "Taking on Cash-Bail Policies, Missouri Supreme Court Aims to End Debtor's Prisons," *Riverfront Times*, January 31, 2019, https://www.riverfronttimes.com/newsblog/2019/01/31/taking-on-cash-bail-policies-missouri-supreme-court-aims-to-end-debtors-prisons.

30. Tony Messenger, "Unconstitutional Application of Cash Bail Makes St. Louis Less Safe, Conservative Group Argues," *St. Louis Post-Dispatch*,

September 27, 2019, https://www.stltoday.com/news/local/columns /tony-messenger/messenger-unconstitutional-application-of-cash-bail -makes-st-louis-less-safe-conservative-group-argues/article_b4777e3c -2b66–5716-afa5-f63c17febfbf.html.

31. Messenger, "Unconstitutional Application of Cash Bail Makes St. Louis Less Safe."

32. *Pretrial Criminal Justice Research* (Laura and John Arnold Foundation, 2013), 5, https://cjcc.doj.wi.gov/sites/default/files/subcommittee/LJAF -Pretrial-CJ-Research-brief_FNL.pdf.

33. Messenger, "Unconstitutional Application of Cash Bail Makes St. Louis Less Safe."

34. "Higginsville, Missouri," City-Data.com, accessed November 3, 2020, http://www.city-data.com/city/Higginsville-Missouri.html.

35. Tony Messenger, "Jailed for Being Poor Is a Missouri Epidemic," *St. Louis Post-Dispatch*, October 9, 2018, https://www.stltoday.com/news/local /columns/tony-messenger/messenger-jailed-for-being-poor-is-a-missouri -epidemic/article_be783c96-e713–59c9–9308–2f8ac5072a0c.html.

36. Mo. Stat. Ann. 1895 § 4990, Missouri Session Laws 1895 at 178, available at https://mdh.contentdm.oclc.org/digital/collection/molaws/id/15351.

37. Tony Messenger, "St. Charles County Points the Way as Lawmakers Seek to End Debtors Prisons in Missouri," *St. Louis Post-Dispatch*, December 9, 2018, https://www.stltoday.com/news/local/columns/tony-messenger/messenger-st -charles-county-points-the-way-as-lawmakers-seek-to-end-debtors-prisons -in/article_337547b9-cca9–5f53–91ec-bd1fe9ae6965.html.

38. *The Andy Griffith Show*, produced by Sheldon Leonard and Danny Thomas, featuring Andy Griffith, Ronny Howard, Don Knotts, Frances Bavier, Elinor Donahue, and Jim Nabors, aired October 3, 1960–April 1, 1968, on CBS. Otis Campbell was played by Hal Smith.

39. Messenger, "St. Charles County Points the Way."

40. Messenger, "Jailed for Being Poor."

41. Tony Messenger, "New Attorney General Joins the Fight Against Debtors Prisons in Missouri," *St. Louis Post-Dispatch*, January 8, 2019, https:// www.stltoday.com/news/local/columns/tony-messenger/messenger-new -attorney-general-joins-the-fight-against-debtors-prisons-in-missouri /article_7f77d9ce-e7e2–5ff5-b905-e034a6c1ceb8.html.

42. *State v. Richey*, 569 S.W.3d 420, 421 (Mo. banc 2019).

43. Titus Wu and Jennifer Mosbrucker, "In Rural Missouri, Going to Jail Isn't Free. You Pay for It," *Columbia-Missourian*, December 19, 2018, https://www.columbiamissourian.com/news/state_news/in-rural-missouri -going-to-jail-isnt-free-you-pay-for-it/article_613b219a-f4d7–11e8 -bf90–33125904976d.html.

44. Wu and Mosbrucker, "In Rural Missouri, Going to Jail Isn't Free."

45. Tony Messenger, "Missouri Supreme Court Draws a Line in the Sand on Rising Court Costs," *St. Louis Post-Dispatch*, April 12, 2017, https://www

.stltoday.com/news/local/columns/tony-messenger/messenger-missouri
-supreme-court-draws-a-line-in-the-sand/article_ab3d630f-908a
-57a5–80c6–713bb45e6cfd.html; Editorial Board, "Missouri Supreme
Court Must End the Ferguson Shake-Down," *St. Louis Post-Dispatch*,
March 6, 2015, https://www.stltoday.com/opinion/editorial/editorial
-missouri-supreme-court-must-end-the-ferguson-shake-down/article
_91dd939f-9454–570d-9741-d98a637699bc.html.

46. Tony Messenger, "Under Fire During Ferguson, Judge Waged Battle Behind the Scenes," *St. Louis Post-Dispatch*, March 28, 2017, https://www
.stltoday.com/news/local/columns/tony-messenger/messenger-under
-fire-during-ferguson-judge-waged-battle-behind-the/article_e0d017c7
-c653–53c4–85bc-1383439d9695.html.

47. Messenger, "Under Fire During Ferguson."

48. Tony Messenger, "Cities Look Foolish Fighting Against Higher Police Standards," *St. Louis Post-Dispatch*, December 20, 2015, https://www
.stltoday.com/news/local/columns/tony-messenger/messenger-cities-look
-foolish-fighting-against-higher-police-standards/article_6b6225b1–928a
-5f97–84fc-1585624826fc.html.

49. Messenger, "Cities Look Foolish Fighting Against Higher Police Standards."

50. Chief Judge Mary R. Russell, "State of the Judiciary," January 22, 2015,
https://www.courts.mo.gov/page.jsp?id=82876; Tony Messenger, "Time for
Missouri's Leaders to Put the Debtors' Prison Band Back Together," *St.
Louis Post-Dispatch*, November 22, 2018, https://www.stltoday.com/news
/local/columns/tony-messenger/messenger-time-for-missouris-leaders-to
-put-the-debtors-prison-band-back-together/article_a0d035e0-e972–53be
-84b1-b5754f3373e1.html.

51. Editorial Board, "Missouri Supreme Court Wades into Ferguson. Excel-
lent," *St. Louis Post-Dispatch*, January 7, 2015, https://www.stltoday.com
/opinion/editorial/editorial-missouri-supreme-court-wades-into-ferguson
-excellent/article_28660c33–6f16–55d5–815f-a728d729dc78.html.

52. S.B. 5 (2015); Mo. Rev. Stat. § 67.287.

53. *State v. Richey*, 569 S.W.3d 420, 420 (Mo. banc 2019).

54. "Photography Staff of *St. Louis Post-Dispatch*," The Pulitzer Prizes, accessed
October 23, 2020, https://www.pulitzer.org/winners/photography-staff-1.

55. Kim Bell, "Protester Featured In Iconic Ferguson Photo Found Dead of
Self-Inflicted Gunshot Wound," *St. Louis Post-Dispatch*, May 5, 2017,
https://www.stltoday.com/news/local/crime-and-courts/protester-featured
-in-iconic-ferguson-photo-found-dead-of-self-inflicted-gunshot-wound
/article_072602fb-99f1–531f-aa1c-b971e8b32566.html.

56. Tony Messenger, "Lines Drawn in Missouri Debtors Prison Debate: Extortion vs. Freedom," *St. Louis Post-Dispatch*, February 7, 2019, https://
www.stltoday.com/news/local/columns/tony-messenger/messenger-lines
-drawn-in-missouri-debtors-prison-debate-extortion-vs-freedom/article
_71931341–9202–538b-aaa7–535b4d3f9047.html.

57. *State v. Richey,* 569 S.W.3d at 425.

58. *State v. Richey,* 569 S.W.3d at 425.

59. *State v. Richey,* 569 S.W.3d at 425.

60. *Timbs v. Indiana,* 139 S. Ct. 682 (2019).

61. *State v. Richey,* 569 S.W.3d at 425–26.

62. Tony Messenger, "Veteran Who Spurred Historic Missouri Debtors Prison Ruling Finds Himself Back Behind Bars," *St. Louis Post-Dispatch,* February 5, 2020, https://www.stltoday.com/news/local/columns/tony -messenger/messenger-veteran-who-spurred-historic-missouri-debtors -prison-ruling-finds-himself-back-behind-bars/article_85a36bb3–749c -5eae-8231–3771d19593cf.html.

63. Jesse Bogan and Kurt Erickson, "Missouri Faces Choice: Improve Prison System or Build Two New Lockups, Task Force Warns," *St. Louis Post-Dispatch,* January 4, 2018, https://www.stltoday.com/news/local/state -and-regional/missouri-faces-choice-improve-prison-system-or-build -two-new-lockups-task-force-warns/article_22a8a62f-9ddb-58e2-bbdc -df396b1020cd.html.

64. *State v. Richey,* 569 S.W.3d at 425; Tony Messenger, "Rural Missouri Judges Are Still Holding on to Debtors Prison Scheme," *St. Louis Post-Dispatch,* May 10, 2019, https://www.stltoday.com/news/local/columns/tony-messenger /messenger-rural-missouri-judges-are-still-holding-on-to-debtors-prison -scheme/article_9a0a5e65–097c-588f-9214-bc003df86bcc.html.

65. "Confined and Costly: How Supervision Violations Are Filling Prisons and Burdening Budgets," Justice Center, Council of State Governments, June 18, 2019, https://csgjusticecenter.org/publications/confined-costly/.

66. Tony Messenger, "A Happy Ending for St. Louis Woman Who Faced Six Months in Rural Jail Over Speeding Ticket," *St. Louis Post-Dispatch,* January 27, 2019, https://www.stltoday.com/news/local/columns/tony-messenger /messenger-a-happy-ending-for-st-louis-woman-who-faced-six-months -in-rural-jail/article_9a1d621e-d1f5–591b-99d5–3353439f0e93.html.

CHAPTER 7: JUDGES VS. JUDGES

1. Tony Messenger, "Two Days After Debtors Prison Ruling, Missouri Judge Tries to Collect Pay-to-Stay Bills," *St. Louis Post-Dispatch,* March 22, 2019, https://www.stltoday.com/news/local/columns/tony-messenger/messenger -two-days-after-debtors-prison-ruling-missouri-judge-tries-to-collect-pay -to-stay/article_4e735ee5–1744–5ef4-a7b1-c3c73b2adeb8.html.

2. Messenger, "Two Days After Debtors Prison Ruling."

3. Messenger, "Two Days After Debtors Prison Ruling."

4. Messenger, "Two Days After Debtors Prison Ruling."

5. Tony Messenger, "With Unified Voice, Missouri Supreme Court Signals an End to Debtors Prison Scheme," *St. Louis Post-Dispatch,* March 20, 2019,

https://www.stltoday.com/news/local/columns/tony-messenger/messenger
-with-unified-voice-missouri-supreme-court-signals-an-end-to-debtors
-prison-scheme/article_fd1f0999–667c-5a8d-91d5-de9f69d37539.html.

6. Messenger, "With Unified Voice."

7. Tony Messenger, "A Tale of Two Counties on Opposite Ends of Missouri's Debtors' Prison Cycle," *St. Louis Post-Dispatch*, November 30, 2018, https:// www.stltoday.com/news/local/columns/tony-messenger/messenger-a-tale -of-two-counties-on-opposite-ends-of-missouris-debtors-prison-cycle /article_a182e3eb-a974–5f99–9ff0–72fb7de6e031.html.

8. Messenger, "Two Days After Debtors Prison Ruling."

9. Tony Messenger, "Public Defender Alleges Missouri Judge Is Ignoring Double Jeopardy Protections," *St. Louis Post-Dispatch*, February 22, 2019, https://www.stltoday.com/news/local/columns/tony-messenger/messenger -public-defender-alleges-missouri-judge-is-ignoring-double-jeopardy -protections/article_bfd61703–7785–5907-a853-af46eec0fdf9.html.

10. Messenger, "Public Defender Alleges Missouri Judge Is Ignoring Double Jeopardy Protections."

11. Tony Messenger, "With Smart Move on Child Support, Bell Joins Battle Against Debtors' Prisons," *St. Louis Post-Dispatch*, January 11, 2019, https:// www.stltoday.com/news/local/columns/tony-messenger/messenger-with -smart-move-on-child-support-bell-joins-battle-against-debtors-prisons /article_6bc3e9e6-ffd2–5e60–935e-bdfc4610252d.html.

12. Messenger, "Two Days After Debtors Prison Ruling."

13. "Nonpartisan Court Plan," Missouri Courts, accessed October 27, 2020, https://www.courts.mo.gov/page.jsp?id=297.

14. "Nonpartisan Court Plan," Missouri Courts.

15. "Celebrating 75 Years of the Missouri Plan," Missouri Bar, November 5, 2015, http://missourilawyershelp.org/celebrating-75-years-of-the-missouri -plan/.

16. "Historic Missourians: Thomas J. Pendergast," State Historical Society of Missouri, accessed October 27, 2020, https://historicmissourians.shsmo.org /historicmissourians/name/p/pendergast/index.html.

17. William Worley, "The Decline and Fall of the Pendergast Machine," The Pendergast Years, Kansas City Public Library, https://pendergastkc.org /article/decline-and-fall-pendergast-machine.

18. Worley, "The Decline and Fall of the Pendergast Machine."

19. Worley, "The Decline and Fall of the Pendergast Machine."

20. "Celebrating 75 Years of the Missouri Plan," Missouri Bar.

21. "The Missouri Plan," Your Missouri Judges, accessed October 27, 2020, http://www.yourmissourijudges.org/missouri-plan/.

22. Tony Messenger, "Missouri Plan for Selecting Judges Faces New Challenge," *St. Louis Post-Dispatch*, November 27, 2010, https://www.stltoday.com/news /local/govt-and-politics/missouri-plan-for-selecting-judges-faces-new -challenge/article_7fb91810-c4da-5957–951d-daec4f112746.html.

23. "The Missouri Plan."
24. James A. Gleason, "State Judicial Selection Methods as Public Policy: The Missouri Plan" (dissertation, Purdue University, December 2016), 90, https://docs.lib.purdue.edu/cgi/viewcontent.cgi?article=2147&context=open_access_dissertations.
25. Adam Liptak, "U.S. Voting for Judges Perplexes Other Nations," *New York Times*, May 25, 2008, https://www.nytimes.com/2008/05/25/world/americas/25iht-judge.4.13194819.html.
26. Liptak, "U.S. Voting for Judges Perplexes Other Nations."
27. "Fact Sheet: California Judicial Branch," Judicial Council of California, October 2020, https://www.courts.ca.gov/documents/California_Judicial_Branch.pdf.
28. Reece Trevor, "Judicial Selection: A Look At California," Brennan Center for Justice, August 7, 2017, https://www.brennancenter.org/our-work/research-reports/judicial-selection-look-california.
29. "Judicial Selection in California," Ballotpedia, accessed October 30, 2020, https://ballotpedia.org/Judicial_selection_in_California.
30. "How Judges Are Elected in South Carolina," South Carolina State House, updated January 11, 2010, https://www.scstatehouse.gov/JudicialMeritPage/HowJudgesAreElectedInSC011110.pdf.
31. Joseph Cranney, "These SC Judges Can Have Less Training Than Barbers But Still Decide Thousands of Cases Each Year," *Post and Courier*, September 14, 2020, https://www.postandcourier.com/news/these-sc-judges-can-have-less-training-than-barbers-but-still-decide-thousands-of-cases/article_deeac12e-eb6f-11e9-927b-5735a3edbaf1.html.
32. "How Judges Are Elected in South Carolina."
33. Dwayne McClellan, "Nixon Appoints Baird Associate Circuit Judge," *Salem News*, March 15, 2011, https://www.thesalemnewsonline.com/news/local_news/article_59315bb0-4f1f-11e0-87cf-0017a4a78c22.html.
34. Andrew Sheeley, "Appeal Challenges Local Collection of Board Bills," *Salem News*, October 23, 2018, https://www.thesalemnewsonline.com/news/local_news/article_829c5d4c-d6d0-11e8-98a3-5b9c15af1ab5.html.
35. Sheeley, "Appeal Challenges Local Collection of Board Bills."
36. "Dent County Shows Up Red, and by a Longshot," *Salem News*, November 6, 2018, https://www.thesalemnewsonline.com/news/local_news/article_6f4ead5c-e22f-11e8-b2f4-a7f794fcc6fc.html.
37. Bob Davis and Dante Chinni, "America's Factory Towns, Once Solidly Blue, Are Now a GOP Haven," *Wall Street Journal*, July 19, 2018, https://www.wsj.com/articles/americas-manufacturing-towns-once-solidly-blue-are-now-a-gop-haven-1532013368.
38. "2016 Missouri Presidential Election Results," *Politico*, updated December 13, 2016, https://www.politico.com/2016-election/results/map/president/missouri/.

39. "Baird Announces as Republican Candidate for Circuit Judge," *Salem News*, March 3, 2020, https://www.thesalemnewsonline.com/news/local_news /article_cdcfeb04–5d6a–11ea-a26c-affcf02c8a69.html.

40. Elizabeth Crisp, "Groups Battle Over How to Pick Judges in Missouri," *St. Louis Post-Dispatch*, October 27, 2012, https://www.stltoday.com/news/local /crime-and-courts/groups-battle-over-how-to-pick-judges-in-missouri /article_4edfdd77-a054–5322-a02b-557bb27aea7f.html.

41. Tony Messenger, "Why Is Mega-Donor Investing in Missouri AG Candidate? Check the Court Records," *St. Louis Post-Dispatch*, October 11, 2016, https://www.stltoday.com/news/local/columns/tony-messenger/messenger -why-is-mega-donor-investing-in-missouri-ag-candidate-check-the-court -records/article_b8571bef-8e84–5d3a-b1d9–91ead3b6b59d.html.

42. Crisp, "Groups Battle Over How to Pick Judges in Missouri"; Marshall Griffin, "Battles Over Mo.'s Non-Partisan Court Plan Not Over," *St. Louis Public Radio*, November 9, 2012, https://news.stlpublicradio.org /government-politics-issues/2012–11–09/battles-over-mo-s-non-partisan -court-plan-not-over.

43. "Nonpartisan Court Plan," Missouri Courts, accessed October 27, 2020, https://www.courts.mo.gov/page.jsp?id=297.

44. Messenger, "Missouri Plan for Selecting Judges Faces New Challenge."

45. A. G. Sulzberger, "Ouster of Iowa Judges Sends Signal to Bench," *New York Times*, November 3, 2010, https://www.nytimes.com/2010/11/04/us /politics/04judges.html.

46. Sulzberger, "Ouster of Iowa Judges Sends Signal to Bench."

47. Tim Anderson, "Supreme Costs: 5 Midwestern States Have Among Most Expensive Judicial Elections in Nation," The Council of State Governments, Midwest, November 2011, https://www.csgmidwest.org/policyresearch /1111judicialraces.aspx.

48. Anderson, "Supreme Costs."

49. Anderson, "Supreme Costs."

50. Sulzberger, "Ouster of Iowa Judges Sends Signal to Bench."

51. Mary R. Russell, "State of the Judiciary," January 22, 2015, https://www .courts.mo.gov/page.jsp?id=82876.

52. Tony Messenger, "Missouri Supreme Court Faces Its Reputation-Defining Moment," *St. Louis Post-Dispatch*, February 19, 2016, https://www.stltoday .com/news/local/columns/tony-messenger/messenger-missouri-supreme -court-faces-its-reputation-defining-moment/article_0a26f1a9-f1d7–505b -90d2–0aff4c642644.html.

53. Cranney, "These SC Judges Can Have Less Training Than Barbers."

54. Cranney, "These SC Judges Can Have Less Training Than Barbers."

55. Cranney, "These SC Judges Can Have Less Training Than Barbers."

56. Cranney, "These SC Judges Can Have Less Training Than Barbers."

57. Cranney, "These SC Judges Can Have Less Training Than Barbers."

CHAPTER 8: THE COURTHOUSE

1. "Nusrat Choudhury," American Civil Liberties Union, accessed November 4, 2020, https://www.aclu.org/news/by/nusrat-choudhury.

2. Joseph Cranney, "These SC Judges Can Have Less Training Than Barbers But Still Decide Thousands of Cases Each Year," *Post and Courier*, September 14, 2020, https://www.postandcourier.com/news/these-sc-judges -can-have-less-training-than-barbers-but-still-decide-thousands-of-cases /article_deeac12e-eb6f-11e9–927b-5735a3edbaf1.html.

3. Class Action Second Amended Complaint at ¶ 1, *Brown v. Lexington County*, No. 3:17-cv-01426-MBS-SVH (D.S.C. October 19, 2017), available at https://www.aclu.org/legal-document/brown-v-lexington-county -et-al-class-action-second-amended-complaint; "ACLU Sues Lexington County for Running 'Modern-Day Debtors' Prison,'" American Civil Liberties Union, June 1, 2017, https://www.aclusc.org/en/news/aclu-sues -lexington-county-running-modern-day-debtors-prison.

4. Nusrat Choudhury, "Single Moms Get Sucked Into the Cruelest Debtors' Prison We've Ever Seen," *American Civil Liberties Union* (Blog), December 21, 2018, https://www.aclu.org/blog/racial-justice/race-and-criminal -justice/single-moms-get-sucked-cruelest-debtors-prison-weve.

5. Class Action Second Amended Complaint at ¶¶ 10, 14, *Brown v. Lexington County*.

6. Amended Complaint with Jury Demand, *Graff v. Aberdeen Enterprizes, Inc.*, No. 4:17-CV-606-CVE-JFJ (February 1, 2018), available at https://www .documentcloud.org/documents/4365230-Oklahoma-Aberdeen-Lawsuit .html.

7. Curtis Killman, "Every Sheriff in Oklahoma Being Sued Over Unpaid Fees Going to Collection," *Tulsa World*, November 6, 2017, https://tulsaworld .com/news/local/crime-and-courts/every-sheriff-in-oklahoma-being-sued -over-unpaid-fees-going-to-collection/article_ffae758c-1287–5791-b7ea -eff2dde4bd03.html.

8. Killman, "Every Sheriff in Oklahoma Being Sued Over Unpaid Fees Going to Collection."

9. Amended Complaint with Jury Demand at ¶ 181, *Graff v. Aberdeen Enterprizes, Inc.*, No. 4:17-CV-606-CVE-JFJ.

10. Amended Complaint with Jury Demand at ¶ 22, *Graff v. Aberdeen Enterprizes, Inc.*, No. 4:17-CV-606-CVE-JFJ.

11. Killman, "Every Sheriff in Oklahoma Being Sued Over Unpaid Fees Going to Collection."

12. Amended Complaint with Jury Demand at ¶¶ 8–10, *Graff v. Aberdeen Enterprizes, Inc.*, No. 4:17-CV-606-CVE-JFJ.

13. Nolan Clay, "Oklahoma Judge Requires Offenders to Go to Company that Pays Him Rent," *Oklahoman*, February 4, 2013, https://oklahoman.com /article/3751749/oklahoma-judge-requires-offenders-to-go-to-company -that-pays-him-rent.

14. Clay, "Oklahoma Judge Requires Offenders to Go to Company that Pays Him Rent."

15. Michael Zuckerman, "Criminal Injustice," *Harvard Magazine*, September–October 2017, https://harvardmagazine.com/2017/09/karakatsanis -criminal-justice-reform.

16. "Our Work," Civil Rights Corps, accessed November 4, 2020, https://www .civilrightscorps.org/work.

17. Zuckerman, "Criminal Injustice."

18. *Mitchell v. City of Montgomery*, No. 2:14cv186-MHT, 2014 U.S. Dist. LEXIS 195207 (M.D. Ala. 2014).

19. Paul Hampel, "Lawsuits Call Ferguson, Jennings Jails Debtors' Prisons," *St. Louis Post-Dispatch*, February 9, 2015, https://www.stltoday.com/news/local /crime-and-courts/lawsuits-call-ferguson-jennings-jails-debtors-prisons /article_a4360994-f557–5ae9–8080–8840e2724891.html.

20. Amended Complaint with Jury Demand at ¶¶ 3–4, *Graff v. Aberdeen Enterprizes, Inc.*, No. 4:17-CV-606-CVE-JFJ.

21. John Steinbeck, *Grapes of Wrath* (New York: The Viking Press, 1939).

22. "Brown v. Lexington County, et al," American Civil Liberties Union, accessed November 5, 2020, https://www.aclu.org/cases/brown-v-lexington -county-et-al.

23. "Graff v. Aberdeen Enterprizes II, Inc.," Institute for Constitutional Advocacy and Protection, Georgetown Law, accessed November 5, 2020, https://www.law.georgetown.edu/icap/our-work/police-and-criminal -justice-reform/graff-v-aberdeen-enterprizes-ii-inc/ (compiling filings in *Graff v. Aberdeen Enterprizes II, Inc.*, No. 4:17-CV-606-CVE-JF, including briefs in response to motions to dismiss from defendants claiming immunity).

24. Tony Messenger, "St. Louis Case of Prone Restraint Jail Death Could Affect Outcome of George Floyd Civil Action," *St. Louis Post-Dispatch*, June 4, 2020, https://www.stltoday.com/news/local/columns/tony-messenger /messenger-st-louis-case-of-prone-restraint-jail-death-could-affect -outcome-of-george-floyd/article_f9eb9290-ce1e-514f-8c63-f899e9d326d7 .html.

25. Hailey Fuchs, "Qualified Immunity Protection for Police Emerges as Flash Point," *New York Times*, July 20, 2020, https://www.nytimes.com/2020/06 /23/us/politics/qualified-immunity.html.

26. April Rodriguez, "Lower Courts Agree—It's Time to End Qualified Immunity," American Civil Liberties Union, September 10, 2020, https://www .aclu.org/news/criminal-law-reform/lower-courts-agree-its-time-to-end -qualified-immunity/.

27. "Graff v. Aberdeen Enterprizes II, Inc.," Institute for Constitutional Advocacy and Protection.

28. "Graff v. Aberdeen Enterprizes II, Inc.," Institute for Constitutional Advocacy and Protection.

29. *Rodriguez v. Providence Community Corrections, Inc.*, No. 3:15-cv-01048 (M.D. Tenn. 2018); "Rutherford County, TN: Private Probation," Civil Rights Corps, accessed November 5, 2020, http://www.civilrightscorps.org /work/criminalization-of-poverty/rutherford-county-tn-private-probation.

30. "QuickFacts: Rutherford County, Tennessee; Murfreesboro, Tennessee," U.S. Census Bureau, accessed November 5, 2020, https://www.census.gov /quickfacts/fact/table/rutherfordcountytennessee,murfreesborocitytenness ee/PST045219.

31. First Amended Class Action Complaint at 1, *Rodriguez v. Providence Community Corrections, Inc.*, No. 3:15-cv-01048, available at https://cdn .buttercms.com/BGlqwjugTuBhqghCFrGZ.

32. "Rutherford County, TN: Private Probation."

33. *Thomas v. Haslam*, 329 F. Supp. 3d 475, 543 (M.D. Tenn. 2018).

34. *Thomas v. Haslam*, 329 F. Supp. 3d at 483–84.

35. *Robinson v. Purkey*, 326 F.R.D. 105, 121 (M.D. Tenn. 2018).

36. *Robinson v. Long*, 814 Fed. Appx. 991, 997 (2020).

37. Tony Messenger, "Missouri Among Worst in Nation for Unconstitutional Driver's License Suspensions, Attorneys Say," *St. Louis Post-Dispatch*, March 4, 2019, https://www.stltoday.com/news/local/columns/tony-messenger /messenger-missouri-among-worst-in-nation-for-unconstitutional -drivers-license-suspensions-attorneys-say/article_e3d7541b-d2b1–52dc -9e45–9f59e9078d86.html.

38. "About the Campaign," Free to Drive, accessed November 5, 2020, https:// www.freetodrive.org/about.

39. Mo. H.B. 192 (2019), Missouri House of Representatives, https://house.mo .gov/Bill.aspx?bill=HB192&year=2019&code=R.

CHAPTER 9: THE CAPITOL

1. Tony Messenger, "Lines Drawn in Missouri Debtors Prison Debate: Extortion vs. Freedom," *St. Louis Post-Dispatch*, February 7, 2019, https:// www.stltoday.com/news/local/columns/tony-messenger/messenger-lines -drawn-in-missouri-debtors-prison-debate-extortion-vs-freedom/article _71931341–9202–538b-aaa7–535b4d3f9047.html.

2. Messenger, "Lines Drawn in Missouri Debtors Prison Debate"; "Representative Shamed Dogan," Missouri House of Representatives, accessed November 4, 2020, https://house.mo.gov/MemberDetails.aspx?year =2019&code=R&district=098.

3. Messenger, "Lines Drawn in Missouri Debtors Prison Debate."

4. Jack Suntrup, "Missouri Outlaws Jail Debt Turning into Jail Time, Following Action by Gov. Mike Parson," *St. Louis Post-Dispatch*, July 10, 2019, https:// www.stltoday.com/news/local/govt-and-politics/missouri-outlaws-jail-debt -turning-into-jail-time-following-action/article_26b4fa38–3437–502e -9f4a-49c4302e1f37.html.

5. Tony Messenger, "Amid Turbulent Political Times, Criminal Justice Reform Forges Common Ground," *St. Louis Post-Dispatch*, July 11, 2019, https://www.stltoday.com/news/local/columns/tony-messenger/messenger-amid-turbulent-political-times-criminal-justice-reform-forges-common-ground/article_65230f12-39b7-5180-bbd7-69df19879bf2.html.

6. Tony Messenger, "Missouri Lawmaker Switches Teams, Files Bill to Help Debt-Collector Clients," *St. Louis Post-Dispatch*, April 23, 2017, https://www.stltoday.com/news/local/columns/tony-messenger/messenger-missouri-lawmaker-switches-teams-files-bill-to-help-debt-collector-clients/article_e9b41a91-51af-594d-ac47-aaf7802d004a.html.

7. "How Debt Collectors Are Transforming the Business of State Courts," Pew Charitable Trusts, May 6, 2020, https://www.pewtrusts.org/en/research-and-analysis/reports/2020/05/how-debt-collectors-are-transforming-the-business-of-state-courts.

8. Messenger, "Missouri Lawmaker Switches Teams."

9. Messenger, "Missouri Lawmaker Switches Teams."

10. Daniel P. Mehan, "Tonight's Program Is Sponsored by Missouri's Booming Lawsuit Industry," *St. Louis Post-Dispatch*, September 25, 2018, https://www.stltoday.com/opinion/columnists/tonight-s-program-is-sponsored-by-missouri-s-booming-lawsuit/article_44f0de07-d12e-5e25-8946-a421cf6ee4d0.html.

11. Tony Messenger, "Fake Emails on Chamber-Pushed Tort Reform Prompt Allegation of Identity Theft in Missouri," *St. Louis Post-Dispatch*, September 30, 2018, https://www.stltoday.com/news/local/columns/tony-messenger/messenger-fake-emails-on-chamber-pushed-tort-reform-prompt-allegation-of-identity-theft-in-missouri/article_31801e5c-9e88-58a2-973e-2aa80e6e4974.html.

12. Messenger, "Missouri Lawmaker Switches Teams."

13. Messenger, "Missouri Lawmaker Switches Teams."

14. Tony Messenger, "Judge Tries to Block Access to Debtors' Prison Hearings in Dent County," *St. Louis Post-Dispatch*, November 5, 2018, https://www.stltoday.com/news/local/columns/tony-messenger/messenger-judge-tries-to-block-access-to-debtors-prison-hearings-in-dent-county/article_ec6a9526-e652-5819-88b0-b5e8fd3b28dc.html.

15. "Representative Bruce DeGroot," Missouri House of Representatives, accessed October 28, 2020, https://www.house.mo.gov/MemberDetails.aspx?year=2019&code=R&district=101.

16. Mo. H.B. 192 (2019), Missouri House of Representatives, https://house.mo.gov/Bill.aspx?bill=HB192&year=2019&code=R.

17. Messenger, "Amid Turbulent Political Times, Criminal Justice Reform Forges Common Ground."

18. Lauren-Brooke Eisen, "Paying for Your Time: How Charging Inmates Fees Behind Bars May Violate the Excessive Fines Clause," Brennan Center for Justice at NYU School of Law, July 31, 2014, https://www.brennancenter

.org/our-work/research-reports/paying-your-time-how-charging-inmates-fees-behind-bars-may-violate.

19. *Timbs v. Indiana*, 139 S. Ct. 682, 686 (2019).
20. *Timbs v. Indiana*, 139 S. Ct. at 689.
21. Tony Messenger, "Supreme Court 'Adds Teeth' to Criminal Justice Reform in Missouri," *St. Louis Post-Dispatch*, February 21, 2019, https://www.stltoday.com/news/local/columns/tony-messenger/messenger-supreme-court-adds-teeth-to-criminal-justice-reform-in-missouri/article_0395d988-e769-54fe-b731-0b497d671bc4.html.
22. Tony Messenger, "Supreme Court 'Adds Teeth.'"
23. Tony Messenger, "Supreme Court 'Adds Teeth.'"
24. Tony Messenger, "Supreme Court 'Adds Teeth.'"
25. Mo. H.B. 192 (2019).
26. *Mystic River*, directed by Clint Eastwood, starring Sean Penn, Tim Robbins, Kevin Bacon, and Laurence Fishburne (Warner Bros., 2003); *A Perfect World*, directed by Clint Eastwood, starring Kevin Costner, Clint Eastwood, and Laura Dern (Warner Bros., 1993); *Gran Torino*, directed by Clint Eastwood, starring Clint Eastwood, Christopher Carley, Bee Vang, and Ahney Her (Warner Bros., 2008).
27. Mo. H.B. 192 (2019).
28. Messenger, "Amid Turbulent Political Times, Criminal Justice Reform Forges Common Ground."
29. "Rep. John Lesch," Minnesota House of Representatives, accessed November 4, 2020, https://www.house.leg.state.mn.us/members/profile/10773.
30. "2020 State Payables List Traffic/Criminal," Minnesota Judicial Branch, 2 https://www.mncourts.gov/mncourtsgov/media/scao_library/Statewide%20Payables/2020-Traffic-Criminal-Payables-List-Rev-2-2020.pdf.
31. Jonathan Avise, "'Vicious Cycle' of License Suspension for Unpaid Fines Would Stop Under House Bill," Minnesota House of Representatives, March 14, 2018, https://www.house.leg.state.mn.us/SessionDaily/Story/13102.
32. "Cash Register Justice Round II: Covering the Hidden Costs of the Justice System," John Jay College of Criminal Justice, https://thecrimereport.org/wp-content/uploads/2019/09/CRJ-Program-Final.pdf.
33. Minn. S.F. 3656 (2018), vetoed May 23, 2018, available at "Minnesota Session Laws—2018, Regular Session," https://www.revisor.mn.gov/laws/2018/0/Session+Law/Chapter/201/.
34. "Free to Drive: About the Campaign," Free to Drive Coalition, accessed October 5, 2020, https://www.freetodrive.org/maps/#page-content.
35. "Free to Drive: State Laws," Free to Drive Coalition, accessed October 5, 2020, https://www.freetodrive.org/maps/#page-content.
36. "Free to Drive: About the Campaign."
37. "Mississippi Department of Public Safety Declines to Enforce Statute That Permits Driver's License Suspension for Failure to Pay Fines and Fees," Fines

and Fees Justice Center, April 7, 2017, https://finesandfeesjusticecenter.org
/articles/mississippi-drivers-license-suspension-fines-fees/.

38. "Mississippi Department of Public Safety Declines to Enforce Statute," Fines and Fees Justice Center.

39. "Mississippi HB 1352: The Criminal Justice Reform Act," Fines and Fees Justice Center, March 28, 2019, https://finesandfeesjusticecenter.org/articles /mississippi-hb-1352-the-criminal-justice-reform-act-ends-drivers-license -suspension-for-unpaid-fines-and-fees-failure-to-appear/.

40. "Driving for Opportunity Act of 2020," Fines and Fees Justice Center, July 2, 2020, https://finesandfeesjusticecenter.org/articles/driving-for-opportunity -act-of-2020/.

41. *Driving Toward Justice* (San Francisco: Financial Justice Project, April 2020), 2, https://sftreasurer.org/sites/default/files/2020–04 /DrivingTowardJustice.pdf.

42. Free to Drive, "Bipartisan U.S. Senate Bill Targets Debt-Based Driver's License Suspensions," press release, July 2, 2020, https://www.freetodrive.org /2020/07/02/press-release-bipartisan-u-s-senate-bill-targets-debt-based -drivers-license-suspensions/.

43. Jon A. Carnegie and Alan M. Voorhees, *Driver's License Suspensions, Impacts and Fairness Study* (New Jersey: Rutgers University, New Jersey Department of Transportation, New Jersey Motor Vehicle Commission, and U.S. Department of Transportation, August 2007), 2, 5, 56, available at https://www .politico.com/states/f/?id=00000174-fabe-d951-a77f-fbfedef80000.

44. *Report on the Statewide Collection of Delinquent Court-Ordered Debt for 2017–18* (Judicial Council of California, December 2018), 2, https://www .courts.ca.gov/documents/lr-2018-statewide-court-ordered-debt-2017–18 -pc1463_010.pdf.

45. Michael Zuckerman, "Criminal Injustice: Alec Karaktsanis Puts 'Human Caging' and 'Wealth-Based Detention' in America on Trial," *Harvard Magazine*, September–October 2017, https://harvardmagazine.com/2017/09 /karakatsanis-criminal-justice-reform.

46. Diana Dabruzzo, "New Jersey Set Out to Reform Its Cash Bail System. Now, the Results Are In," *Arnold Ventures*, November 14, 2019, https://www .arnoldventures.org/stories/new-jersey-set-out-to-reform-its-cash-bail -system-now-the-results-are-in/.

47. Christopher Porrino and Elie Honig, "New Jersey's Former Top Prosecutors: Bail Reform Isn't Easy, But It Works," *Westlaw, Thomson Reuters,* November 21, 2018, 1, https://www.lowenstein.com/media/4708/wlj_wcc3303 _-porrinohonig.pdf.

48. Eric Rosenbaum, "Millions of Americans Are Only $400 Away from Financial Hardship. Here's Why," *CNBC*, May 23, 2019, https://www.cnbc.com /2019/05/23/millions-of-americans-are-only-400-away-from-financial -hardship.html.

49. Porrino and Honig, "Bail Reform Isn't Easy, But it Works," 2.

50. Porrino and Honig, "Bail Reform Isn't Easy, But it Works," 2–3.

51. Porrino and Honig, "Bail Reform Isn't Easy, But it Works," 3.

52. *Dog the Bounty Hunter*, produced by Daniel Elias, David Houts, David McKillop, and Neil A. Cohen, starring Duane Chapman, Beth Chapman, Leland Chapman, and Lyssa Chapman, aired August 31, 2004–June 23, 2012, on A&E.

53. "California: State-wide Bail," Civil Rights Corps, accessed October 30, 2020, https://www.civilrightscorps.org/work/wealth-based-detention/california-state-wide-bail.

54. *In re Humphrey*, 19 Cal. App. 5th 1006, 1016–17, 1040 (2018).

55. "California: State-wide Bail."

56. *In re Humphrey*, 19 Cal. App. 5th at 1049.

57. *In re Humphrey*, 19 Cal. App. 5th at 1048–49.

58. *In re Humphrey*, 19 Cal. App. 5th at 1049.

59. Vanessa Romo, "California Becomes First State to End Cash Bail After 40-Year Fight," *NPR*, August 28, 2018, https://www.npr.org/2018/08/28/642795284/california-becomes-first-state-to-end-cash-bail.

60. "Edmund G. Brown Jr., State of the State Address, Delivered: January 16, 1979," The Governors' Gallery, California State Library, updated 2019, https://governors.library.ca.gov/addresses/s_34-JBrown4.html.

61. "Edmund G. Brown Jr., State of the State Address."

62. Jazmine Ulloa, "California's Historic Overhaul of Cash Bail Is Now On Hold, Pending a 2020 Referendum," *Los Angeles Times*, January 16, 2019, https://www.latimes.com/politics/la-pol-ca-bail-overhaul-referendum-20190116-story.html.

63. "California: State-wide Bail."

64. Taryn A. Merkl, "New York's Latest Bail Law Changes Explained," Brennan Center for Justice, April 16, 2020, https://www.brennancenter.org/our-work/analysis-opinion/new-yorks-latest-bail-law-changes-explained.

65. Merkl, "New York's Latest Bail Law Changes Explained."

66. "Michael Milton," The Bail Project, Our Team, accessed October 30, 2020, https://bailproject.org/team/michael-milton/.

67. Editorial Board, "Jail or Bail? Common Sense Must Be Part of The Bail Project's Mission," *St. Louis Post-Dispatch*, April 27, 2019, https://www.stltoday.com/opinion/editorial/editorial-jail-or-bail-common-sense-must-be-part-of-the-bail-projects-mission/article_ad317604–6d63–5eb6–9bf0–26fe002a1dda.html.

68. Tony Messenger, "'Defund the Police' Is About Reimagining Public Safety, Not Dystopian Lawlessness," *St. Louis Post-Dispatch*, June 15, 2020, https://www.stltoday.com/news/local/columns/tony-messenger/messenger-defund-the-police-is-about-reimagining-public-safety-not-dystopian-lawlessness/article_eea721d8-c805–500c-9308-e4a58e35a905.html.

69. *After Cash Bail: A Framework for Reimagining Pretrial Justice* (The Bail Project, 2020), accessed October 30, 2020, https://bailproject.org/after-cash-bail/.

70. Tony Messenger, "In Virtual Secret, Missouri Lawmaker Tries to Unravel Court Ruling on Debtors Prisons," *St. Louis Post-Dispatch*, May 5, 2020, https://www.stltoday.com/news/local/columns/tony-messenger/messenger-in-virtual-secret-missouri-lawmaker-tries-to-unravel-court-ruling-on-debtors-prisons/article_8ce8ba47–4cae-5aa4-bcc7-d468816ce4ec.html.

71. Cameron Gerber, "SB 600, Missouri's Controversial Crime Bill, Explained," *Missouri Times*, June 25, 2020, https://themissouritimes.com/sb-600-missouris-controversial-crime-bill-explained/.

72. Ulloa, "California's Historic Overhaul of Cash Bail Is Now On Hold"; Merkl, "New York's Latest Bail Law Changes Explained."

73. Minn. S.F. 3656 (Minnesota 2018), vetoed May 23, 2018.

74. Alec Karakatsanis, *Usual Cruelty* (New York: The New Press, 2019), 15.

75. Karakatsanis, *Usual Cruelty*, 16.

76. Karakatsanis, *Usual Cruelty*, 15.

77. Tony Messenger, "Veteran Who Spurred Historic Missouri Debtors Prison Ruling Finds Himself Back Behind Bars," *St. Louis Post-Dispatch*, February 5, 2020, https://www.stltoday.com/news/local/columns/tony-messenger/messenger-veteran-who-spurred-historic-missouri-debtors-prison-ruling-finds-himself-back-behind-bars/article_85a36bb3–749c-5eae-8231–3771d19593cf.html.

CHAPTER 10: THE KOCH BROTHERS MEET THE ACLU

1. "Thomas Jefferson Statue," Lewis and Clark Trail, accessed October 30, 2020, http://www.lewisandclarktrail.com/section1/mocities/jeffersoncity/jeffersonstatue.htm.

2. "Missouri History: Missouri State Capitol," Missouri Secretary of State, accessed October 30, 2020, https://www.sos.mo.gov/archives/history/capitol.

3. Tony Messenger, "Sarah Palin, 'Mine, Baby, Mine,'" *St. Louis Post-Dispatch*, November 3, 2008, https://www.stltoday.com/news/local/govt-and-politics/sarah-palin-mine-baby-mine/article_4ee27b3f-8293–5602–9aae-04711f2fc62a.html.

4. Tony Messenger, "Nanny State Champion Josh Hawley Takes On Snapchat So We Don't Have To," *St. Louis Post-Dispatch*, August 1, 2019, https://www.stltoday.com/news/local/columns/tony-messenger/messenger-nanny-state-champion-josh-hawley-takes-on-snapchat-so-we-dont-have-to/article_1b7ab2ea-1ffe-52ec-b8e2-cab31e0f32cf.html.

5. Tim Dickinson, "Inside the Koch Brothers' Toxic Empire," *Rolling Stone*, September 24, 2014, https://www.rollingstone.com/politics/politics-news/inside-the-koch-brothers-toxic-empire-164403/.

6. Dickinson, "Inside the Koch Brothers' Toxic Empire."

7. Tony Messenger, "Dishonest Campaign Tries to Pit Union Workers Against the Middle Class," *St. Louis Post-Dispatch*, July 29, 2018, https://www

.stltoday.com/news/local/columns/tony-messenger/messenger-dishonest
-campaign-tries-to-pit-union-workers-against-the-middle-class/article
_714496e4–3063–531f-a0f6-ed5ea60feba8.html; Kevin McDermott, "$1.84
Gas Briefly Coming to St. Louis Friday—Courtesy of Koch Brothers," *St.
Louis Post-Dispatch*, October 17, 2012, https://www.stltoday.com/news/local
/govt-and-politics/1–84-gas-briefly-coming-to-st-louis-friday-courtesy-of
-koch-brothers/article_7b66fad6–18aa-11e2–80fe-0019bb30f31a.html.

8. Jeremy Cady, email message to author, December 2018.
9. Michael M. Grynbaum, "Trump Calls the News Media the 'Enemy of the
American People,'" *New York Times*, February 17, 2017, https://www.nytimes
.com/2017/02/17/business/trump-calls-the-news-media-the-enemy-of-the
-people.html; "Trump Calls CNN 'Fake News,'" *New York Times*, January
11, 2017, https://www.nytimes.com/video/us/politics/100000004865825
/trump-calls-cnn-fake-news.html.
10. "St. Louis Globe-Democrat Collection," St. Louis Mercantile Library,
accessed October 30, 2020, https://www.umsl.edu/mercantile/collections
/mercantile-library-special-collections/special_collections/slma-112.html.
11. Editorial Board, "Times Have Changed, But Pulitzer's Platform Remains
Our Rock of Truth," *St. Louis Post-Dispatch*, January 1, 2020, https://www
.stltoday.com/opinion/editorial/editorial-times-have-changed-but-pulitzers
-platform-remains-our-rock-of-truth/article_8407d26c-8867–5e81-b8af
-16c40172dcaa.html.
12. "St. Louis Post-Dispatch Platform," *St. Louis Post-Dispatch*, April 20, 2010,
stltoday.com/opinion/columnists/st-louis-post-dispatch-platform/article
_d48be4ae-4cca-11df-a08e-0017a4a78c22.html.
13. Tony Messenger, "Missouri Gov. Mike Parson Wants to Close a Prison. It's a
Good Start," *St. Louis Post-Dispatch*, January 17, 2019, https://www.stltoday
.com/news/local/columns/tony-messenger/messenger-missouri-gov-mike
-parson-wants-to-close-a-prison-its-a-good-start/article_ad3125c9-a2ae
-5093-a147-cf1aedade99f.html.
14. "Missouri Profile," Prison Policy Initiative, accessed October 30, 2020,
https://www.prisonpolicy.org/profiles/MO.html.
15. Barb Rosewicz, Justin Theal, and Alexandre Fall, "Decade After Recession,
Tax Revenue Higher in 45 States," Pew Charitable Trusts, January 9, 2020,
https://www.pewtrusts.org/en/research-and-analysis/articles/2020/01/09
/decade-after-recession-tax-revenue-higher-in-45-states; "Fiscal 50: State
Trends and Analysis," Pew Charitable Trusts, Pew Center for the States,
last updated September 4, 2020, https://www.pewtrusts.org/en/research
-and-analysis/data-visualizations/2014/fiscal-50#ind0.
16. Phil Oliff, Chris Mai, and Vincent Palacios, "States Continue to Feel Recession's Impact," Center on Budget and Policy Priorities, updated June 27,
2012, https://www.cbpp.org/research/states-continue-to-feel-recessions
-impact.

17. Tony Messenger, "Charlie Shields Calls for Special Budget-Cutting Session of Missouri Senate," *St. Louis Post-Dispatch*, March 17, 2010, https://www.stltoday.com/news/local/govt-and-politics/charlie-shields-calls-for-special-budget-cutting-session-of-missouri-senate/article_5681bfe1–7a8f-596d-80e2-b09a9e0ecd05.html.

18. Messenger, "Charlie Shields Calls for Special Budget-Cutting Session."

19. "Missouri History: Why is Missouri Called the 'Show-Me' State?," Missouri Secretary of State, accessed October 30, 2020, https://www.sos.mo.gov/archives/history/slogan.asp.

20. "Missouri History: Why is Missouri Called the 'Show-Me' State?"

21. Emma Green, "In the Age of Trump, No Wonder Republicans Miss William F. Buckley," *Atlantic*, October 20, 2016, https://www.theatlantic.com/politics/archive/2016/10/debate-william-f-buckley/504620/.

22. Messenger, "Charlie Shields Calls for Special Budget-Cutting Session."

23. "Missouri Profile."

24. Tracey Kyckelhahn, *State Corrections Expenditures, FY 1982–2010* (U.S. Department of Justice, Bureau of Justice Statistics, April 30, 2014), 7, https://www.bjs.gov/content/pub/pdf/scefy8210.pdf.

25. Messenger, "Missouri Gov. Mike Parson Wants to Close a Prison."

26. Heather Ratcliffe, "Missouri Judges Get Penalty Cost Before Sentencing," *St. Louis Post-Dispatch*, September 14, 2010, https://www.stltoday.com/news/local/crime-and-courts/missouri-judges-get-penalty-cost-before-sentencing/article_924097a5–9f4d-54bb-80ca-4cc4160dde7c.html.

27. Tony Messenger, "After State Pays Jail Bill of Indigent Felon, Lewis County Seeks Even More," *St. Louis Post-Dispatch*, December 7, 2018, https://www.stltoday.com/news/local/columns/tony-messenger/messenger-after-state-pays-jail-bill-of-indigent-felon-lewis-county-seeks-even-more/article_6c63c58d-3b9d-5031–8806–9ef762e74b41.html.

28. "Missouri Profile."

29. Wendy Sawyer, "The Gender Divide: Tracking Women's State Prison Growth," Prison Policy Initiative, January 9, 2018, https://www.prisonpolicy.org/reports/women_overtime.html.

30. Peter Wagner and Leah Sakala, "Mass Incarceration: The Whole Pie," Prison Policy Initiative, March 12, 2014, https://www.prisonpolicy.org/reports/pie.html.

31. Campbell Robertson, "Crime Is Down, Yet U.S. Incarceration Rates Are Still Among the Highest in the World," *New York Times*, April 25, 2019, https://www.nytimes.com/2019/04/25/us/us-mass-incarceration-rate.html.

32. E. Ann Carson, "Prisoners in 2018," U.S. Department of Justice, Bureau of Justice Statistics, April 2020, https://www.bjs.gov/content/pub/pdf/p18.pdf.

33. Peter Wagner and Wendy Sawyer, "States of Incarceration: The Global Context 2018," Prison Policy Initiative, June 2018, https://www.prisonpolicy.org/global/2018.html.

34. Kurt Erickson, "Parson Calls for More Downsizing in Missouri Prison System," *St. Louis Post-Dispatch*, January 20, 2020, https://www.stltoday.com/news/local/crime-and-courts/parson-calls-for-more-downsizing-in-missouri-prison-system/article_70e3f602-4e35-5432-973c-da8e5c4180ae.html.

35. Pat Bradley, "Prison Closure Proposals Concern North Country Officials," *WSKG*, April 5, 2019, https://wskg.org/uncategorized/prison-closure-proposals-concern-north-country-officials/.

36. Wes Venteicher, "Gavin Newsom Wants to Close a California State Prison. It Won't Be Easy," *Sacramento Bee*, November 24, 2019, https://www.sacbee.com/news/politics-government/the-state-worker/article237689339.html.

37. Bob Christie, "Arizona Governor to Close Prison, Calls for Veteran Tax Cut," Associated Press, January 13, 2020, https://apnews.com/article/2de6de412d39d2fe76f88ff89fffbc9d.

38. Josiah Bates, "'We Can Do Better.' Mississippi Governor Orders Closure of State Prison's Ward After String of Deaths," *Time*, January 28, 2020, https://time.com/5773059/mississippi-governor-closure-parchman-prison-ward/.

39. Bradley, "Prison Closure Proposals Concern North Country Officials."

40. Ryan Tarinelli, "Cuomo Wants Quicker Process for Closing New York Prisons," *NBC New York*, January 22, 2020, https://www.nbcnewyork.com/news/cuomo-wants-quicker-process-for-closing-new-york-prisons/2263465/.

41. Rosie Perper, "Trump's Super Bowl Ad Featured Alice Johnson, Who Kim Kardashian West Campaigned to Free from Prison," *Business Insider*, February 2, 2020, https://www.businessinsider.com/donald-trump-super-bowl-2020-campaign-ad-alice-johnson-2020-2.

42. Emanuella Grinberg, Jamiel Lynch, and Nick Valencia, "Alice Marie Johnson to President Trump: 'I Am Going to Make You Proud,'" *CNN*, June 7, 2018, https://www.cnn.com/2018/06/06/us/alice-marie-johnson-leaves-prison/index.html.

43. Perper, "Trump's Super Bowl Ad Featured Alice Johnson."

44. Ames Grawert and Tim Lau, "How the FIRST STEP Act Became Law—and What Happens Next," Brennan Center for Justice, January 4, 2019, https://www.brennancenter.org/our-work/analysis-opinion/how-first-step-act-became-law-and-what-happens-next.

45. "Conservatives Send Letter to President Trump in Support of FIRST STEP Act," Right on Crime, August 22, 2018, http://rightoncrime.com/2018/08/conservatives-send-letter-to-president-trump-in-support-of-first-step-act/.

46. S. A. Miller, "Donald Trump MAGA Hat Powerful Political Symbol," Associated Press, February 24, 2019, https://apnews.com/article/1aeaf746236b18137a211589677d75a2.

47. Erica Werner and John Wagner, "Trump Says He's Canceling Pelosi's Foreign Trip a Day After She Asked Him to Delay His State of the Union Speech," *Washington Post*, January 17, 2019, https://www.washingtonpost

.com/politics/trump-says-hes-canceling-pelosi-foreign-trip-a-day-after
-she-asked-him-to-delay-his-state-of-the-union-speech/2019/01/17
/75acf6c2–1a8d-11e9–9ebf-c5fed1b7a081_story.html.

48. "Representative Tony Lovasco," Missouri House of Representatives, accessed October 30, 2020, https://house.mo.gov/memberdetails.aspx?year
=2020&district=064.

49. "QuickFacts: St. Charles County, Missouri," U.S. Census Bureau, accessed November 4, 2020, https://www.census.gov/quickfacts/fact/table
/stcharlescountymissouri/PST120219.

50. "Quick Facts: St. Louis City, Missouri," U.S. Census Bureau, accessed November 4, 2020, https://www.census.gov/quickfacts/fact/table
/stlouiscitymissouri/PST120219.

51. Malcolm Gay, "White Flight and White Power in St. Louis," *Time*, August
13, 2014, https://time.com/3107729/michael-brown-shooting-ferguson
-missouri-white-flight/.

52. Walter Johnson, *The Broken Heart of America: St. Louis and the Violent History
of the United States* (New York: Basic Books, 2020), 252–53.; Gay, "White
Flight and White Power in St. Louis."

53. "Soil Survey of St. Charles County Missouri," U.S. Department of Agriculture (May 1982), 1–2, https://www.nrcs.usda.gov/Internet/FSE
_MANUSCRIPTS/missouri/StCharlesMO_1982/StCharlesMO_1982.pdf.

54. "The New Town at St. Charles," Homes by Whittaker, accessed November
5, 2020, https://www.newtownstcharles.com/.

55. "How Much Are My Taxes," St. Charles County, accessed November 4,
2020, https://www.sccmo.org/Faq.aspx?QID=61.

56. "2016 Missouri Presidential Election Results," *Politico*, updated December
13, 2016, https://www.politico.com/2016-election/results/map/president
/missouri/.

57. Tony Messenger, "St. Charles County Points the Way as Lawmakers Seek
to End Debtors Prisons in Missouri," *St. Louis Post-Dispatch*, December
9, 2018, https://www.stltoday.com/news/local/columns/tony-messenger
/messenger-st-charles-county-points-the-way-as-lawmakers-seek/article
_337547b9-cca9–5f53–91ec-bd1fe9ae6965.html.

58. Messenger, "St. Charles County Points the Way."

59. Sarah Solon, "'You Have the Right to an Attorney . . .' We All Know the
Hollywood Version, But What's the Real Story?," American Civil Liberties
Union, March 15, 2013, https://www.aclu.org/blog/criminal-law-reform
/public-defense-reform/you-have-right-attorney-we-all-know-hollywood
-version.

60. Messenger, "St. Charles County Points the Way."

61. Mo. H.B. 192 (2019), Missouri House of Representatives, https://house.mo
.gov/Bill.aspx?bill=HB192&year=2019&code=R.

62. Americans for Prosperity, "AFP Announces Criminal Justice Reform Tour:
First Steps to Reform: The Matthew Charles Story," press release, November

5, 2019, https://americansforprosperity.org/afp-announces-criminal-justice -reform-tour-first-steps-to-reform-the-matthew-charles-story/.

63. Americans for Prosperity, "AFP Announces Criminal Justice Reform Tour."

64. Jon Schuppe, Kim Cornett, and Michelle Cho, "'I Refused to Be Bitter or Angry': Matthew Charles, Released from Prison and Sent Back Again, Begins Life As A Free Man," *NBC News*, January 8, 2019, https://www .nbcnews.com/news/us-news/i-refuse-be-bitter-or-angry-matthew-charles -released-prison-n955796.

65. "Cash Register Justice Round II: Covering the Hidden Costs of the Justice System," John Jay College of Criminal Justice, https://thecrimereport.org /wp-content/uploads/2019/09/CRJ-Program-Final.pdf.

66. "The Cost of Child Care in Missouri," Economic Policy Institute, accessed October 27, 2020, https://www.epi.org/child-care-costs-in-the-united -states/#/MO.

67. "QuickFacts: Caldwell County, Missouri," U.S. Census Bureau, ac- cessed October 30, 2020, https://www.census.gov/quickfacts/fact/table /caldwellcountymissouri/PST120219.

68. "Marc Levin, J.D.," Texas Public Policy Foundation, accessed October 30, 2020, https://www.texaspolicy.com/about/staff/marc-levin/.

69. "Cash Register Justice."

70. Samuel Brooke, "The Hidden Costs of U.S. Justice" (panel presentation, "Cash Register Justice," John Jay College, New York, NY, September 26, 2019).

71. Marc A. Levin, "The Hidden Costs of U.S. Justice" (panel presentation, "Cash Register Justice," John Jay College, New York, NY, September 26, 2019).

72. Tony Messenger, "Of Billy Graham, Gateway Pundit and Guns. Ameri- ca's Need for Amazing Grace," *St. Louis Post-Dispatch*, February 22, 2018, https://www.stltoday.com/news/local/columns/tony-messenger/messenger -of-billy-graham-gateway-pundit-and-guns-americas-need-for-amazing -grace/article_b725ecc6-3dc0-5f8c-a2aa-8e9cb736d13a.html.

73. Messenger, "Of Billy Graham, Gateway Pundit and Guns."

74. Messenger, "Of Billy Graham, Gateway Pundit and Guns."

75. Messenger, "Of Billy Graham, Gateway Pundit and Guns."

76. "QuickFacts: Caldwell County, Missouri," U.S. Census Bureau, ac- cessed October 30, 2020, https://www.census.gov/quickfacts/fact/table /caldwellcountymissouri/PST120219.

77. "QuickFacts: Dent County, Missouri," U.S. Census Bureau, accessed Octo- ber 30, 2020, https://www.census.gov/quickfacts/dentcountymissouri.

78. "QuickFacts: St. Francois County, Missouri," U.S. Census Bu- reau, accessed October 30, 2020, https://www.census.gov/quickfacts /stfrancoiscountymissouri.

79. Tony Messenger, "Latest Debtors' Prison Lawsuit Straddles Missouri's Urban-Rural Divide," *St. Louis Post-Dispatch*, December 15, 2018, https://

www.stltoday.com/news/local/columns/tony-messenger/messenger-latest
-debtors-prison-lawsuit-straddles-missouris-urban-rural-divide/article
_c0ea89b0-a271–59ce-95a4-aaae96e0d535.html.

80. *Targeted Fines and Fees Against Communities of Color: Civil Rights & Consti-tutional Implications* (Washington, DC: U.S. Commission on Civil Rights, September 2017), 3, 36, https://www.usccr.gov/pubs/2017/Statutory_Enforcement_Report2017.pdf.

81. Tony Messenger, "St. Louis Woman Did 20 Days In Jail for Speed-ing; Now Rural Missouri Judge Wants Her for 6 More Months," *St. Louis Post-Dispatch*, November 25, 2018, https://www.stltoday.com/news/local/columns/tony-messenger/messenger-st-louis-woman-did-20-days-in-jail-for-speeding-now-rural-missouri-judge/article_3aca26a5-dca7–5103–8b0e-0fd1b6179b82.html.

82. Tony Messenger, "Missouri Judge Skips Court Date of Man Who Went to Jail for Skipping Court Date," *St. Louis Post-Dispatch*, November 26, 2018, https://www.stltoday.com/news/local/columns/tony-messenger/messenger-missouri-judge-skips-court-date-of-man-who-went-to-jail-for-skipping-court/article_719b8821-dbbe-5430-add4-d904730a6314.html.

83. Messenger, "Latest Debtors' Prison Lawsuit Straddles Missouri's Urban-Rural Divide."

84. Messenger, "Latest Debtors' Prison Lawsuit Straddles Missouri's Urban-Rural Divide."

85. "Black Jeopardy with Tom Hanks," *Saturday Night Live*, featuring Sasheer Zamata, Leslie Jones, and Tom Hanks, aired October 22, 2016, on NBC, https://www.youtube.com/watch?v=O7VaXlMvAvk&index=1807&list=LLYM7hZtbHvQG9idkpf-Dvpg.

86. "Black Jeopardy with Tom Hanks," *Saturday Night Live*.

87. "Black Jeopardy with Tom Hanks."

88. Peter B. Edelman, "Criminalization of Poverty: Much More to Do," *Duke Law Journal Online* 69 (April 2020): 117, https://dlj.law.duke.edu/2020/04/criminalizationofpoverty/.

89. Peter Edelman, *Not a Crime to Be Poor: The Criminalization of Poverty in America* (New York: The New Press, 2017); Peter Edelman, *So Rich, So Poor: Why It's So Hard to End Poverty in America* (New York: The New Press, 2012).

CHAPTER 11: A TALE OF TWO LETTERS

1. Tony Messenger, "She Was Late to a Hearing, So a Dent County Judge Tossed Her in Jail. Then She Got the Bill," *St. Louis Post-Dispatch*, No-vember 16, 2018, https://www.stltoday.com/news/local/columns/tony-messenger/messenger-she-was-late-to-a-hearing-so-a-dent-county-judge-tossed-her-in/article_03e2a934-c094–5cb4-bf18–15bce4b825d4.html.

2. Tony Messenger, "Private Probation Company Tries to Shame Dent County Woman Back to Jail," *St. Louis Post-Dispatch*, November 8, 2018, https://www.stltoday.com/news/local/columns/tony-messenger/messenger-private-probation-company-tries-to-shame-dent-county-woman-back-to-jail/article_6c5e866e-44ef-5567–8740-d6a2c992bed2.html.

3. Messenger, "Private Probation Company Tries to Shame Dent County Woman."

4. Messenger, "Private Probation Company Tries to Shame Dent County Woman."

5. Messenger, "Private Probation Company Tries to Shame Dent County Woman."

6. Tony Messenger, "Battle Against Mass Incarceration Is Making a Dent in Missouri's Prison Population," *St. Louis Post-Dispatch*, April 24, 2019, https://www.stltoday.com/news/local/columns/tony-messenger/messenger-battle-against-mass-incarceration-is-making-a-dent-in-missouris-prison-population/article_8552e14e-9f78–5e0e-9a39–66c8bf5d097a.html.

7. Craig Montgomery, "Jail Population Drops Due to New Bonding Guidelines, Court Ruling," *Salem News*, April 30, 2019, https://www.thesalemnewsonline.com/news/local_news/article_2374e2d2–6b52–11e9–81ea-a7e455119e4d.html.

8. Montgomery, "Jail Population Drops Due to New Bonding Guidelines."

9. Tony Messenger, "Rural Missouri Judges Are Still Holding On to Debtors Prison Scheme," *St. Louis Post-Dispatch*, May 10, 2019, https://www.stltoday.com/news/local/columns/tony-messenger/messenger-rural-missouri-judges-are-still-holding-on-to-debtors-prison-scheme/article_9a0a5e65–097c-588f-9214-bc003df86bcc.html.

10. Judge David A. Dolan, email to author, May 2019.

11. "QuickFacts: Scott County, Missouri," U.S. Census Bureau, accessed October 30, 2020, https://www.census.gov/quickfacts/scottcountymissouri.

12. Tony Messenger, "A Tale of Two Counties on Opposite Ends of Missouri's Debtors' Prison Cycle," *St. Louis Post-Dispatch*, November 30, 2018, https://www.stltoday.com/news/local/columns/tony-messenger/messenger-a-tale-of-two-counties-on-opposite-ends-of-missouris-debtors-prison-cycle/article_a182e3eb-a974–5f99–9ff0–72fb7de6e031.html.

13. "QuickFacts: Stoddard County, Missouri," U.S. Census Bureau, accessed October 30, 2020, https://www.census.gov/quickfacts/stoddardcountymissouri.

14. "My Congressional District: Missouri Congressional District 8," U.S. Census Bureau, accessed October 30, 2020, https://www.census.gov/mycd/?st=29&cd=08.

15. Messenger, "A Tale of Two Counties."

EPILOGUE: POVERTY IS RELATIVE

1. "Vicksburg Village Ltd.," Public Housing, accessed October 30, 2020, https://www.publichousing.com/details/vicksburg_village_ltd.

2. Tony Messenger, "Predatory Lenders Find Happy Hunting in Missouri," *St. Louis Post-Dispatch*, June 8, 2016, https://www.stltoday.com/news /local/columns/tony-messenger/messenger-predatory-lenders-find-happy -hunting-in-missouri/article_fa64a687–53a0–593d-96b8–1961f14029c3 .html.

INDEX